# MINNIE and HSpice for
# Analogue Circuit Simulation

# MINNIE and HSpice for Analogue Circuit Simulation

## DEREK C. BARKER

*Department of Electrical Engineering and Electronics*
*University of Manchester Institute of Science and Technology*

**CHAPMAN & HALL**
University and Professional Division

London · New York · Tokyo · Melbourne · Madras

**Published by Chapman & Hall, 2–6 Boundary Row, London SE1 8HN**

Chapman & Hall, 2–6 Boundary Row, London SE1 8HN, UK

Van Nostrand Reinhold Inc., 115 5th Avenue, New York NY10003, USA

Chapman & Hall Japan, Thomson Publishing Japan, Hirakawacho Nemoto Building, 7F, 1-7-11 Hirakawa-cho, Chiyoda-ku, Tokyo 102, Japan

Chapman & Hall Australia, Thomas Nelson Australia, 102 Dodds Street, South Melbourne, Victoria 3205, Australia

Chapman & Hall India, R. Seshadri, 32 Second Main Road, CIT East, Madras 600 035, India

First edition 1991

© 1991 Derek C. Barker

MINNIE: Version 7.2.6
Copyright in the basic MINNIE software programs referred to in this book is owned by the National Research Development Corporation and no use may be made of such works without a licence from the NRDC.

HSPICE: Version H8907
© 1985
Metasoftware, 50 Curtner, Ave., Suite 16, Campbell, CA 95008, USA.

Typeset in 10½/12pt Times by Excel Typesetters Company
Printed in England by Clays Ltd., St Ives Plc

0 412 42760 5     0 442 31478 7 (USA)

A catalogue record for this book is available from the British Library

Library of Congress Cataloging-in-Publication data available

∞  Printed on permanent acid-free text paper, manufactured in accordance with the proposed
ANSI/NISO Z 39.48–199X and ANSI Z 39.48–1984

# Contents

# Preface

After many years of teaching circuit theory and analogue electronic circuits the author believes that for most students the main path to obtaining a good understanding of the principles involved, as measured by their ability to apply them in a correct and intelligent manner, is through problem solving and design exercises.

In an ideal world the student would be able to construct the circuit being analysed or designed, and so directly test the calculated or predicted results. Indeed, experience leads to the conclusion that typical students like to see their own circuits perform as intended, with a consequent increase in motivation.

At present, however, time and facility constraints mean that most of this work is of the pencil and paper variety, students having few opportunities to see the consequences of their efforts in a practical situation. At best they have to accept sample solutions or simply numerical answers. This path can seem tedious to all but the most motivated of students, so an alternative which can provide many of the benefits of direct circuit testing within the time and resources available is of immediate interest. This is where the MINNIE and HSpice simulation package can assist the undergraduate teaching activity.

Interest in simulation of analogue electronic circuits has existed for many years both in industry and in educational establishments. Software packages using advanced mathematical techniques allied to reasonable device models are widely available – Spice, HSpice and other Spice derivatives are well known and are not unique. However, the size of these programs and the time required for simulation of even a simple circuit implies computing power until recently available only on mainframes and minicomputers. They were written by and for experienced circuit designers, and did not incorporate the 'user friendly' approach now popular in the personal computer market.

MINNIE provides just such a user friendly interface for HSpice. By accepting circuit information in circuit diagram form (**schematic capture**) it builds directly on students' experience as obtained in lectures and laboratories. Consequently they have immediate understanding of the procedures to be followed to simulate the performance of their circuits. Allied to the vastly increased computing power and greatly improved screen resolutions of the workstations or personal computers now generally available, students have a very powerful tool at their disposal.

When MINNIE/HSpice first arrived at UMIST the author realized that the existing documentation, the *MINNIE User Guide*, was written for experienced users and would not be appropriate for first year undergraduates. This led to the preparation of three introductory tutorial documents aimed specifically at undergraduates. The success of these documents persuaded the author to develop his ideas further, leading to the preparation of this book. It is intended to be an initial guide to circuit simulation using MINNIE/HSpice, aimed at undergraduates (and any other interested readers), and does not attempt to replace the *MINNIE User Guide*. Consequently some of the more advanced features of MINNIE/HSpice, of interest only to experienced circuit designers, have been omitted in the interest of brevity.

The author has adopted a self-teaching approach in order to reduce the demands that would otherwise be made on already heavily loaded staff. The reader proceeds at his or her own pace, avoiding periods of peak usage of terminals or workstations and dispensing with the necessity for scheduled formal lectures. First year students are soon brought up to the point at which they are able to confirm the theoretical circuit behaviour described in textbooks and lectures, the answers obtained analytically for set problems, or the results obtained experimentally in the laboratories. The tutorial (demonstration) examples and the exercises used were selected bearing in mind the progress of students as they advance through their courses, so they will be able to simulate the standard circuits they meet in the second and third years as well as the more complex ones they may design for undergraduate and postgraduate project work.

In Chapter 1 the author is concerned with introducing the beginner to the rudiments of MINNIE/HSpice and the host system. Some items are specific to the Apollo system installed at UMIST, and are mentioned only as being representative of the systems the user is likely to encounter.

The next six chapters, dealing with the response of linear systems to sinusoidal stimulation, form the bulk of the book. While Chapter 2 deals exclusively with passive components (linear circuit theory), the next five, Chapters 3 to 7, deal mainly with circuits which include active devices (electronic circuits). The electronic circuit used for tutorial purposes is the standard bipolar common emitter, so the discussions are accessible to the typical second year (and in many cases first year) undergraduate. The exercises cover a wider range of achievement, some being taken from second and third year design exercises as implemented at UMIST. Due to the inherent similarities between bipolars and FETs, students will have little difficulty in adapting to the latter and so they are not specifically covered. Operational amplifiers, on the other hand, are introduced because they make possible the discussion of active filters and feedback oscillators (Wien Bridge) in a relatively simple manner, as well as having certain peculiarities of their own.

Many of the techniques introduced in these six chapters are of general application. The reader is introduced to the MINNIE filing and retrieval system and to its post-processing facilities in Chapter 4, while the presentation and 'measurement' of simulation results is discussed in Chapter 5. Of particular interest is Chapter 6 covering independently variable passive components – though specific to variable resistors the reader can immediately extend the procedures to capacitors, etc. Finally, Chapter 7 is devoted to the single most useful activity in the electronics laboratory: the presentation and examination of waveforms. This chapter includes four quite comprehensive analysis/design exercises suitable for second/third year undergraduates (and postgraduates).

Chapter 8 forms a third part concerned with the response of linear circuits to square waves and step functions. It commences with passive circuits directly relevant to transient analysis as covered in basic circuit theory, and then proceeds to the response of the common emitter stage operating in its linear region. The transient responses are drawn and the harmonic contents (Fourier analysis) are determined. Typical circuit theory exercises are presented which emphasize the use of initial conditions, the simulation path following closely that of analysis.

Finally, Chapter 9 introduces non-linear circuits through a very comprehensive exercise set to UMIST students during their second year. The reader is guided through a detailed examination and comparison of the response of simple $RC$, diode-capacitor and transistor-capacitor circuits. The concepts of independently variable components, previously introduced for passive components, are extended to include voltage (and, by inference, current) sources.

The tutorial and exercise examples used in this book were primarily selected to demonstrate particular facilities of MINNIE in a logical order. These facilities will individually first be required at different points of the first and second years of the undergraduate course, and it was considered important that the examples should relate to corresponding parts of the syllabus. Design work is encouraged where feasible and a number of questions are asked at various points, answers being provided in the Appendix.

Derek C. Barker

Department of Electrical Engineering and Electronics,
University of Manchester Institute of Science and Technology.

# Using this book

This book is aimed at the beginner – the first year student who is just having an initial organized look at computers, and is meeting circuit theory for the first time. If he or she is not at the same time entering the world of analogue electronic engineering it will not be long before this happens. The student has probably used a personal computer before, at school or at home so is 'computer-aware', not an absolute novice. It is also intended to be of immediate use to second and third year undergraduates.

More experienced users, postgraduates, circuit designers, etc., who are interested in the MINNIE/HSpice simulation package, will also find this book to be a useful introduction.

To meet the needs of all readers, within this book the material is presented in three different forms.

1. Guides to specific MINNIE facilities: these are comprehensive and detailed, and each step is illustrated with the relevant screen picture, so that it is clear at all times exactly what to do and what results should be obtained.
2. Tutorials: these are fully documented simulations, in which the reader is taken step by step through each stage, from setting up the initial circuit to presenting the final results. Again each step is fully documented with all the relevant screen pictures. The problem and any relevant issues are discussed, with particular attention to factors affecting the analysis. Where appropriate the commonality between simulation and laboratory procedures is emphasized.

   The choice of demonstration circuits is based on the author's experience and should provide additional insights into important topics in both circuit theory and analogue electronics.
3. Exercises: as the name implies they are presented to give further experience in the use of the facilities presented in the immediately preceding guide sections or tutorials. The assistance provided is less comprehensive than in the other sections, but is still sufficient to lead the student to the correct results.

   In several of these exercises design work is encouraged. The problem is set and one may then proceed to one's own design and simulation or alternatively use the sample solution provided. Where suitable these problems intentionally leave considerable scope for making decisions – a good incentive to understanding the factors influencing circuit performance.

Beginners should not attempt to work their way through all the chapters of this book immediately, but should start by familiarizing themselves with the local system, with the contents of Chapter 1 and with the first parts of Chapter 2. Then this experience can be added to as other topics are covered in the circuit theory or electronic engineering lectures.

There are opportunities offered by laboratory work, set tutorial questions, old examination papers, etc. to increase familiarity with this very powerful aid to design work. It is only through active use that the expertise necessary for efficient use of the MINNIE/HSpice package is acquired.

It should be noted that the sequence of topics, though quite logical from the organizational viewpoint of the book, is not necessarily the chronological order in which they appear in courses. Thus parts of Chapters 8 and 9 could be encountered in the first year, much earlier than the circuits of Chapter 7. Consequently progress through the book need not be strictly sequential.

Finally, do persevere. When you achieve familiarity with MINNIE you will have at your disposal a very powerful tool for all your analogue design work.

Derek C. Barker

# Getting started  | 1

## 1.1  THE SYSTEM

A typical suite of workstations dedicated to undergraduate CAD activities might consist of a network of 30 Apollo (or similar) monochrome computers. Each computer or 'node' would operate independently using its own processor and memory, but have free access to files or directories belonging to any other node via a high speed communications network. This arrangement gives the user the ability to work from any node and 'transparently' use the collection of nodes as one large computer. MINNIE (and HSpice) would run on this system, together with a variety of other software packages.

The UMIST system, based on Apollo DN3000 monochrome computers, has at present about 1.4 G of disk storage capacity, which is not sufficient to meet the requirements of nearly 600 undergraduates plus interested postgraduates and academic staff. Consequently it is necessary to restrict the individual's overall memory requirements, and users are strongly encouraged to store files on personal floppy disks. This also has the virtue of protecting data from unauthorized entry.

Experience also shows that it is desirable to limit student output. It is easy and very tempting to request a screen dump for every circuit change or new result, but uncontrolled output leads to long print queues.

## 1.2  INITIAL CONDITIONS

The procedures described here are for an Apollo DN3000 network. Other installations will have similar start up sequences.

1. When you arrive at the workstation it should already be on. They are normally left on all the time, to reach and maintain stable operating conditions.

   If the screen is blank, press any key on the keyboard or move the mouse to wake up the terminal (the screen is blanked if it is not used within a time limit).

2. At the bottom of the screen you will see the **display command line**. On it you are asked to login. Use the mouse to move the arrow cursor to the display command line and type in the user name you have been given. Thus if your user name is 'apprentice', you will have

**Login: apprentice**

3. Then, the machine will ask for your **password**. You will have been given an initial password so at least one other person knows it. (Facilities exist for you to change it to a private code, but if you make use of them do not forget the new password you have selected). If your initial password is 'plumber', type it and you will then have

**Password:** .......

Note that the password that you typed is not shown on the screen. If you make a mistake you will be asked to **Login** again.

4. If you are successful in completing steps 1–3 the rest of the screen comes into use. At the bottom of the **main display**, just above the display command line, you will see a **dollar ($) prompt**. Let us:

(a) **adjust the screen display mode**. The monochrome Apollos will present either white lines on a black background or black lines on a white background.

To change between modes, place the cursor on the command line (bottom line). Then use the command **inv** (**invert**):

**command: inv**

and when you press **return** the display will change. (For these notes I will assume that you have selected black lines on white background. Consequently, the description **inverse video** will always imply a black background, also referred to as **enhanced**.)

(b) **see what directories there are** in your name. Your **user name** (apprentice) and **password** (plumber) have given you access to a working area, which may be compared to a large, multi-drawer, private filing cabinet, having the ability to grow to suit your demands. You could then liken a directory to a drawer within that filing cabinet. You can create new directories as appropriate.

At the **$** prompt use the command **ls** (**list**). NB: use lower case letters.

**$ ls**

You will then see a list of the directories at present in your working area.

(c) **make a working directory** (to put your MINNIE work in). Use the (lower case) command **mkdir** ⟨**directory-name**⟩ (make a directory called, say, kitchen)

**$ mkdir kitchen**

(NB: you only need to make a working directory if you do not have one from a previous use).

(d) **check that the directory was created**. Repeat step (b) and see what directories are listed.

**$ ls**

**kitchen** should now appear in its place on the directory list.

(e) **start to work** in this new directory. Individual jobs – circuits etc. – may be allocated to different **files** within this directory, so you may store a lot of work in it.

Use the (lower case) command **cd** ⟨**directory-name**⟩ (change directory to, in this case, kitchen):

$$\text{\$ cd kitchen}$$

(f) check that you are now in **kitchen**. Use the command **pwd**:

$$\text{\$ pwd}$$

and you should see the full **path** (all the directory names) from the lowest (**root**) level of the operating system up to the level at which you are at present operating. The *last* item in the list is your **current directory** – kitchen in this case.

$$\text{//serf/u/apprentice/kitchen}$$

(g) **call** MINNIE. Just type **minnie** (lower case),

$$\text{\$ minnie}$$

and wait for the MINNIE start-up screen to appear.


## 1.3   START UP SCREEN

When MINNIE appears you will see Fig. 1.3-1, containing

1. A right-hand section full of items and functions to be used for laying out your circuit.
2. A larger left-hand area for drawing your circuit. This area is covered with a regular array (grid) of points. (NB: this is only a small section of the total drawing area available).
3. A small black/white two-coloured square in the centre of the screen, on one of the grid points. This square, your **current position marker**, indicates your actual working point on the screen. Components will attach to the long edge of the black half of this marker.
4. A circle with a cross in it. This is your **cursor** or **pointer**. Note that in some modes it will change shape (a dagger, a pen, a magnifying glass, etc.).

   (If this cursor is not visible it may be in the drawing area off screen so move the MOUSE to bring it back into view).
5. At the top of the right-hand area, a **highlighted** (inverse video) box indicating that you are immediately in DRAWING mode. The alternative modes, to be selected as required, are ANALYSIS and RESULTS. In this area you will also find EXIT, CAPTIONS and GLOBALS.

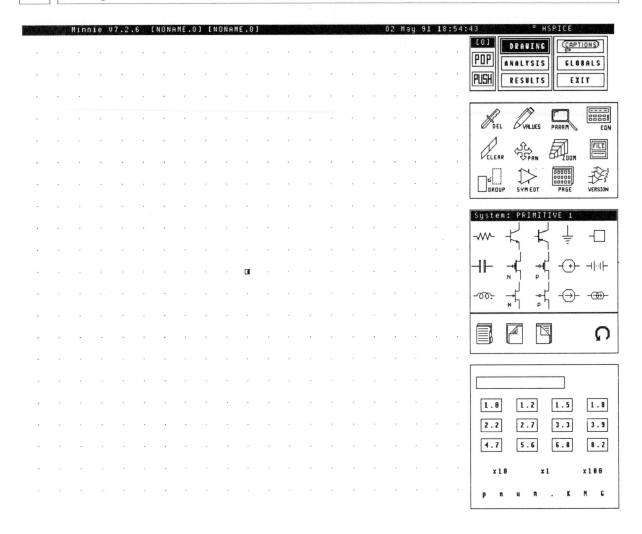

**Fig. 1.3-1** Menu on the MINNIE start-up screen

## 1.4 PRINTING THE SCREEN CONTENTS

To obtain **hard copy** (print out) of your circuits and graphs it is necessary to have a copy of the screen image sent (**dumped**) to a printer.

The **control codes** used depend on the manner in which the local system is set up. The dump procedure may use the local operating system's **printer drivers** or drivers provided by ISL, the suppliers of MINNIE. The local system supervisory staff will know which are being used. The codes are:

|  | System drivers | ISL drivers |
|---|---|---|
| Full screen dump (Fig. 1.4-1) | control-F | control-W |
| Partial screen dump (Fig. 1.4-2) | control-D | control-V |

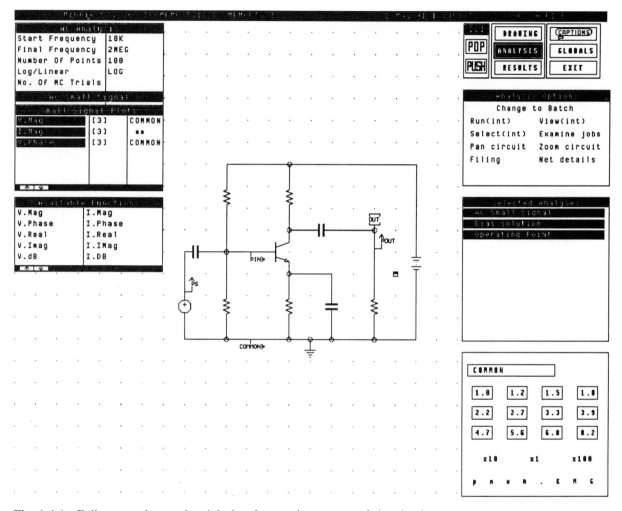

**Fig. 1.4-1**  Full screen dump: the right-hand menu is not part of the circuit or result presentation area, so it can often be discarded

in which **control-F** means hold down the 'control key' while typing 'F'. Note that **control-f** is the same.

## 1.5  DRAW YOUR CIRCUIT

Circuits are drawn by positioning components using a mouse. The mouse has three keys, which have the following functions:

     **L**  left mouse key: rotates position marker
     **M**  middle mouse key: all selection & deselection
     **R**  right mouse key: cursor movement

1. **Cursor movement**: move the mouse, in contact with its mat so that the ball under it rotates, and notice how the cursor (the circle with a cross) moves in response to the mouse movements.

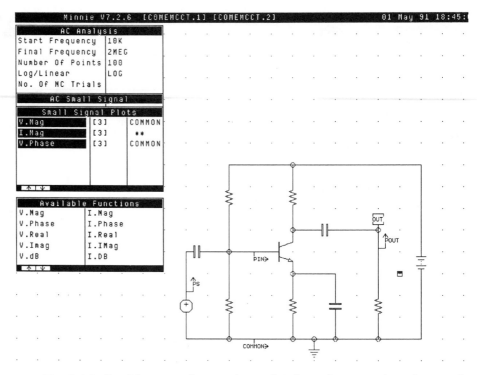

**Fig. 1.4-2** Partial screen dump: when printed on the same size of paper the circuit diagram is 1.5 times larger than in the full screen dump

2. **Position marker rotation (component direction)**: position the cursor anywhere within the drawing area, and press the left mouse key **L**. Watch the current position marker, and notice how it rotates clockwise 90° on each press.

   You can use this technique to determine the direction along which a component will be positioned.

3. **Current position (component position)**. Keep the cursor in the drawing area, and press the middle mouse key **M**. See how the marker moves to the **grid point** closest to the cursor. Move the cursor elsewhere and repeat.

   You use this technique to determine the position of a component (which will grow from the grid point covered by the marker).

4. **Line (conductor) drawing**. Keep the cursor in the drawing area, and press the middle mouse key **M**, *holding it down*. Roll the mouse in all directions. Watch how it draws lines while the **M** key is held down. See how the reverse process can be used to **undraw** lines but only if you start from an *open* end. Notice also how these lines snap to the grid lines.

   These lines are your **electrical conductors**. It is important to note that an electrical connection is made *only* when one conductor terminates on another. Consequently if a conductor is drawn across a central portion of another no connection is made. If a connection is required it is necessary to terminate one conductor (on the other one) and then restart it at the crossing point (or elsewhere).

Connections are indicated by the small diamond shapes drawn where the conductors meet.

5. **Resistor selection/insertion**. Move the cursor to the RESISTOR element in the right-hand section. Select this element by pressing the middle mouse key **M**. Note that:

    (a) a resistor has grown from the grid point previously covered by the current position marker, in the direction determined by the black half of the marker; and

    (b) the marker itself has moved to the far end of the resistor.

6. **Other basic components**. Repeat the selection procedure in (5.) above for the CAPACITOR, and for the VOLTAGE and CURRENT SOURCES.

    Note that the octagonal sources are AC. The other two are DC.

7. **Component rotation**.

    (a) For *immediate* rotation, repeat the selection procedure (5.) for the POLARIZED INDUCTOR. Then as soon as it appears on the drawing grid move the cursor to the Rotation symbol: this is the black counter-clockwise arrow. Press the **M** key and see how the inductor polarity changes.

        NB: this method only works for components immediately after they are selected.

    (b) For *delayed* rotation, first move the current position marker away from any elements in the drawing area. Then move the cursor to the rotation symbol. Press the **M** key to select it. This time it should change to reverse video. Now move the cursor onto any of the polarized elements you have on the drawing grid, and press the **M** key. See how the polarization changes. Note that you can do as many elements as you wish at one time.

        When you are satisfied, move the cursor back to the rotation symbol, and press **M** to deselect it.

8. **Component deletion**. Select the dagger symbol (DEL). It changes to inverse video, and the cursor changes to a dagger. Place the dagger on the element you wish to delete and select it by pressing **M**. Notice that the selected element is now drawn in dotted lines. If no such change occurs, the dagger may not be *on* the element, so try again.

    Select other items for deletion in the same way. When you have selected all the items you want deleted (and they are all drawn in dotted lines), move the dagger cursor back to the dagger symbol and press **M**. All the selected (dotted) components should vanish, the dagger symbol and the cursor revert to their normal conditions.

9. **Component values**. Select the pen symbol (VALUES). It changes to reverse video, and the cursor changes to a pen. Notice that all the elements which have not been assigned values are now drawn with thicker lines to make their condition clear.

    Look at the bottom right corner to the VALUES MENU. You

will see the standard range of component values (1.0  1.2  1.5  1.8  etc.), value multipliers ($\times 1$  $\times 10$  $\times 100$) and unit multipliers (p = pico, n = nano, u = micro, m = milli, K = kilo, M = mega, and G = giga).

MINNIE automatically assumes the correct *type* of unit (ohm, volt, farad, etc.) for each component, so you do not need to specify the type of unit. Note also that all values are written in upper case (capitals) on the circuit diagrams. Consequently it is difficult to differentiate between m (mili) and M (mega). For this reason MINNIE writes MIL instead of m and MEG instead of M. The other letters are self-evident.

You can set the value of a component using either the mouse or the keyboard:

(a) *Mouse*: use the cursor and the mouse **M** key to select appropriate values. The values you select will appear in the box in this menu.

When the correct quantity appears in the box, move the cursor on to the actual circuit element, and press **M** key. The component will revert to normal line thickness and the value will appear on it.

(b) *Keyboard*: this is probably the faster method – it is certainly more flexible offering greater variety of values.

Place the pen cursor on the selected component, but do *not* press. Instead, type in the value you want, remembering to use MIL and MEG instead of m and M. (MINNIE will not differentiate between m and M). The value will appear in the same box as for (a) above.

Now press **M**, and the value will appear on the circuit as above.

Now deselect **VALUES**. The cursor reverts to its normal form and the component values vanish from the circuit diagram for better clarity.

Note that as long as **VALUES** is selected the component values are shown. When **VALUES** is deselected, the component values are no longer shown, but they remain valid until you decide to change them. Consequently, if you wish to check on your component values, select **VALUES**, always remembering to deselect afterwards.

10. **Fast cursor movement.** The right mouse key **R** moves the cursor sequentially between its most recent position on the drawing area and its most recently *used* position(s) on the menu(s).

This can be a time saver when laying out circuits, but requires a bit of practice. It is not essential, but it is very useful.

# Passive circuits | 2

## 2.1 TUTORIAL: FREQUENCY RESPONSE OF THE LOW-PASS RC CIRCUIT

Using the techniques described in the previous pages, draw the circuit of Fig. 2.1-1. Do not forget the component values.

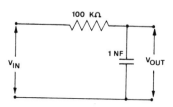

**Fig. 2.1-1** Simple low pass RC filter (also known as the RC integrating circuit)

MINNIE analyses a circuit by calculating the results caused by the application of a **stimulus**. Consequently it cannot do anything until:

1. appropriate stimulus is connected (voltage and/or current sources, AC or DC); and
2. it is told exactly which results are required.

MINNIE cannot analyse Fig. 2.1-1 until you satisfy (1.) and (2.) above. So connect an AC voltage source as in Fig. 2.1-2. Also attach a label to the output as shown. Either immediately type **VOUT** (followed by **return**) or else, later, use the **VALUES** (pen) facility to enter **VOUT** (via the keyboard, remembering to press the **return** key). You must also add an **EARTH** (or **COMMON**, or **GROUND**) connection as shown.

   A result you might want MINNIE to calculate and plot is the output voltage as a function of frequency. For comparison purposes you might also want to plot the input voltage on the same set of graphs.

   You achieve this by attaching **measurement probes** to the relevant parts of the circuit. Remember two points:

1. voltage measurements require two physical connections, because voltage is always measured with respect to a reference potential (such as earth, or zero, or common). Hence for each voltage analysis/measurement you must place a probe to indicate:

   (a) where you want to calculate/measure the voltage; and
   (b) where the reference potential is.

2. current measurements do not require reference points, and hence only one connection (probe) is required.

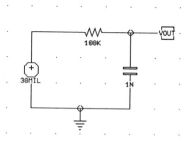

**Fig. 2.1-2** The RC filter with a voltage source. Note MINNIE's representation of AC voltage sources. Also note the earth connection.

It is important to note also that MINNIE does not like loose wires or components hanging around. It will interpret them as incomplete circuitry and refuse to analyse. This is why the output conductor in Fig. 2.1-2 has a label attached to it. MINNIE can recognize it as not requiring further components or connections.

```
┌────────────────────────────────┐
│      Analysis Options          │
│ AC Analysis                    │
│ DC Analysis                    │
│ Transient Analysis             │
│ Temperature Sweep              │
│ Parameter Sweep                │
└────────────────────────────────┘
```

**Fig. 2.1-3**  Analysis Options

```
┌──────────────────────────────┐
│        AC Analysis           │
│ Start Frequency     │10      │
│ Final Frequency     │1MEG    │
│ Number Of Points    │50      │
│ Log/Linear          │LOG     │
│ No. Of MC Trials    │        │
├──────────────────────────────┤
│ AC Small Signal              │
│ Bias solution                │
│ AC Noise Analysis            │
│ AC Distortion Analysis       │
└──────────────────────────────┘
```

**Fig. 2.1-4**  AC Analysis

*Analysis*

Select **ANALYSIS** mode (shown in the top right corner menu) and be patient because it may take a short while to react! Note that if you deselect (press **M** on an enhanced/selected item) the **DRAWING** mode MINNIE automatically enters the **ANALYSIS** mode.

A new menu appears on the left side of the screen, headed **Analysis Options** (Fig. 2.1-3). To determine the frequency response of your circuit you require an AC analysis so press **M** on **AC Analysis**.

You now have the menu of Fig. 2.1-4. This is suitable for your purpose, so accept it, and proceed to set up your **measurement ranges**. You want to do an AC analysis so first set the frequency range and the number of analysis points as follows:

1. Select the 10 (**Start Frequency** = 10 Hz) box by pressing **M** (mouse middle key) on it. It becomes enhanced.
2. Type **1K** (for 1 kHz as a frequency lower limit). Press **M** on the above enhanced box. Note that 1K replaces 10 in the box.
3. Follow the procedure of (1.) above to select the 1MEG (**Final Frequency** = 1 MHz) box and the procedure of (2.) above to replace it with a 100K (100 kHz) frequency upper limit.
4. Select the 50 (**Number of Points** (frequencies) between the above limits at which the results should be calculated), and assuming you do not need such resolution, change it to 30.
5. Leave the **LOG** (for logarithmic scale) alone. This is the normal scale used for ALL frequency plots.
6. Also leave **No. of MC Trials** alone.

*Results*

Having set up your measurement ranges you must now specify the results you want, so look at the types of AC analysis available to you. **AC Small Signal** seems most appropriate, so select it by pressing **M** on **AC Small Signal** to get the menu of Fig. 2.1-5. It requires filling, so to see the options available press **M** on **Small Signal Plots** and a menu of **Available Functions** appears, as shown in Fig. 2.1-6.

In the **Small Signal Plots** menu there are three columns, the left one

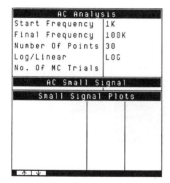

**Fig. 2.1-5** Small Signal Plots selection pad

**Fig. 2.1-6** Available Functions for selection

containing the active choices which must be selected. In the middle column you indicate where you want MINNIE to produce results (where you would make your measurements on an actual circuit) while in the right column you indicate any necessary reference points (as for voltages).

Now, assume that you wish to measure magnitude and phase of voltages and currents:

1. Press **M** to select: **V.Mag  V.Phase  I.Mag  I.Phase**. Note that the items selected appear under Small Signal Plots in inverse video. These are your **active choices**, as shown in Fig. 2.1-7. (To deselect simply press **M** on the active choice – it now reverts to normal. This indicates that it will not be used.)

2. Move the cursor arrow to the middle column next to **V.Mag**. Note that a normal box appears, and press **M** to select this box. It should then change to be enhanced.

   Note that any probes already selected for this quantity (**V.Mag**), will appear *enhanced* (thicker) on the circuit diagram. This way you can check on your measuring arrangements.

   Now move the cursor to a section of conductor (not a component's lead) on which you wish to measure the output voltage, and leave it there.

   Type **POUT** (for output probe, or any other name you wish). Note that only upper case letters are available, and, if you leave out this step, MINNIE will use the default names **P1**, **P2**, **P3**, etc.

   Press **M**, and

   (a) a probe appears, with the name you have typed (or the default name), in the position where you left the cursor, (but if it does

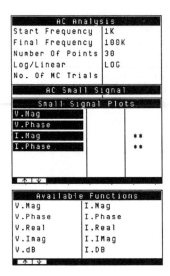

**Fig. 2.1-7** The functions **V.Mag**, **V.Phase**, **I.Mag** and **I.Phase** have been selected for analysis

**Fig. 2.1-8** The function **V.Mag** will be 'measured' at the position defined by **POUT**

not appear you have not selected a piece of conductor so try again, avoiding the end leads of components); and

(b) the probe name (**POUT**) appears in the enhanced box, as shown in Fig. 2.1-8.

Now move the cursor to a section of conductor on which you wish to measure the input voltage. Type an appropriate name, such as **PIN**, press **M**, and this time:

(c) a probe **PIN** appears in the relevant place, in enhanced form; and

(d) **PIN** replaces **POUT** in the selection box as shown in Fig. 2.1-9 (but **POUT** is *not* forgotten).

(e) now return the cursor to the centre column box (currently enhanced) and deselect it by pressing **M**.

Only one name can appear in the box (because probe names may be quite long), so when more than one probe has been selected for a given box the final display is simply the total number of probes selected for this type of quantity, as shown in Fig. 2.1-10.

3. For **V.Phase**, select the appropriate box in the middle column. Then move the cursor to where one of the probes connects to a conductor and select (press **M**). Repeat with the other probe. Return cursor to the enhanced box and deselect it.

4. Are **POUT** and/or **PIN** suitable for current measurement? If so, repeat (3.) above for **I.Mag** and **I.Phase**. Otherwise introduce new probes where appropriate.

5. You have now connected probes at the points at which you wish to

**Fig. 2.1-9** Probe **PIN** is now displayed in the menu (and on the circuit)

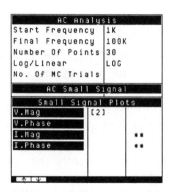

**Fig. 2.1-10** Final display for **V.Mag** only shows number of probes used

measure voltages and currents. You must now specify the **common terminal** with respect to which the voltages should be measured. The procedure is very similar to that above: move the cursor to form a box in the right column on the **V.Mag** row. Select this box and use the above procedure outline to place a probe **PCOM** on the **earth (common) conductor**. Note though that step (e) above is not require.

6. Repeat for **V.Phase**, and then you should have the menu and circuit of Fig. 2.1-11.

*Simulation*
The circuit is now ready so you can tell MINNIE to proceed with the simulation.

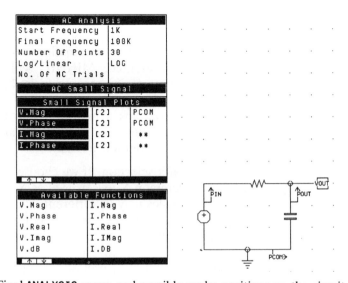

**Fig. 2.1-11** Final **ANALYSIS** menu and possible probe positions on the circuit

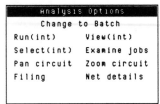

**Fig. 2.1-12** Analysis Options menu (do not confuse with the earlier menu of the same name, in Fig. 2.1-3)

Move the cursor to the **ANALYSIS OPTIONS** menu on the right-hand side, Fig. 2.1-12, then

1. select Run(int) (run interactively), and
2. read the bottom line – you are looking for an instruction to type in a name for your circuit. Do not delay, MINNIE will wait, doing nothing, until it knows your circuit identifier.

MINNIE will use your circuit name to create names for files to be used for processing and storing information related to this particular simulation. Consequently the simulation cannot proceed until the name is typed in.

The name must begin with a letter and may include up to 32 characters, selected from:

all the letters $\quad$ A–Z
all the digits $\quad$ 0–9
the two symbols $\quad$ _ and $

Other symbols have special meanings so do not use them. A space is interpreted as the end of the name, so do not use one as part of a name. Thus:

ccts1sept91a
fred$123b
last_chance$001

are all acceptable names.

Once you have typed in the name (and do not forget to press the **RETURN** key), MINNIE should be left to get on with the job (this simple job should take less than one minute on most systems – mainly file management).

*Presentation of results*

When MINNIE is ready it will require information about the way in which the results should be presented. MINNIE will automatically enter **RESULT MODE** (top right of screen), which brings up the Result Options menu, Fig. 2.1-13.

In this menu you will see five boxes indicating the type of result presentation you can choose, although not all will be appropriate for a given situation. The boxes are, from left to right:

1. $\quad$ **Single graph**: the default selection. If we choose this one all our graphs must have a common Y axis as well as X axis. Of course the Y axis units and scales may be different.
2. $\quad$ **Multiple graph**: With this one we can display up to six separate graphs, but they will all have the same abscissa (X axis). Of course the Y axis will be independent.
3. $\quad$ **Circuit diagram**: indicated by a printed circuit schematic. This is a useful way to present DC values (biasing voltages, etc.)

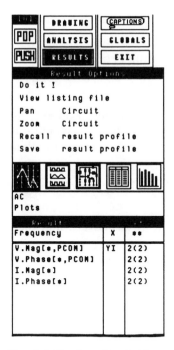

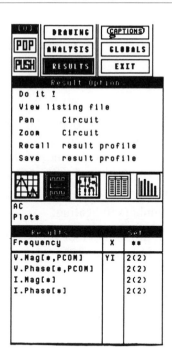

**Fig. 2.1-13** Results Option: Default selection

**Fig. 2.1-14** Results Option: Multiple graph selection

4. + 5. These two display forms, **tabular** and **bar chart**, are of less immediate interest. Leave them for the time being. At a later date you may wish to use them.

For the purposes of this tutorial select option (2.) Multiple graph (press **M** on it). Then, further down in Fig. 2.1-14 you see a menu under the heading Results Set. In the left column you see:

1. The independent variable Frequency. Next to it you see X indicating it is to be plotted along the X axis. You may be happy with this. The right-hand column is not used for Frequency.
2. The dependent variable V.Mag. Next to it you can have:

   (a) YI  the default choice shown in Fig. 2.1-14, indicating it will have an **independent Y axis**; or
   (b) YC  indicating it shares a **common Y axis** with other dependent variables; or
   (c) a blank space, indicating it will *not* be plotted.

   Note that if you press **M** on the present choice of axis it will be replaced by a new option. This way you can set up your graphs.
   Also available, under special conditions, is:

   (d) X  indicating that it is now the **independent variable**, and will be plotted along the X axis.

The conditions are due to the fact that you can only have one independent variable. Hence

(i) it is necessary to remove the X from Frequency, and
(ii) there should be only one member (one quantity) in the set to which X is being assigned.

3. The other dependent variables V.Phase, I.Mag and I.Phase are shown in Fig. 2.1-14 with blank (no Y axis) default conditions. Using the technique described above, press **M** to arrange for them to be plotted with independent Y axis (YI).

In the far right column, next to the above variables, you will find two numbers indicating:

1. the number of probes for which results will be displayed; and then, in brackets,
2. the total number of probes for which results have been obtained.

For the present, these are the same (Fig. 2.1-14).

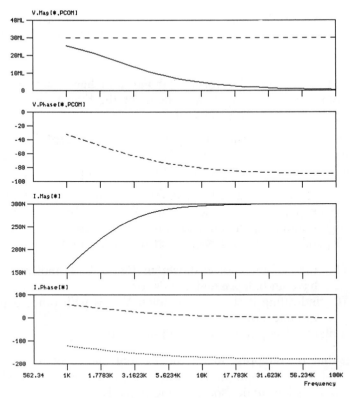

**Fig. 2.1-15** Results: note that MINNIE HSpice initially assume that Iin and Iout have opposing polarities; in fact they are the same, so one result is ±180° with respect to the other

It is evident that you have 8 dependent variables, but as stated earlier you can plot only 6 graphs. To solve this problem you could:

1. remove two dependent variables completely (press **M** on the corresponding Y axis choice until a blank space appears); or
2. plot several variables on the same graph (that is with common Y axis) (press **M** on the corresponding Y axis choice until **YC** appears).

For this tutorial it is left to you to choose how to display the data, so when you are ready, take the cursor up to **Do it!** and press **M**.

MINNIE should now present the results of this simulation. Figure 2.1-15 shows results displayed using **YC** for each of the four types of variable. Examining your circuit you see that at the probe **PIN** the

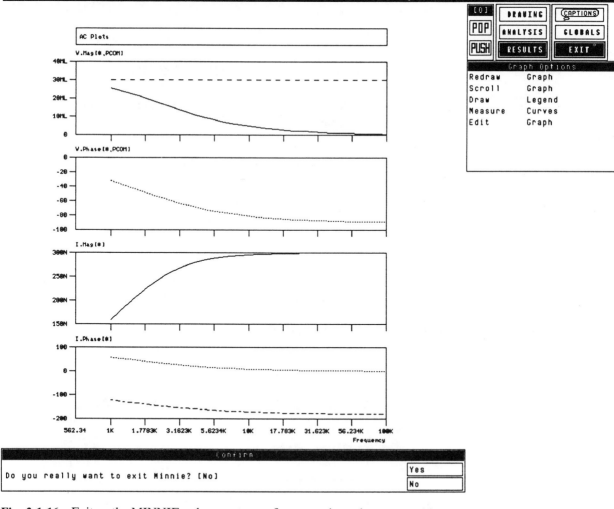

**Fig. 2.1-16** Exit path: MINNIE asks you to confirm your intentions to avoid accidents

voltage magnitude and phase must be constants, 30 mV and 0° respectively, and that the current must be identical at both probe positions. MINNIE agrees (the 180° phase difference is due to the initially assumed polarities of Iin and Iout).

The asterisk in V.Mag[*,PCOM] indicates that V.Mag is being determined at more than one probe. PCOM is the single reference point for V.Mag.

*Exiting from MINNIE and logging out*

To leave MINNIE at any time, first take the cursor to the top right-hand corner and press **M** on the EXIT box, Fig. 2.1-16.

Read the question on the bottom line, take the cursor to the appropriate answer and press **M**. Then wait until MINNIE clears the screen.

Lastly take cursor to bottom (command) line (see Chapter 1) and type **lo** (short for **log out**).

Do not switch off!

## 2.2 EXERCISES: SIMPLE PASSIVE CIRCUITS

### 2.2.1 A simple resistive circuit and its Thevenin equivalent voltage source

*Analysis*

Consider the DC circuit shown in Fig. 2.2-1.

1. Write down the equations required to determine the three loop currents using **Kirchhoff's Voltage Law** (KVL).
2. Use the **Thevenin–Norton** equivalence to replace the two voltage sources by equivalent current sources. Then write down the equations required to determine the node voltages using **Kirchhoff's Current Law** (KCL).
3. Replace the section of the circuit to the left of labels A and B by its Thevenin equivalent circuit, and then determine the current through the 40 V battery.
4. Confirm your numerical results by simulation.

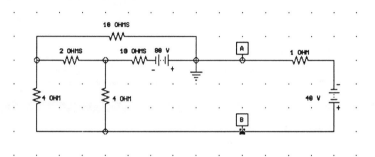

**Fig. 2.2-1**

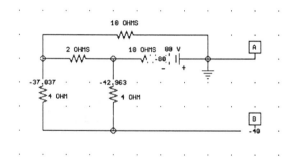

**Fig. 2.2-2** Results of simulation with open circuit across A − B

*Simulation*

To determine the Thevenin equivalent circuit use the standard open circuit and short circuit tests. Then

$$V_{\text{Thevenin}} = \text{Output open circuit voltage}$$

$$R_{\text{Thevenin}} = \frac{\text{Output open circuit voltage}}{\text{Output short circuit current}}$$

The open circuit results are shown in Fig. 2.2-2. The output voltage at terminal B is −40 V. Terminal A is obviously at 0 V.

The short circuit results are shown in Fig. 2.2-3. The output current clearly is the sum of the two currents through the 4 Ω resistors:

$$I_{\text{(short circuit)}} = -(8.4656 + 14.392)/4 = -5.7144 \, \text{A}$$

Consequently

$$V_{\text{th}} = -40 \, \text{V}$$
$$R_{\text{th}} = (-40)/(-5.7144) = 7.00 \, \Omega$$

Connecting the rest of the circuit (1 Ω and 40 V source) to the Thevenin equivalent leads directly to a 10 A current in the load. This is confirmed by direct simulation, as in Fig. 2.2-4.

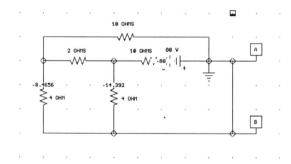

**Fig. 2.2-3** Results of simulation with short circuit across A − B

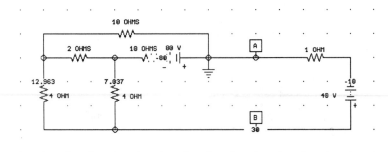

**Fig. 2.2-4**   Overall circuit voltages

### 2.2.2   A series – parallel *RLC* circuit

*Analysis*

Consider the circuit shown in Fig. 2.2-5. Sinusoidal voltage and current magnitudes are *always* given as root-mean-square (RMS) quantities unless otherwise specified. However, MINNIE requires, and produces, **peak** values (i.e. $\sqrt{2} \times$ RMS).

1. Determine the effective (root-mean-square) value of the current delivered by the source.
2. Determine the RMS (effective) value of the voltage across the load, and its phase relative to that of the source.
3. Determine the RMS value of the current through the load, and its phase relative to that of the source.
4. Confirm your numerical results by simulation.

When setting up your analysis profile you should consider carefully your frequency range requirements. A possible analysis profile is shown in Fig. 2.2-6. Note the restricted frequency range and number of points, and the linear scale. A single frequency, one point profile could also be used.

Figure 2.2-7 shows the source and load current magnitudes and

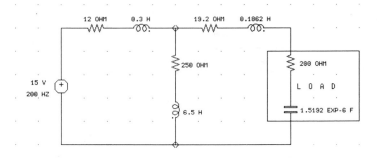

**Fig. 2.2-5**

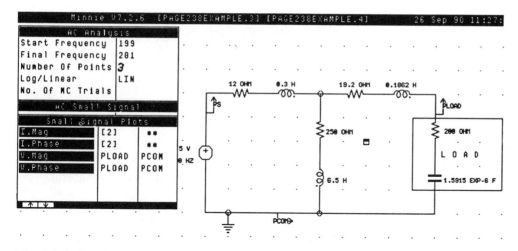

**Fig. 2.2-6**   Possible analysis profile

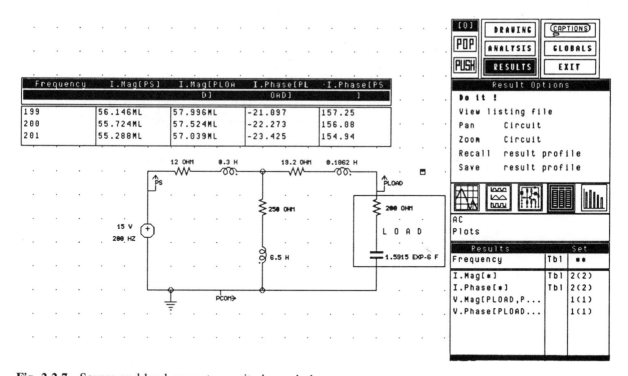

**Fig. 2.2-7**   Source and load current magnitudes and phases

| Frequency | V.Mag[PLOH D.PCOM] | V.Phase[PL OAD.PCOM] |
|---|---|---|
| 199 | 31.359 | -89.389 |
| 200 | 30.97 | -90.466 |
| 201 | 30.577 | -91.519 |

**Fig. 2.2-8** Load voltage magnitude and phase

phases, and Fig. 2.2-8 shows the load voltage magnitude and phase. When displaying results you may find **TABULAR** presentation useful.

## 2.3 TUTORIAL: MUTUAL INDUCTANCE AND TRANSFORMERS

### 2.3.1 Discussion and definitions

Consider the two coils A and B in Fig. 2.3-1. When a current flows through A it produces a magnetic field. This field is proportional to the magnitude of the current, expanding, contracting, going through zero and reversing polarity as appropriate. It will follow the cyclic nature of an alternating current.

A proportion $k_{AB}$ of this field will pass though coil B as it expands and contracts. It will cause an **induced current** in B. Consequently it can be said to **link** or **couple** the two coils. We define

$k_{AB}$: coefficient of coupling of coil A to coil B, giving the proportion of a field produced by coil A which passes through coil B as it expands and then contracts.

In similar manner we define

$k_{BA}$: coefficient of coupling of coil B to coil A, giving the proportion of a field produced by coil B which passes through coil A as it expands and then contracts.

We can now define the overall **Coefficient of Coupling** $k$ for the pair of coils:

$$k = (k_{AB} k_{BA})^{\frac{1}{2}}. \qquad (2.3-1)$$

It should be clear that the coefficients $k$, $k_{AB}$ and $k_{BA}$ *cannot* exceed 1. This fact sets an upper limit to the value of mutual inductance between any pair of coils.

The **mutual inductance** $M$ between the coils A and B may be calculated from their **self inductances** $L_A$ and $L_B$ using the expression

$$M = k(L_A L_B)^{\frac{1}{2}}. \qquad (2.3-2)$$

When $k = 1$ the ratio of turns $n$ is related to the self inductances by the expression

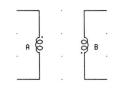

**Fig. 2.3-1**

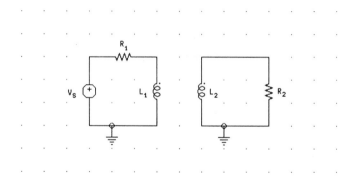

**Fig. 2.3-2** Two loop circuit: the magnetic link between the two inductances has not yet been defined

$$n = N_A/N_B = (L_A/L_B)^{\frac{1}{2}}.\tag{2.3-3}$$

MINNIE will ask you to provide both self inductances and the coefficient of coupling. The mutual inductance is then derived using Eq. 2.3-2 as required.

A consequence of this is that you must be prepared to calculate an appropriate value for $k$ (use Eq. 2.3-2) even though a given problem specifies $M$. However it does have the advantage of ensuring that the resultant values of $M$ are realistic.

### 2.3.2 Procedure

*Setting up the circuit*
In **DRAWING** mode, use the techniques described in section 2.1 to draw the simple two loop circuit shown in Fig. 2.3-2. Notice that both parts of the circuit should be connected to ground. Then use the **VALUES** facility (the **PEN** symbol) to set:

$$V_s = 1\,\text{V} \quad R_1 = 1000\,\Omega \quad R_2 = 10\,\Omega$$

as indicated in Fig. 2.3-2. (You will be shown how to put names and captions on your components and circuits later, in section 3.3.)

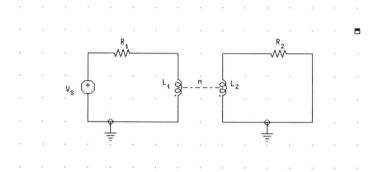

**Fig. 2.3-3** Dashed line joining $L_1$ to $L_2$ showing that these inductances are linked

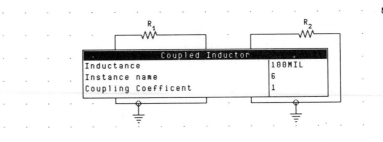

**Fig. 2.3-4** Coupled Inductor menu

Now take the cursor to the centre of $L_1$, press the middle mouse button **M** and *hold it down* while you draw a line to the centre of $L_2$. It is a dashed line, as shown in Fig. 2.3-3. This line informs MINNIE that the coils are linked.

Now press **M** on the **magnifying glass** (PARAM) to select this function. (Note that the cursor takes the shape of the magnifying glass.) Move the cursor to $L_1$ and press **M** to select this component. A Coupled Inductor menu appears across your circuit, as Fig. 2.3-4 but *without values*. This menu has two columns, the right-hand one for you to insert appropriate values (MINNIE will determine the **instance** of a component it is using unless you specify otherwise – for the present ignore this entry).

Press **M** on the right-hand column next to Inductance. The box is highlighted. Then type the required value, $L_1 = 100\,\mathrm{MIL}$. It appears in the input box in the Components Values section at the bottom of the right-hand menu, so press **M** on the highlighted box to accept this value. The box reverts to normal and $100\,\mathrm{MIL}$ appears next to Inductance.

Press **M** on the right-hand column next to Coupling Coefficient. The box is highlighted. Then type the required coupling coefficient – for this tutorial $k = 1$ is satisfactory. Press **M** on the highlighted box to accept this value.

The Coupled Inductor menu will now be as shown in Fig. 2.3-4 (Instance name does not concern you at the moment). Press **M** on the Coupled Inductor menu heading. It vanishes, but the selected values are accepted.

Move the cursor (still the magnifying glass) to $L_2$ and press **M** to select it. This time a larger Inductor menu appears, as Fig. 2.3-5 but *without any values*.

Press **M** on the right-hand column next to Inductance (nominal). The box is highlighted. Type the appropriate value: $L_2 = 1\,\mathrm{MIL}$. Press **M** on the highlighted box. It reverts to normal and the $1\,\mathrm{MIL}$ appears next to Inductance (nominal). The inductor menu should now be as shown in Fig. 2.3-5.

Press **M** on the Inductor menu heading. The menu vanishes, and your circuit should now be ready. As a check, select Values to display all

```
┌──────────────────────▇Inductor▇──────────────────────┬─────────┐
│Inductance (nominal)                                   │1MIL     │
│Instance name                                          │         │
│1st order temperature compensation coefficient [0]     │         │
│2nd order temperature compensation coefficient [0]     │         │
│Initial current through inductor           [0]         │         │
│Number of turns ( * Inductance = Effective)   [1]      │         │
│Non-linear inductor coefficients (Esc., then %)        │         │
│Inductor tolerance (between 0.0 and 1.0)    [0]        │         │
│Inductance designable                       [NO]       │         │
└───────────────────────────────────────────────────────┴─────────┘
```

**Fig. 2.3-5**  Inductor menu

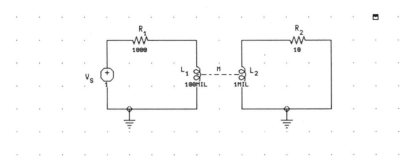

**Fig. 2.3-6**  Coupled circuit ready for testing

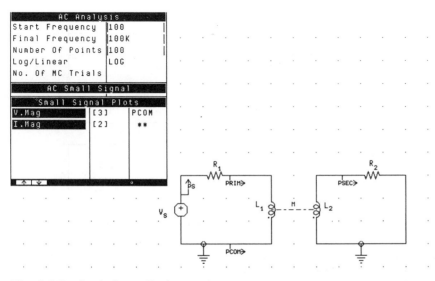

**Fig. 2.3-7**  Analysis profile (you only require AC analysis)

your component values, and you should have Fig. 2.3-6. No value is given for the mutual inductance, but if you have omitted *k* MINNIE will let you know.

*Analysis*

Enter **ANALYSIS** mode, and the `Analysis Options` menu, shown earlier in Fig. 2.1-3, will appear on the top left of the screen. Follow the procedure outlined in section 2.1 to set up the `AC Analysis` profile shown in Fig. 2.3-7.

Press **M** on `Run(int)` to select it and start the simulation. Let MINNIE get on with the simulation – if it is a new circuit MINNIE will ask you for a name (which will be used to identify this circuit and all its derivatives – see section 4.1). When ready, MINNIE will enter `Results` mode.

*Results*

Display your results following the procedures of section 2.1. A possible display is shown in Fig. 2.3-8.

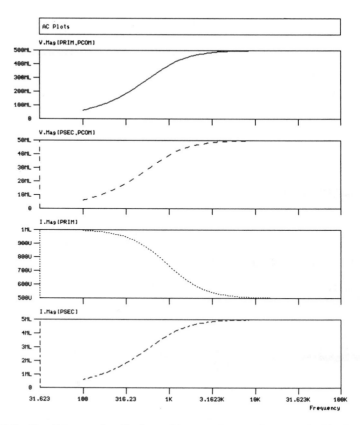

**Fig. 2.3-8**  Possible results display: this transformer is not suitable for use in this circuit at frequencies much below 10 kHz

### 2.3.3 Comments

Note the poor low frequency performance of this transformer. It is due to the relatively high value of the source and load resistances compared with the magnitudes of the inductive reactances $X = j\omega L$.

The defining requirements of an ideal transformer are:

1. the coefficient of coupling $k$ is unity;
2. there are no losses associated with the coils; that is, the coils have no ohmic resistance, and no energy is dissipated in the form of hysteresis or eddy current losses;
3. the self-inductances $L_1$ and $L_2$ are infinite, so that the impedances of any circuit elements in series with $L_1$ and $L_2$, are negligible compared with $X_1$ and $X_2$ respectively.

Conditions (1.) and (2.) are satisfied by this transformer for all frequencies, but condition (3.) is only approximated above about 10 kHz. Note that due to the quadrature relationship between resistance and reactance the approximate requirement set by (3.) is, in this case, less stringent than might be thought. It is

$$(j\omega L)^2 >> R^2$$

and, taking $>>$ as meaning not less than a $\times 10$ ratio, is satisfied in this circuit when $f > 5$ kHz.

## 2.4 EXERCISE: A TWO LOOP *RLC* AND *M* NETWORK

1. Set up the circuit shown in Fig. 2.4-1. The component names are for identification only (you will learn how to set them up later, in section 3.3).

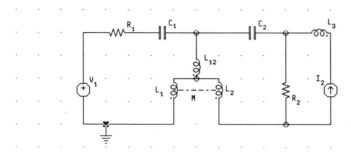

**Fig. 2.4-1** Circuit with mutual inductance

| Coupled Inductor | |
|---|---|
| Inductance | 10 MIL |
| Instance name | 9 |
| Coupling Coefficent | 0.2 |

| Inductor | | |
|---|---|---|
| Inductance (nominal) | | 15 MIL |
| Instance name | | 1 |
| 1st order temperature compensation coefficient | [0] | |
| 2nd order temperature compensation coefficient | [0] | |
| Initial current through inductor | [0] | |
| Number of turns ( * Inductance = Effective) | [1] | |
| Non-linear inductor coefficients (Esc., then %) | | |
| Inductor tolerance (between 0.0 and 1.0) | [0] | |
| Inductance designable | [NO] | |

**Fig. 2.4-2**  Menus for setting up $L_1$, $L_2$ and $M$

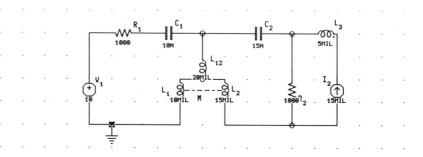

**Fig. 2.4-3**  Circuit showing component values (excepting $M$)

2. Use the **VALUES** facility to set the following component values:

$R_1$ = 1000 Ω      $R_2$ = 1000 Ω
$C_1$ =    10 nF    $C_2$ =    15 nF
$L_{12}$ =   20 mH   $L_3$ =     5 mH
$V_1$ =    10 V     $I_2$ =    15 mA      (AC voltage and current source amplitudes).

3. Use the **PARAM** facility to set

$$L_1 = 10\,\text{mH} \quad L_2 = 15\,\text{mH} \quad M = 2.45\,\text{mH}$$

(work out the required coupling coefficient – see section 2.3).

4. Set up a **RESULTS** profile (similar to Fig. 2.4-4) to determine, over the 100 Hz to 100 kHz frequency range

   (a) magnitudes and phases of voltages at points between $R_1$ and $C_1$, between $C_1$, $C_2$ and $L_{12}$, and between $C_2$, $R_2$ and $L_3$; and
   (b) magnitudes and phases of currents flowing through $C_1$, $C_2$ and $L_{12}$.

(continued on p. 31)

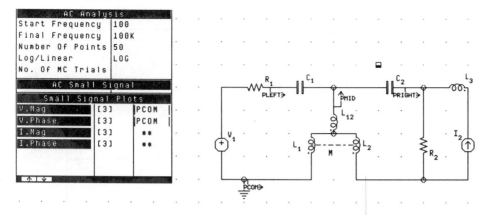

**Fig. 2.4-4**   Possible results profile and probe positions

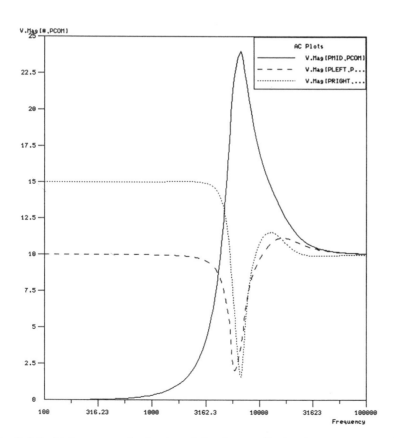

**Fig. 2.4-5**   Voltage magnitudes (graph has been edited to improve presentation, see Chapter 5)

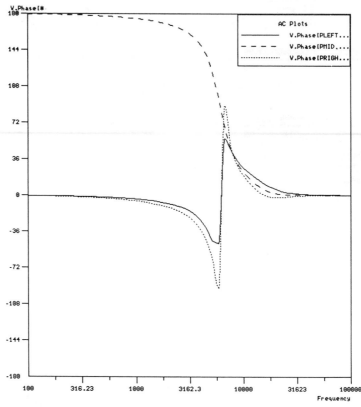

**Fig. 2.4-6**  Voltage phase shifts

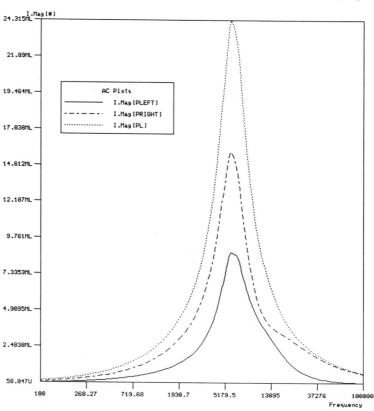

**Fig. 2.4-7**  Current magnitudes

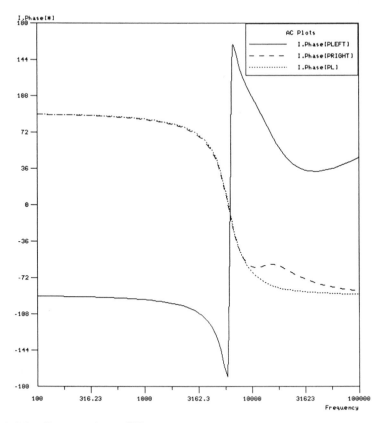

**Fig. 2.4-8**   Current phase shifts

(Measure voltage with respect to ground. Note that as you have not said otherwise MINNIE will assume that the two sources are sinusoids and are in phase. Should you wish to introduce phase differences between the sources you would have to use the **PARAM** facility to set them up)
5. Display your results, similar to those in Figs. 2.4-5, 2.4-6, 2.4-7 and 2.4-8.

# 3 Introducing active devices

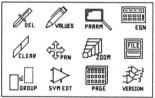

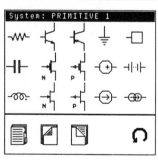

**Fig. 3.1-1** MINNIE start up screen

## 3.1 THE AVAILABLE COMPONENTS

On the start-up screen, Figs. 1.3-1 and 3.1-1, we see the menu headed **System: PRIMITIVE 1**, from which we have already taken components.
Directly below it are three symbols representing:

1. a closed notebook;
2. the notebook with a page turning *backwards*; and
3. the notebook with a page turning *forwards*.

Select (by pressing **M**) **PRIMITIVE 1** *or* the closed notebook, and obtain the list of **Component Pages** of Fig. 3.1-2. The asterisks indicate the pages at present available to us (which at this stage is only **PRIMITIVE 1**). (To deselect this menu, press **M** anywhere outside its box).
Press **M** on the page-turning symbols. The menu vanishes, but the other device pages do *not* appear because we have not yet made them available. Re-open the list, and this time select **PRIMITIVE 2**. Repeat (re-open as necessary) for **PRIMITIVE 3** and for **Discrete Components**. The page contents (components) are shown in Fig. 3.1-3.
The last item on the **Component Pages** list is **Local : Page**

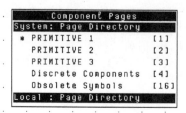

**Fig. 3.1-2** Component Pages list

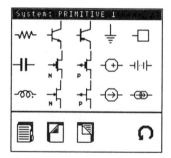

**Fig. 3.1-3(a)** Primitive 1

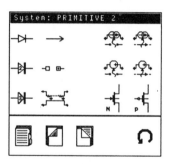

**Fig. 3.1-3(b)** Primitive 2

**Fig. 3.1-3(c)** Primitive 3

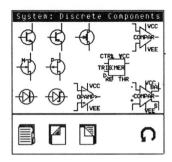

**Fig. 3.1-3(d)** Discrete Components

Directory. The advanced user may create new pages of components which will be listed here – for details see the *User Guide*[1].

## 3.2 DRAWING ACTIVE DEVICES

Remember the mouse keys available to you:

        **L**: left mouse key rotates position marker
        **M**: middle mouse key *all* selection and deselection
        **R**: right mouse key cursor movement

Now enter the start up screen, and then proceed as described below.

### *Active elements*

Move the position marker to some empty region of the screen, and note its position and orientation.

   Move the cursor to a **bipolar transistor symbol (npn** or **pnp)** on the **PRIMITIVE 1** component menu. Press **M**, and note that the device ap-

---

[1] *MINNIE User Guide*: should be available in your system room or from your system advisory staff.

**Fig. 3.2-1** (a) Initial position and orientation of marker (b) First position of npn bipolar

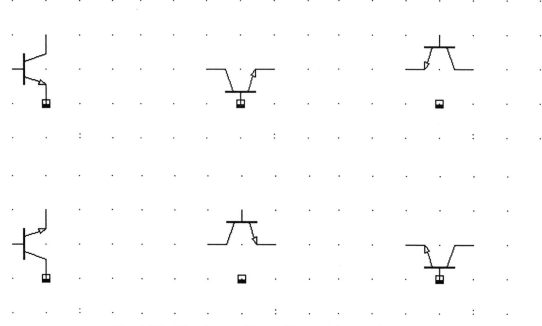

**Fig. 3.2-2** The six possible positions of the npn bipolar of Fig. 3.2-1

pears with its base connected to the grid point where the position marker was, and that the marker itself moves to the *emitter's* grid point, as shown in Fig. 3.2-1. Note how the device orientation is determined by the original position of the black half of the marker.

Now use the rotation procedure described in section 1.5. Observe how the device rotates, as shown in Fig. 3.2-2 and note particularly:

1. that each time a different terminal attaches to the marker's original grid point;
2. that the six possible device positions consistent with the original orientation of the marker are all available; and

3. that the marker remains stationary during device rotations, so that its position with respect to the device changes.

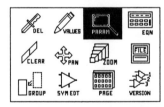

*Device type*
You must tell MINNIE what the active device can do (i.e. what its characteristics are). It is possible to enter device characteristics (in terms of physical data, not 4-terminal parameters (h-parameters etc.)). However it is easier for us to make use of **default devices** or of **library devices**.

Move the cursor to the magnifying lens (**PARAM**) and select it, as shown in Fig. 3.2-3.

Now move the cursor (magnifying lens) on to your transistor, and press **M**. A menu will appear in the middle of the screen, dependent on the type of device (npn, pnp, etc.). For npn bipolars it is shown in Fig. 3.2-4.

Most of the items on this menu are irrelevant to your purpose (you may use them some time, when you have more experience) so concentrate on the first one: **Model Name**.

Move the cursor to this choice (in the left column) and note how a box appears round it, as shown in Fig. 3.2-4. Select it (by pressing **M**), and a new menu appears, as shown in Fig. 3.2-5.

Under **Examine** you will find a list of items, some of which appear highlighted – these are the names of the three libraries available to you:

**Fig. 3.2-3** Select **PARAM** to specify active device characteristics (and also characteristics of AC voltage or current sources)

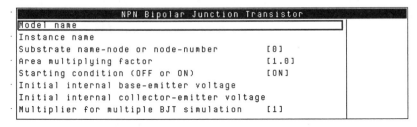

**Fig. 3.2-4** Initial menu for npn bipolar model selection

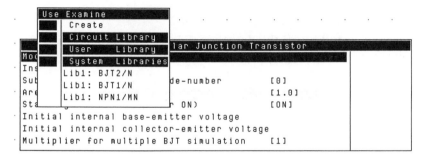

**Fig. 3.2-5** Libraries and device models associated with System: PRIMITIVE 1

```
                    NPN Bipolar Junction Transistor
Model name                                                BJT1/N
Instance name
Substrate name-node or node-number          [0]
Area multiplying factor                     [1.0]
Starting condition (OFF or ON)              [ON]
Initial internal base-emitter voltage
Initial internal collector-emitter voltage
Multiplier for multiple BJT simulation      [1]
```

**Fig. 3.2-6**   As Fig. 3.2-4, but now showing device model selected

1. **Circuit Library**. As you have not yet chosen any devices (from the system library or user library) for the current circuit it is empty.
2. **User Library**. This refers to models of devices (in this case, npn bipolars) which are available only to those who are working within the current user directory. At present it is empty.
3. **System Libraries**. These libraries are available to all users of MINNIE on a given system (such as the one you are on at the moment). Under it you will probably find the three npn bipolars shown in Fig. 3.2-5.

You will also find **Create** for defining your own devices. You can leave that for later.

If you select an available item in this right-hand (**Examine**) column you can examine its parameters. This is not too helpful at this stage. If instead you press **M** in the left-hand column, under **Use**, you are choosing it for your active device. Note that you are returned to the previous menu, but with the device type you have selected now inserted in the right-hand column next to **Model name**, as shown in Fig. 3.2-6.

(Note that the next time you look at the Fig. 3.2-5 menu the device you have selected for your circuit will appear in the **Circuit Library**.)

Now move the cursor to the menu heading and press **M** to deselect it. The menu should then vanish. Move the cursor to the magnifying lens (**PARAM**) and press **M** to deselect it too.

The device type should now be stuck to your device, but is not visible, so to check this select **VALUES**. All values *and* device types should now appear on your circuit as selected. You can then de-select **VALUES**.

*Practice session*
Work your way through the demonstration of this chapter using an npn bipolar from the **Discrete Components** menu. You should get the results

```
      DCL NPN Bipolar Junction Transistor
Model name                        T2N2222
Instance name
BEFAF
TAUF
```

**Fig. 3.2-7**   **Discrete Components**: npn bipolar menu

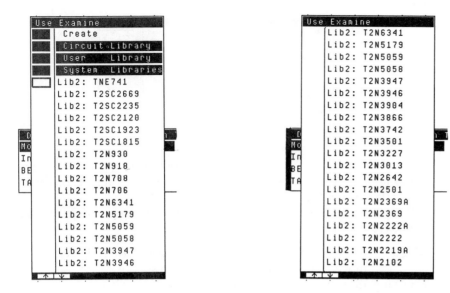

**Fig. 3.2-8** `Discrete Components`: system library (in two sections – use the small arrows at the bottom to scroll the list)

shown in Figs. 3.2-7 and 3.2-8. Note how the little arrows at the bottom of the `System Libraries` menu can be used: press **M** *carefully* on them to **scroll** the device list. This technique is used extensively by MINNIE.

## 3.3   CAPTIONS

Without identification your hard copy (printer output) will be lost in the paper mountain, so put your name on all your diagrams. For this you need to use **captions**.

*Adding captions*
You can now think of adding captions to your circuits. To illustrate the process you might add a title to a circuit. For simplicity use the previous low pass *RC* circuit.

1. Select **CAPTIONS** from the top right-hand menu. The `Captions` menu appears at the top right of the screen. The choices are reasonably obvious so this menu is not shown here.

**Fig. 3.3-1**   Captions working area: the choices are `SMALL/BIG` and `FLOAT/FIX`

**Fig. 3.3-2**

2. Select **ADD** (to add a caption). The caption working area appears in the middle of the screen, as shown in Fig. 3.3-1. Press **M** on **Small** and **FLOAT** to see the alternatives.

   We want a circuit title so it should be rather large, and we want it to **FLOAT**, rather than be **FIXED**.

   **FIXED**    titles are fixed in the drawing area, so if the circuit is moved the caption remains behind.
   **FLOAT**ing titles move with the circuit.

3. Select **BIG** and **FLOAT**.
4. Move the cursor to the left-hand area, under the word **Caption**. Type in your title for the circuit, similar to the example shown in Fig. 3.3-2.
5. When you are happy with your caption deselect the menu head and follow the instructions given on the screen to **drag** the title box to its required position, e.g. as shown in Fig. 3.3-3.

   Drag: press **M** and *keep it pressed* while moving the mouse and hence the title box.

6. When you are happy with the positioning deselect **CAPTIONS**.

*Deletions*
To delete a caption, select the **DELETE** option instead of **ADD**, and proceed as appropriate.

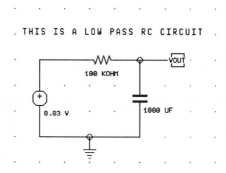

**Fig. 3.3-3** Low pass circuit with title: captions have also been used to show component values

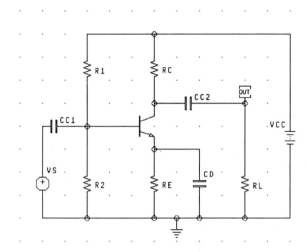

**Fig. 3.4-1.** Single stage common emitter amplifier

*Alterations*
To move, correct or change an existing caption select the **EDIT** option and proceed.

*Additional captions*
You may wish to use a number of captions on your circuit, as shown in Fig. 3.4-1. To do this, immediately after you have finished adding one caption, reselect **ADD** and proceed as above. (Each caption is a separate event.)

## 3.4 TUTORIAL: FREQUENCY RESPONSE OF A SIMPLE COMMON EMITTER AMPLIFIER

*Setting up the circuit*
You now have sufficient information to look at circuits including active devices. Use your expertise to draw a basic common emitter amplifying stage, as shown in Fig. 3.4-1.
   Use the values listed below.

| | | |
|---|---|---|
| $R_1 = 10\,k\Omega$ | $C_{C1} = 0.01\,\mu F$ | $V_{CC} = 15\,V$ |
| $R_2 = 3.9\,k\Omega$ | $C_{C2} = 0.01\,\mu F$ | $V_S = 20\,mV$ |
| $R_E = 680\ \Omega$ | | |
| $R_C = 1.2\,k\Omega$ | $C_D = 10\,\mu F$ | |
| $R_L = 1\,k\Omega$ | | |

Bipolar: **BJT1/N**, npn from the **Primitives 1** system library

Do not forget to put an earth symbol on the common (ground) line. Note that if this earth symbol is not included the analysis is aborted.

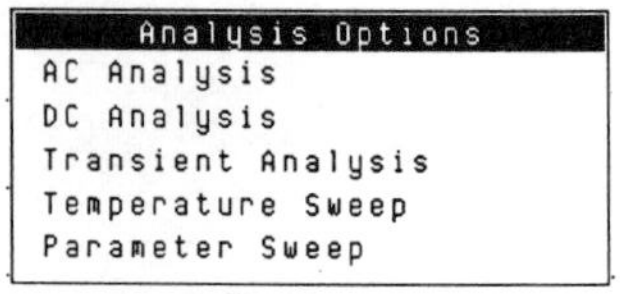

```
    Analysis Options
 AC Analysis
 DC Analysis
 Transient Analysis
 Temperature Sweep
 Parameter Sweep
```

**Fig. 3.4-2** Analysis Options menu

```
       DC Analysis
 DC Transfer Function
 Operating Point
 DC Sensitivities
```

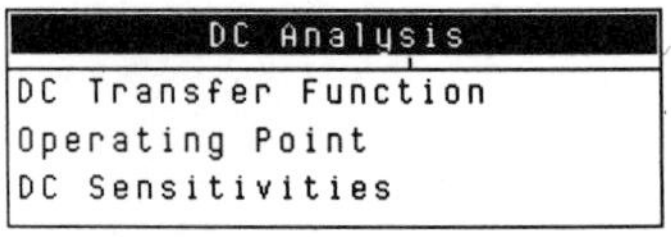

**Fig. 3.4-3** DC Analysis menu

```
       DC Analysis
    Operating Point
```

**Fig. 3.4-4** The DC Operating Points (Bias Conditions) have been selected and will be calculated.

```
        AC Analysis
 Start Frequency  10K
 Final Frequency  2MEG
 Number Of Points 100
 Log/Linear       LOG
 No. Of MC Trials
 AC Small Signal
 Bias solution
 AC Noise Analysis
 AC Distortion Analysis
```

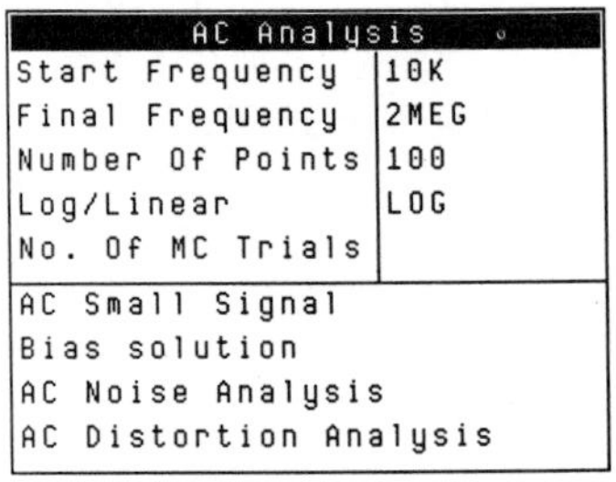

**Fig. 3.4-5** Analysis to be performed at 100 frequencies in the 10 kHz – 2 MHz range; also shows next set of options

(You may get an error message to the effect that there are less than two connections to node 0:0, or something similar.)

*Analysis*
As in section 2.1 you are automatically placed into Analysis Options, as shown in Fig. 3.4-2.

This time you want to look at *both* AC Analysis and DC Analysis. DC Analysis gives you the circuit's biasing conditions which are of fundamental importance in all circuits employing active devices, while AC Analysis gives you the frequency response you are looking for.

It is quite pointless to look at AC performance if the DC conditions are not correct. Consequently, a competent designer of analogue circuits *always* measures the DC biasing voltages first. Only if they agree with the designed or predicted values will the designer proceed to test for AC performance.

The steps to follow are listed below.

1. Select DC Analysis and you will be presented with the menu shown in Fig. 3.4-3.
2. Select Operating Point, as shown in Fig. 3.4-4.
3. Cancel DC Analysis and return to Analysis Options, as shown in Fig. 3.4-2.

   At this point you could, if you so wished, proceed directly to RESULTS mode. In a laboratory situation you would measure the **bias voltages** as soon as possible (to avoid wasting time preparing for useless **signal measurements**).

   With MINNIE, however, the time considerations are somewhat different, and it is quick and easy to set up the AC Analysis immediately. However, do remember that the actual simulation time will be much longer, so for complex circuits it could be just as important to check **bias conditions** first.

   In this instance the circuit is relatively simple, so you can do DC and AC together.
4. Select AC Analysis. Follow the procedure of section 2.1 to set a 10 kHz – 2 Mhz frequency range and a suitable number of frequency points, as shown in Fig. 3.4-5.
5. Select AC Small Signal and you now have the Small Signal Plots menu seen in Fig. 2.1-5. On it specify the analysis results you want and follow the procedure of section 2.1 to select voltage magnitudes, current magnitudes and voltage phases at circuit input (probe Ps), device input (probe Pin) and circuit output (probe Pout).
6. Set voltage gain (dB). At the bottom of the Available Functions menu, hidden in its lower margin, you will find two scrolling arrows. MINNIE uses this scrolling technique whenever menus are too long. Select (by pressing **M**) the upward arrow, the Available Functions should scroll upwards, and V. Gain (dB) should appear.

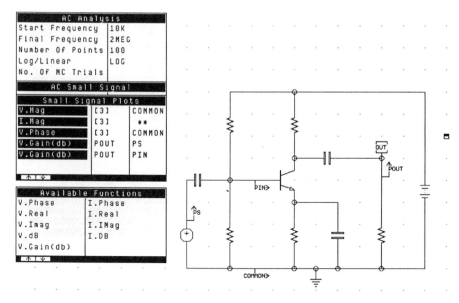

**Fig. 3.4-6** AC results requests; these are the requests MINNIE will send to HSpice.

Select **V.Gain** twice (so that you can define two separate gain functions, **Circuit Voltage** gain $v_{OUT}/v_S$, and **Device Voltage** gain $v_{OUT}/v_{IN}$).

In the **Small Signal Plots** menu you must specify the probes involved in determining **V.Gain (dB)**. In the centre column insert the probes for the corresponding *numerator* voltages (in this case **Pout** for both), while in the right column insert the probes for the *denominator* voltages (**Ps** and **Pin** respectively), and you now have the situation shown in Fig. 3.4-6. (MINNIE will not accept multiple probes in either column for this function).

7. Cancel **AC Small Signal** and Fig. 3.4-5 reappears.
8. Select **Bias solution** and the menus of Fig. 3.4-7 appear. Look at the right-hand side menus and notice that your selections from steps (2.), (5.) and (8.) have appeared (at the appropriate times) under **Selected Analyses**.
9. If you are happy with the situation ask MINNIE to initiate the analysis. On the right-hand menu, under **Analysis Options**, select **Run(int)** (run interactively). Now let MINNIE/HSpice get on with the job, but read the notices MINNIE puts on the screen.

    (a) If this is a new circuit MINNIE will ask for a name (to identify the necessary files). (MINNIE will wait until you take action).
    (b) If there are obvious errors in the work you have done MINNIE will inform you and ask you to take action. Normally it would be appropriate to abort the analysis and proceed to correct the errors.

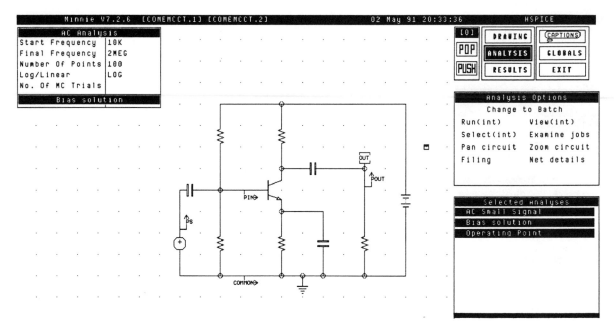

**Fig. 3.4-7** Analysis options have been selected; if no errors have been made you are ready to request the commencement of the analysis

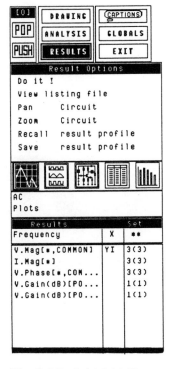

**Fig. 3.4-8** Initial (AC) menu

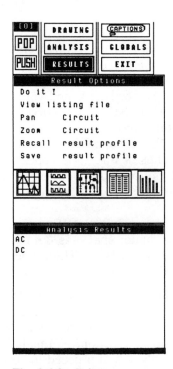

**Fig. 3.4-9** Primary menu

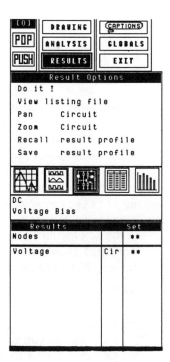

**Fig. 3.4-10** DC results menu

At this point you will know if your circuit is as complete as you think it is. It is my experience that the computer is *never* wrong, and while bugs may well exist in the software, few people ever find them.

10. If everything is okay, **RESULTS** mode is automatically selected for you, as in Fig. 3.4-8. MINNIE assumes that you wish to look at AC results immediately. However, it is better to examine the bias conditions first.

11. Cancel **AC**, and you should now have a screen display similar to that shown in Fig. 3.4-9.

12. Select **DC** and you have Fig. 3.4-10. Note that **Voltage Bias** has been selected for you, and that **Voltage** will be displayed on the circuit diagram at the appropriate points.

13. Select **Do it!**

    The DC voltages (**bias conditions**, **quiescent conditions**) appear directly on your circuit, as shown in Fig. 3.4-11. Check these values with particular care. Is your active device correctly biased?

14. Alternative **Display Options**: MINNIE can provide a more graphic representation of circuit voltages. At the bottom of the right-hand menu on Fig. 3.4-11, select **Boxes**. We now get Fig. 3.4-12, in which the magnitudes of voltages are represented by black squares. The *sides* of the squares (*not* their areas) are proportional to the voltage magnitudes. This gives a visual (but inaccurate) representation which can be useful for fault finding in complex circuits.

15. When you are satisfied that the DC conditions are correct it is time to examine the AC performance, so display **Small Signal** results:

    (a) Cancel **Results** on circuit option (because you now want to display AC responses on graphs). You are returned to the menu of Fig. 3.4-10.

    (b) Cancel **DC**. You are returned to the primary menu of Fig. 3.4-9.

    (c) Cancel **AC**. You are now back to the **AC** menu of Fig. 3.4-8, where MINNIE had first placed you when entering **Results** mode.

    Refer back to section 2.1 and display your results. Typical displays are shown in Figs. 3.4-13, 3.4-14 and 3.4-15.

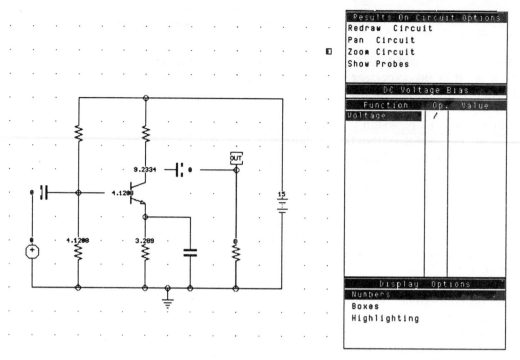

**Fig. 3.4-11**   DC bias results: $V_B = 4.1208\,\text{V}$, $V_E = 3.289\,\text{V}$, $V_C = 9.2334\,\text{V}$

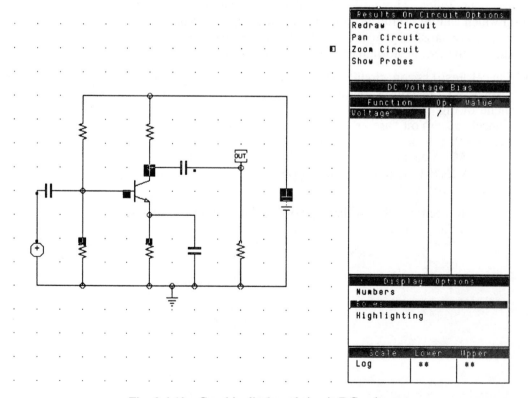

**Fig. 3.4-12**   Graphic display of circuit DC voltages

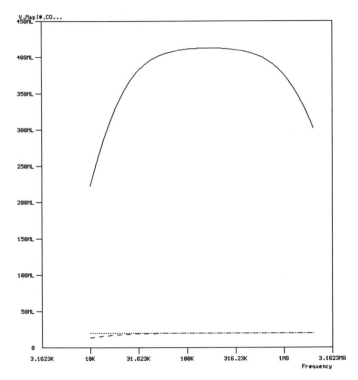

**Fig. 3.4-13**   Circuit signal voltages; single plot option, common Y axis

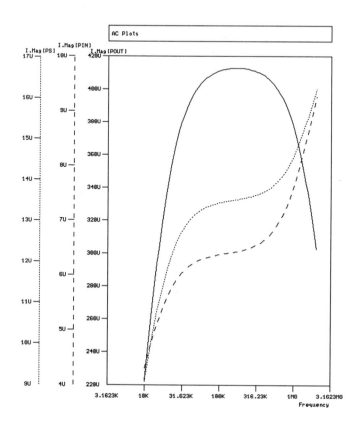

**Fig. 3.4-14**   Circuit current magnitudes; single plot option, independent Y axis; the type of line used – continuous, dotted or dashed – links each curve to its Y axis scale

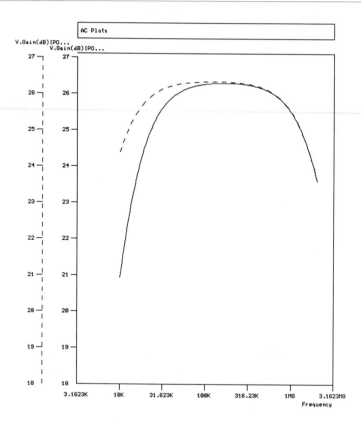

**Fig. 3.4-15** Circuit and device voltage gains, dB; single plot option, independent Y axis

# File and analysis features $\boxed{4}$

## 4.1 FILING SYSTEM

### 4.1.1 File organization and identification

The MINNIE file structure is based on the separate storage of circuits, analysis profiles and results, and it is possible to call independently for these different parts of a previous simulation.

This organization permits considerable flexibility. For example, it is possible, where suitable, to use an analysis profile, set up for one version of a circuit, with a different version of the circuit (although both circuit and analysis profile must belong to the same `Design Directory` – see Fig. 4.1-1 below). It is also possible to look at existing results without having to call for the corresponding circuit and for the analysis profile.

The first time you run an analysis on a *new* circuit MINNIE asks you to give it a **name**. (The rules governing names are set out in section 2.1.) This name identifies a `Design Directory`, which will contain *all* files (drawing, analysis and results) relating to that circuit, and to its future modifications. If the chosen name is **comem** (for **com**mon **emi**tter), the `Design Directory` will be `COMEM.PKG.DESIGN` where:

`COMEN` is the chosen name;
`PKG` is a three letter identifier for the simulator **pack**age e.g. hsp for HSpice, phi for Philpac, etc., and
`DESIGN` is the word to identify *all* `Design Directories`.

Within this directory you find:

1. **Circuit files** as in Fig. 4.1-2, of the form `COMEM.m.CIR`, where

   `COMEM` is the name;
   `m` is the number of this version of this circuit; and
   `CIR` identifies this as a circuit file.

   New circuit files are usually created manually or automatically.

   (a) Manually created circuit files.

       (i) For *new* designs, use the `Write` facility. This enables a new design to be saved without performing an analysis. MINNIE will request a new name, and create a new design directory for this circuit and its future modifications.

```
Design Directories
COMEM.HSP.DESIGN
LOWPASS.HSP.DESIGN
```

**Fig. 4.1-1**

(a)

(b)

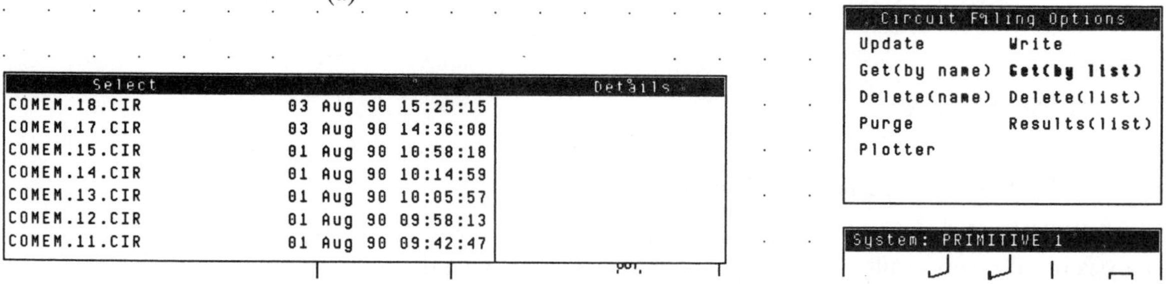

```
Select                                    Details
COMEM.18.CIR        03 Aug 90 15:25:15
COMEM.17.CIR        03 Aug 90 14:36:08
COMEM.15.CIR        01 Aug 90 10:58:18
COMEM.14.CIR        01 Aug 90 10:14:59
COMEM.13.CIR        01 Aug 90 10:05:57
COMEM.12.CIR        01 Aug 90 09:58:13
COMEM.11.CIR        01 Aug 90 09:42:47
```

```
Circuit Filing Options
Update          Write
Get(by name)    Get(by list)
Delete(name)    Delete(list)
Purge           Results(list)
Plotter
```

```
System: PRIMITIVE 1
```

**Fig. 4.1-2** (a) On the left are listed circuit files, most recent version on top, with the date and time created. The right column will either be blank or contain a brief Circuit Title. (b) This menu shows the file handling options available in Drawing mode. Get (by list) was used to obtain the list of circuit files.

    (ii) For *modifications* to existing designs, use the Update facility. When a design is changed you can save these changes, creating a new version of the circuit. The name of the circuit does not change, but the version number is incremented.

        Note that Update will, if requested, prepare a new file even when there are *no* changes to the circuit. The date remains unchanged though the version number is, of course, updated.

During both these processes you are given the opportunity to add (or modify) first a brief Circuit Title, and then a longer (up to three lines) Circuit Description, useful for outlining the changes made.

(b) Automatically created circuit files.

    (i) *New* designs: when you select Run(int) you are asked for a name, as outlined in section 2.1. If the analysis is successfully completed a new Design Directory is created as well as the new file.

    (ii) *Modifications* to existing designs: when you change the circuit, select Run(int), and the analysis is then successfully completed.

(c) Optionally, when you change the circuit and then exit, or clear the circuit, before performing an update. MINNIE will offer you the option to perform an automatic update.

2. **Analysis profile files** as in Fig. 4.1-3, of the form COMEM.n.ANA, where

    COMEM is the name;

    n is the number of this version of the results profile for this circuit; and

(a) (b)

| Select | | Details |
|---|---|---|
| COMEM.30.ANA | 03 Aug 90 15:39:51 | Automagically filed |
| COMEM.29.ANA | 03 Aug 90 15:34:50 | Automagically filed |
| COMEM.28.ANA | 03 Aug 90 15:30:18 | Automagically filed |
| COMEM.27.ANA | 03 Aug 90 15:19:10 | Automagically filed |
| COMEM.26.ANA | 03 Aug 90 14:34:33 | Automagically filed |
| COMEM.23.ANA | 01 Aug 90 11:28:44 | Automagically filed |
| COMEM.22.ANA | 01 Aug 90 11:24:07 | Automagically filed |
| COMEM.21.ANA | 01 Aug 90 10:07:08 | Automagically filed |
| COMEM.20.ANA | 01 Aug 90 10:07:08 | Automagically filed |



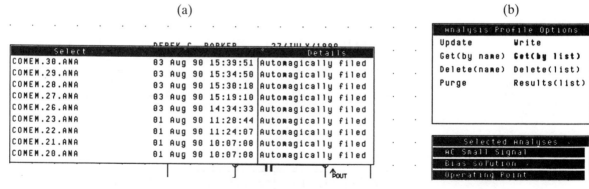

**Fig. 4.1-3** (a) On the left are listed the analysis files, with creation date and time. The right column indicates filing process used. (b) `Analysis` mode filing options are the same as for `Drawing` mode but without the `Plotter` option.

`ANA` identifies this as an analysis profile file.

New analysis profile files are created manually or automatically.

(a) Manually

   (i) with a *new* name, using the `Write` facility when first creating the analysis profile, or when you wish to save it under another name; or

   (ii) with the *current* name, using the `update` facility to create new versions of the analysis file.

   Again you are offered the opportunity to add a description to each new file.

(b) Automatically, when a new analysis is successfully completed and you then `exit` without performing an update.

3. **Result files** as in Fig. 4.1-4. These files are not directly visible to the user. They may be called from the `Drawing` and the `Analysis` mode

Results available for COMEM

| Cir:Ana: Creation date | Circuit details | Analysis details |
|---|---|---|
| 18: 30: 03 Aug 90 15:42:39 | | Automagically filed |
| 18: 29: 03 Aug 90 15:37:24 | | Automagically filed |
| 18: 28: 03 Aug 90 15:33:15 | | Automagically filed |
| 18: 27: 03 Aug 90 15:27:46 | | Automagically filed |
| 17: 26: 03 Aug 90 14:46:20 | | Automagically filed |
| 15: 23: 01 Aug 90 11:39:05 | | Automagically filed |
| 15: 22: 01 Aug 90 11:29:23 | | Automagically filed |
| 14: 21: 01 Aug 90 10:21:59 | | Automagically filed |
| 13: 20: 01 Aug 90 10:13:50 | | Automagically filed |



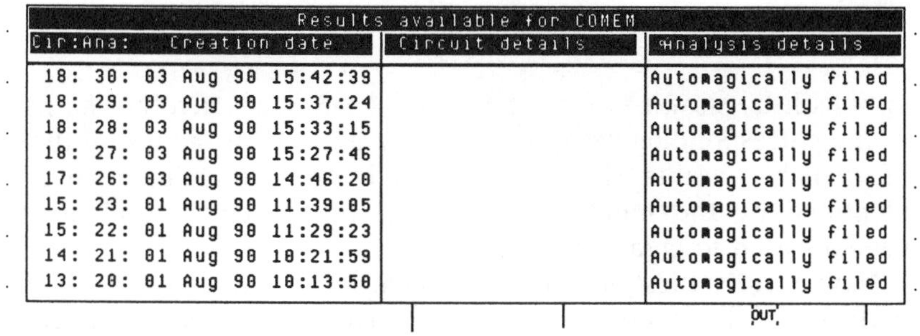

**Fig. 4.1-4** 18:30 in the top set indicates that the result was created by circuit `Comem.18.CIR` and analysis profile `Comem.30.ANA.`, at the time also given. In the other two columns you can access details for the circuit and analysis profile files respectively.

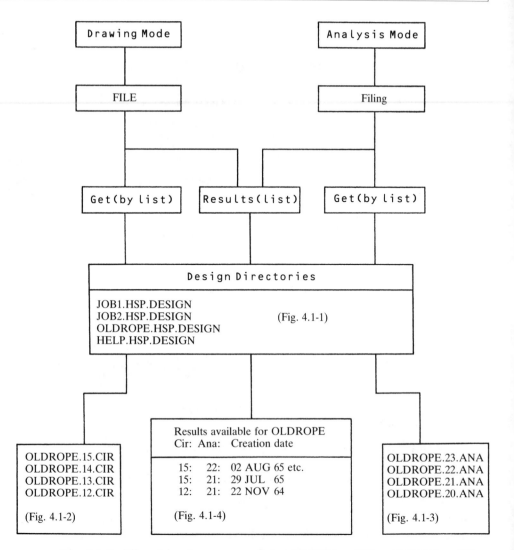

**Fig. 4.1-5** File retrieval sequences. Select `OLDROPE.m.CIR` or `OLDROPE.n.ANA` or `m: n: date` as appropriate.

options lists, shown in Figs. 4.1-2 and 4.1-3, respectively. The name of the corresponding `Design Directory` appears at the top of the list of available results. These are listed in the left column, and are identified by the numbers, $m$ and $n$, of the circuit and analysis versions used to create them.

New results files are created whenever a successful analysis is performed. They are automatically saved, with the identification described above. However, as running a given analysis profile on a given circuit must always yield the same results, MINNIE will only save one result file for this pair.

### 4.1.2  Retrieving circuits, analysis profiles and results

The retrieval procedure is similar for all situations. The sequence of events and the detailed differences are shown schematically in Fig. 4.1-5.

## 4.2  CALCULATING GAINS, INPUT IMPEDANCES AND OTHER FUNCTIONS

In the `Analysis` mode you instruct MINNIE to prepare analysis requests to be sent to HSpice. Though you have great flexibility in the type of circuit you wish to have analysed, and in the number of points (probes) for which you would like to have the results prepared, you are quite restricted in the types of results you can request from HSpice (basically just magnitude and phase for voltage and current plus voltage gain).

To resolve this problem MINNIE has the ability to **post-process** the results it receives from HSpice: it can perform mathematical operations on these results. These operations are defined and carried out in `RESULTS` mode. When you get to the point at which you are considering how to display the results you can instruct MINNIE to carry out fairly complex mathematical operations.

The mathematical functions available are listed below.

| Functions | Representations |
|---|---|
| Basic arithmetic | $+$  $-$  $*$  $/$ |
| Square root | SQRT |
| Absolute value | ABS |
| | |
| Exponential | EXP |
| Natural (base e) logarithm | LN |
| Base 10 logarithm | LOG |
| | |
| Sine | SIN |
| Cosine | COS |
| Tangent | TAN |
| | |
| arc Sine   $(\sin^{-1})$ | ARCSIN |
| arc Cosine   $(\cos^{-1})$ | ARCCOS |
| arc Tangent   $(\tan^{-1})$ | |
| for $0° < \theta < 90°$ | ARCTAN |
| for $0° < \theta < 180°$ | ARCTAN2 |
| | |
| Hyperbolic Sine | SINH |
| Hyperbolic Cosine | COSH |
| Hyperbolic Tangent | TANH |
| | |
| Differentiation $(dy/dx)$ where: | DIFF $(y,x)$ |
| $y$ is a result (a *dependent* variable); | |
| $x$ is the *independent* variable (if more than one, the first one listed). | |
| $\pi = 3.141592654359$ | PI |

For many purposes you will want more than the HSpice results. You will want the other **transfer functions** (current gain $A_i$, forward transfer conductance $g_m$ and forward transfer resistance $r_m$) and the **impedances** (input impedance $Z_{IN}$ and output impedance $Z_{OUT}$). Note that the magnitudes of *all* the transfer functions and of $Z_{IN}$ can be calculated from the results MINNIE can obtain directly from HSpice.

However, the magnitude of $Z_{OUT}$ cannot be calculated from this data – $V_{OUT}/I_{OUT}$ simply yields the effective load impedance (Ohm's Law). Other techniques are required, such as the measurement of $V_{OUT}$ for two different load conditions, so MINNIE is not be able to produce $Z_{OUT}$ without your external help. (See section 4.4.)

## 4.3 TUTORIAL: CURRENT GAIN AND INPUT IMPEDANCES OF THE COMMON EMITTER

Set up the common emitter amplifier as in section 3.4, and arrange the same probes and analysis requests.

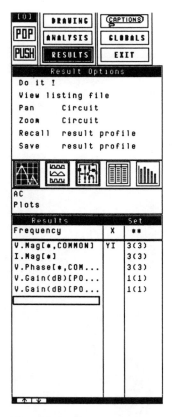

**Fig. 4.3-1** Box set up in results menu

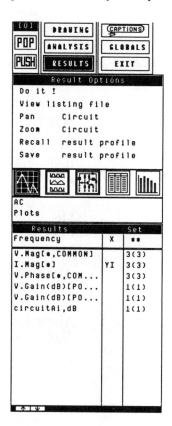

**Fig. 4.3-2** Circuit gain (dB) appears in results menu

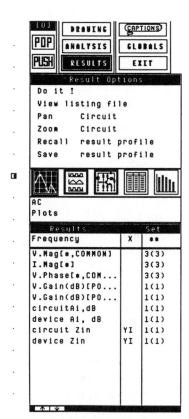

**Fig. 4.3-3** The full set of requests appear in results menu

*Current gain in decibels*

When the analysis is finished MINNIE automatically goes to **RESULTS** mode, **AC**, **Plots**, as in Fig. 3.4-8. Move the cursor to form the empty box as shown in Fig. 4.3-1. Select this box, and another, larger, box appears across the circuit.

Type in

$$\text{circuit} A_i \text{ (dB)} = 20 * \text{LOG(I.MAG[Pout]/I.MAG[Ps])}$$

(If you are using other probe names modify as appropriate).

Press **M** on this large box's heading, and see that circuit current gain appears in the original small box, and thus is added to your list of items that may be displayed, as in Fig. 4.3-2.

Repeat this procedure for

Device $A_i$ (dB) = 20 * log($\langle$collector current$\rangle$ / $\langle$base current$\rangle$)
$Z_{IN}$ (device)    = $\langle$base voltage$\rangle$ / $\langle$base current$\rangle$
$Z_{IN}$ (circuit)    = $\langle$base voltage$\rangle$ / $\langle$circuit input current$\rangle$

remembering that dBs are only appropriate for voltage, current and power ratios. Do not use them for impedances!

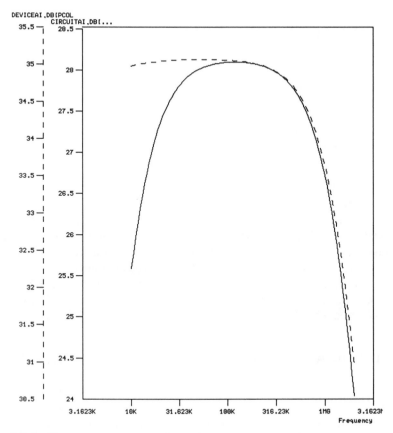

**Fig. 4.3-4** Frequency response of a common emitter amplifier. Current gains, dB. Note the effect of the bias resistors.

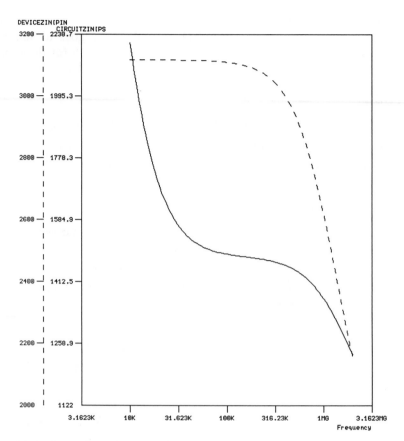

**Fig. 4.3-5** Input impedances. Note the effect of the input coupling capacitor at low frequencies – change it!

It is important to note also that the voltages must be fully defined – the reference probe must not be forgotten.

You should now have something like Fig. 4.3-3. So, now decide how you wish to display these results. As the actual magnitudes of voltages and currents are not too important (since it is the transfer functions and the impedances that you really want), it is reasonable to plot only the calculated values (just as you would normally do in a laboratory situation). Set up appropriate choices for type of display and Y axis, and then select Do it! Typical results are shown in Figs. 4.3-4 and 4.3-5.

## 4.4 TUTORIAL: SOURCE AND/OR OUTPUT IMPEDANCE

### 4.4.1 Discussion

All *linear* circuits, when viewed into any two terminals, can be represented by a Thevenin equivalent circuit (or a Norton equivalent circuit if preferred). The only difference between passive circuits and

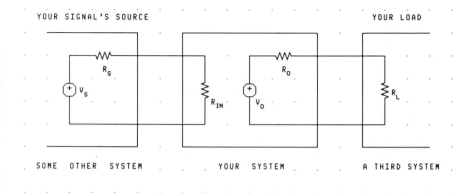

YOUR SIGNAL'S SOURCE                                    YOUR LOAD

SOME   OTHER   SYSTEM              YOUR   SYSTEM          A THIRD SYSTEM

**Fig. 4.4-1** Source voltage $V_S$ and source resistance $R_S$. Output voltage $V_O$ and output resistance $R_O$

those containing active elements is that in the former case the Thevenin voltage source (or Norton current source) is a constant, while for the latter case the source is a variable, a function of some other parameter.

When a linear circuit is acting as a *signal source* its Thevenin voltage source is its effective source voltage $V_S$, while its Thevenin resistance is its effective source resistance $R_S$. Alternatively its Norton current source would be its effective source current $I_S$ (of course the source resistance $R_S$ does not change).

This source resistance $R_S$ is often referred to by the alternative and equally correct name of **output resistance** $R_O$ (or $R_{OUT}$). However, when you are dealing with a circuit which receives signal from some other source, processes it, and then passes it on to a load, it is convenient to use $R_S$ for the Thevenin resistance of the other source, and keep $R_O$ for the Thevenin resistance seen by the load looking into the output terminals of the circuit, as shown in Fig. 4.4-1.

### 4.4.2 Measurement Technique

In Fig. 4.4-1 current in the output circuit is

$$I_O = V_O/(R_O + R_L) = V_L/R_L.$$

Clearly $I_O$ and $V_L$ will change if $R_L$ is changed. This can be used to determine $R_O$ as follows:

1. using $R_{L1}$: measure $V_{L1}$ and calculate $I_{L1}$; and
2. using $R_{L2}$: measure $V_{L2}$ and calculate $I_{L2}$.

Then

$$R_O = \frac{(V_{L2} - V_{L1})}{(I_{L1} - I_{L2})} \qquad (4.4\text{-}1)$$

(You should derive this equation to gain a better understanding of the method.)

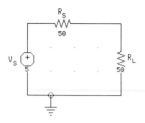

**Fig. 4.4-2**  Test circuit

This is a thoroughly practical method for measuring source/output impedances, and is widely used in laboratory testing. Note that it is the general case of the open-circuit/short-circuit technique ($R_{L1} = \infty$, $R_{L2} = 0$) used for transformer testing and elsewhere.

A simulation on MINNIE is effectively an attempt to do laboratory testing on a computer. Consequently the methodology is the same as that employed on the test bench, and this method is to be used to determine $R_S$ and $R_O$.

Note that *two* measurements/simulation runs are required due to the change of $R_L$. However, the full analysis profile need not be used for the second run as much of the information would have little value.

### 4.4.3  Simulation

*Testing the method*
Set up the simple circuit of Fig. 4.4-2, with $V_S = 5\,V$, $R_S = 50\,\Omega$ and $R_L = 50\,\Omega$, and then using AC Analysis measure the output voltage (probes as shown in Fig. 4.4-3). Present the results in Tabular form, as in Fig. 4.4-4(a).

Change $R_L$ to $25\,\Omega$ and repeat, to obtain data as in Fig. 4.4-4(b). Then calculate $R_S$ from the data and check against circuit value.

*Output impedance of a simple common emitter stage*
Set up a common emitter circuit as shown in Fig. 4.4-5. Note that the capacitor values have been substantially increased to improve low frequency performance. The load resistance is $1\,k\Omega$.

Set up an AC Analysis profile, such as shown in Fig. 4.4-6, to obtain the voltage across the load resistor.

Run the simulation and present your results as graphs as in Fig. 4.4-7 to confirm that your circuit is operating correctly. If satisfied, present them in tabular form to obtain $R_O$ data, as in Fig. 4.4-9(a).

Add a $1\,k\Omega$ parallel to the existing load, as in Fig. 4.4-8, and repeat the simulation. The corresponding results are shown in Figs. 4.4-10 and 4.4-9(b).

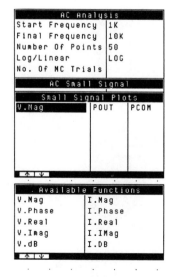

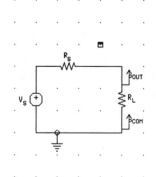

**Fig. 4.4-3**  Analysis profile and probe positions

| Frequency | V.Mag[POUT .PCOM] |
|-----------|-------------------|
| 1000 | 2.5 |
| 1.0471K | 2.5 |
| 1.0965K | 2.5 |
| 1.1482K | 2.5 |
| 1.2023K | 2.5 |
| 1.2589K | 2.5 |
| 1.3183K | 2.5 |
| 1.3804K | 2.5 |
| 1.4454K | 2.5 |
| 1.5136K | 2.5 |
| 1.5849K | 2.5 |
| 1.6596K | 2.5 |
| 1.7378K | 2.5 |
| 1.8197K | 2.5 |
| 1.9055K | 2.5 |
| 1.9953K | 2.5 |
| 2.0893K | 2.5 |
| 2.1878K | 2.5 |
| 2.2909K | 2.5 |
| 2.3988K | 2.5 |
| 2.5119K | 2.5 |
| 2.6303K | 2.5 |
| 2.7542K | 2.5 |
| 2.884K | 2.5 |
| 3.0199K | 2.5 |
| 3.1623K | 2.5 |
| 3.3113K | 2.5 |
| 3.4674K | 2.5 |
| 3.6308K | 2.5 |
| 3.8019K | 2.5 |

| Frequency | V.Mag[POUT .PCOM] |
|-----------|-------------------|
| 1000 | 1.6667 |
| 1.0471K | 1.6667 |
| 1.0965K | 1.6667 |
| 1.1482K | 1.6667 |
| 1.2023K | 1.6667 |
| 1.2589K | 1.6667 |
| 1.3183K | 1.6667 |
| 1.3804K | 1.6667 |
| 1.4454K | 1.6667 |
| 1.5136K | 1.6667 |
| 1.5849K | 1.6667 |
| 1.6596K | 1.6667 |
| 1.7378K | 1.6667 |
| 1.8197K | 1.6667 |
| 1.9055K | 1.6667 |
| 1.9953K | 1.6667 |
| 2.0893K | 1.6667 |
| 2.1878K | 1.6667 |
| 2.2909K | 1.6667 |
| 2.3988K | 1.6667 |
| 2.5119K | 1.6667 |
| 2.6303K | 1.6667 |
| 2.7542K | 1.6667 |
| 2.884K | 1.6667 |
| 3.0199K | 1.6667 |
| 3.1623K | 1.6667 |
| 3.3113K | 1.6667 |
| 3.4674K | 1.6667 |
| 3.6308K | 1.6667 |
| 3.8019K | 1.6667 |

**Fig. 4.4-4**   (a) Results for $R_{L1} = 50\,\Omega$.         (b) Results for $R_{L2} = 25\,\Omega$

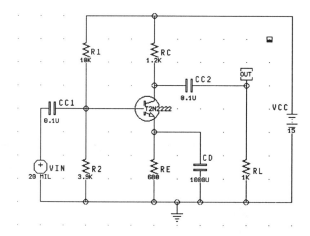

**Fig. 4.4-5**   Common emitter stage, $1\,k\Omega$ load

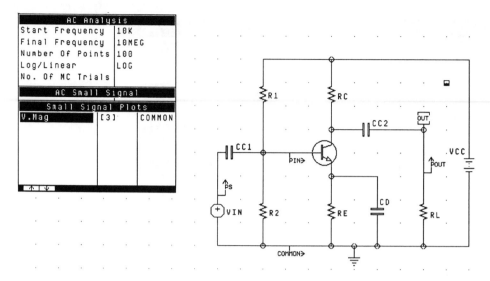

**Fig. 4.4-6**   Possible analysis profile and probes

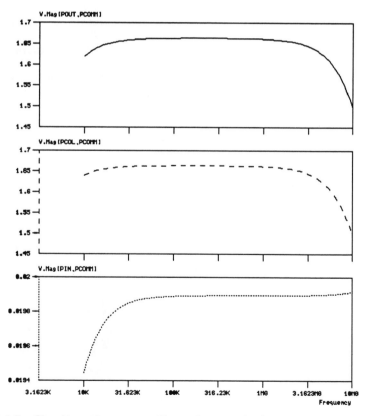

**Fig. 4.4-7**   Circuit performance. Note the greatly improved low frequency results due to increased values of the coupling and emitter bypass capacitors.

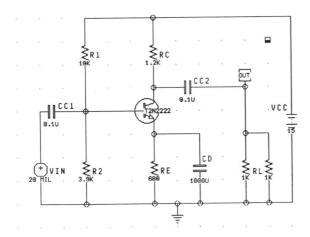

**Fig. 4.4-8** Circuit with $R_\mathrm{L} = 500\,\Omega$

| Frequency | V.Mag[PIN,<br>COMMON] | V.Mag[POUT<br>.COMMON] | V.Mag[PCOL<br>.COMMON] |
|---|---|---|---|
| 28.48K | 19.836ML | 1.6576 | 1.6602 |
| 30.539K | 19.844ML | 1.6583 | 1.6606 |
| 32.745K | 19.85ML | 1.659 | 1.6609 |
| 35.112K | 19.856ML | 1.6595 | 1.6612 |
| 37.649K | 19.861ML | 1.66 | 1.6615 |
| 40.37K | 19.865ML | 1.6604 | 1.6617 |
| 43.288K | 19.869ML | 1.6608 | 1.6619 |
| 46.416K | 19.872ML | 1.6611 | 1.6621 |
| 49.77K | 19.875ML | 1.6614 | 1.6622 |
| 53.367K | 19.877ML | 1.6616 | 1.6623 |
| 57.224K | 19.879ML | 1.6618 | 1.6625 |
| 61.359K | 19.881ML | 1.662 | 1.6626 |
| 65.793K | 19.883ML | 1.6622 | 1.6626 |
| 70.548K | 19.884ML | 1.6623 | 1.6627 |
| 75.646K | 19.885ML | 1.6624 | 1.6628 |
| 81.113K | 19.887ML | 1.6625 | 1.6628 |
| 86.975K | 19.887ML | 1.6626 | 1.6629 |
| 93.26K | 19.888ML | 1.6627 | 1.6629 |
| 100K | 19.889ML | 1.6627 | 1.6629 |
| 107.23K | 19.89ML | 1.6628 | 1.663 |
| 114.98K | 19.89ML | 1.6628 | 1.663 |
| 123.28K | 19.891ML | 1.6629 | 1.663 |
| 132.19K | 19.891ML | 1.6629 | 1.663 |
| 141.75K | 19.891ML | 1.6629 | 1.6631 |
| 151.99K | 19.892ML | 1.663 | 1.6631 |
| 162.97K | 19.892ML | 1.663 | 1.6631 |
| 174.75K | 19.892ML | 1.663 | 1.6631 |
| 187.38K | 19.892ML | 1.663 | 1.6631 |
| 200.92K | 19.892ML | 1.663 | 1.6631 |
| 215.44K | 19.893ML | 1.663 | 1.6631 |

(a)

| Frequency | V.Mag[PIN,<br>COMMON] | V.Mag[POUT<br>.COMMON] | V.Mag[PCOL<br>.COMMON] |
|---|---|---|---|
| 26.561K | 19.851ML | 1.1548 | 1.163 |
| 28.48K | 19.86ML | 1.1554 | 1.1626 |
| 30.539K | 19.867ML | 1.156 | 1.1623 |
| 32.745K | 19.874ML | 1.1565 | 1.162 |
| 35.112K | 19.879ML | 1.157 | 1.1617 |
| 37.649K | 19.884ML | 1.1573 | 1.1615 |
| 40.37K | 19.889ML | 1.1577 | 1.1613 |
| 43.288K | 19.892ML | 1.158 | 1.1611 |
| 46.416K | 19.896ML | 1.1582 | 1.1609 |
| 49.77K | 19.898ML | 1.1584 | 1.1608 |
| 53.367K | 19.901ML | 1.1586 | 1.1607 |
| 57.224K | 19.903ML | 1.1588 | 1.1606 |
| 61.359K | 19.905ML | 1.1589 | 1.1605 |
| 65.793K | 19.906ML | 1.1591 | 1.1604 |
| 70.548K | 19.908ML | 1.1592 | 1.1604 |
| 75.646K | 19.909ML | 1.1593 | 1.1603 |
| 81.113K | 19.91ML | 1.1594 | 1.1602 |
| 86.975K | 19.911ML | 1.1594 | 1.1602 |
| 93.26K | 19.912ML | 1.1595 | 1.1602 |
| 100K | 19.913ML | 1.1595 | 1.1601 |
| 107.23K | 19.913ML | 1.1596 | 1.1601 |
| 114.98K | 19.914ML | 1.1596 | 1.1601 |
| 123.28K | 19.914ML | 1.1597 | 1.16 |
| 132.19K | 19.915ML | 1.1597 | 1.16 |
| 141.75K | 19.915ML | 1.1597 | 1.16 |
| 151.99K | 19.915ML | 1.1597 | 1.16 |
| 162.97K | 19.916ML | 1.1598 | 1.16 |
| 174.75K | 19.916ML | 1.1598 | 1.16 |
| 187.38K | 19.916ML | 1.1598 | 1.1599 |
| 200.92K | 19.916ML | 1.1598 | 1.1599 |

(b)

**Fig. 4.4-9** Tabular presentation of results (a) $R_\mathrm{L} = 1\,\mathrm{k}\Omega$. (b) $R_\mathrm{L} = 500\,\Omega$

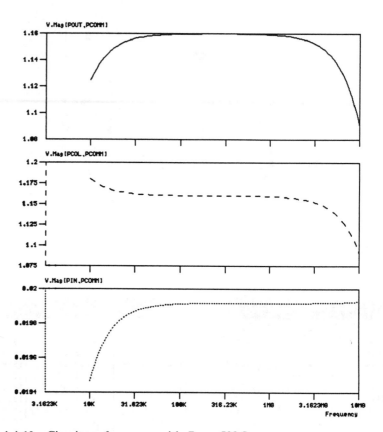

**Fig. 4.4-10**  Circuit performance with $R_L = 500\,\Omega$

Now use Eq. 4.4-1 to calculate the output impedance of the circuit. Assuming that the reactance of the coupling capacitor is negligible, the impedance you have calculated is that of $R_C = 1.2\,\text{k}\Omega$ parallel to the output impedance of the transistor (looking into its collector).

Calculate the output impedance of the bipolar.

### 4.4.4  Comment

The procedure described above is successful in practical applications and is recommended for your laboratory work. However it is showing up what the author believes is an inconsistency in HSpice. Using Eq. 4.4-1 the above results lead to a circuit output impedance of $767\,\Omega$ at $100\,\text{kHz}$, corresponding to a device output impedance of $2123\,\Omega$. This value is too low.

The device used in the simulation is the 2N2222, described in the manufacturer's data books as a silicon planar epitaxial transistor primarily intended for high-speed switching, but also suitable for dc and VHF/UHF amplifiers. It originally appeared in the mid 1960s and is still considered to be suitable for new designs. The data books (1968, 1983) provide the following value ranges for $h_{oe}$:

$$I_C = \quad 1\,\text{mA}: \ 5 < h_{oe} < \ \ 35\,\mu\text{S}$$
$$I_C = 10\,\text{mA}: 25 < h_{oe} < 200\,\mu\text{S}$$

whereas the simulation result leads to

$$h_{oe} = 1/R_{OUT} = 1/2123 = 471\,\mu\text{S} \quad \text{at} \quad I_C = 5\,\text{mA}.$$

If **BJT1/N** from the **PRIMITIVES 1** components page library is used very similar results are obtained for circuit and device output impedances ($782\,\Omega$ and $2236\,\Omega$ respectively).

# 5 Output options

## 5.1 SELECTING YOUR RESULTS FOR DISPLAY

When you enter **RESULTS** mode MINNIE assumes a series of default options. These are unlikely to be the optimum set for your problem. You have already achieved some flexibility by making decisions concerning **single** or **multiple** displays and **independent** or **common** Y axis. You have also decided whether *all* the **V.Mag** results should be displayed or not, *as a group*. This is somewhat limiting when your analysis produces a large set of results, more than can be displayed conveniently on the screen. Ideally you would like to pick and choose *within* a group without having to reset your analysis profile and recalculate your results. MINNIE allows you to do this.

Set up an **AC Analysis** profile for your common emitter circuit as shown in Fig. 5.1-1. For later use also set up, in the **Transient Analysis** menu, a request for **Volt.OutVar** to be simulated at the same four probes (with **COMMON** as reference). You also need the **DC Operating Conditions.** Note the new probe **PCOL** replacing **P5** to permit the

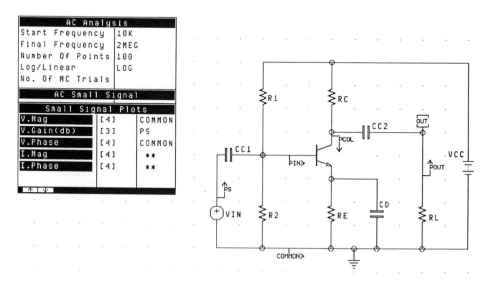

**Fig. 5.1-1** Common emitter circuit and **AC Analysis** profile. Note that probe **P5** used previously has now been replaced by **PCOL**. This is because the currents measured at **P5** would be the same as that measured at **POUT**.

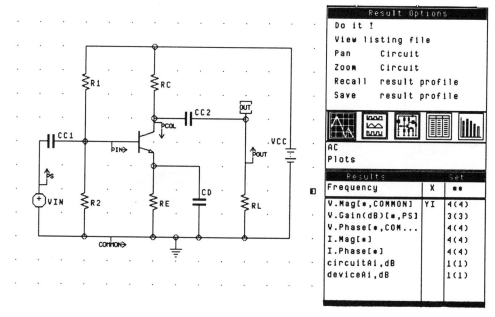

**Fig. 5.1-2** Default Results menu for AC Plots. In Results/Set menu, the third column indicates for each results group the number of probes for which results will be shown, and then the total number for which the result group was calculated.

measurement of the collector current. Run the analysis in the usual way, and MINNIE should present you with the Results menu shown in Fig. 5.1-2.

In the results menu of Fig. 5.1-2, bottom right, you find next to V.Mag[*,COMMON] the default Y axis choice (YI). In the third column you find, under Set, the number of nodes, four, for which MINNIE will display results if requested, followed in brackets by the total number of nodes, also four, for which the variable was calculated.

The equivalent arrangement exists for the other groups of variables, (the Y axis choice is still pending for them).

Obviously you cannot display all the possible plots simultaneously. You would have to decide which ones you want now, and perhaps look at the others later. For this simulation you might wish to display

1. YC   V.Gain(dB)   at **POUT** and **PCOL** with respect to **PS**.
2. YC   V.Phase      at **POUT** and **PCOL**.
3. YC   I.Phase      at **POUT** and **PCOL**.
4. YI   circuit Ai(dB) = 20 * log(I.Mag[POUT]/I.Mag[PS])
5. YI   device Ai(dB) = 20 * log(I.Mag[PCOL]/I.Mag[PIN])

using the Multiple Graph option.

Select the Set box to the right of V.Gain(dB) (press **M** on 3(3)), as shown in Fig. 5.1-3. Note that the relevant probes appear highlighted on the circuit.

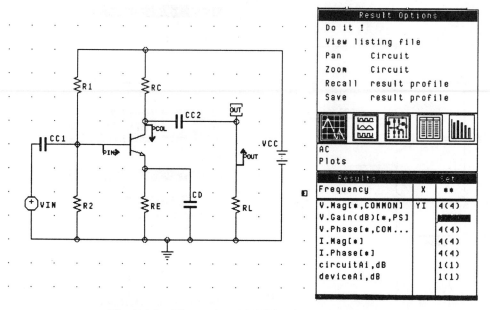

**Fig. 5.1-3** The probes highlighted on the circuit are those for which MINNIE would show results if **V.Gain(dB)** is selected for display

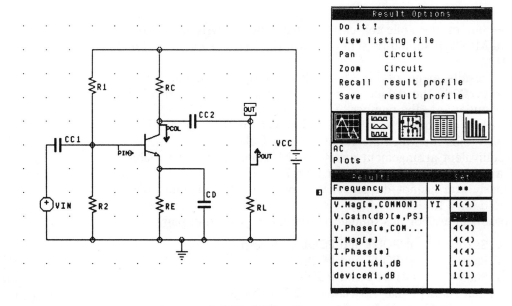

**Fig. 5.1-4** **V.Gain(dB)** will be displayed for two probes only

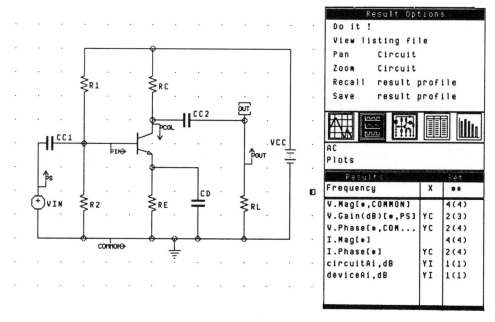

**Fig. 5.1-5**  Final Results display selection menu

Move the cursor to the base of the probe you do not wish to use (**PIN**) and cancel it (press **M** where it joins the circuit). As soon as you cancel a probe it reverts to normal and the **Set** box now reads **2(3)**, as in Fig. 5.1-4. We still have results for three probes, but MINNIE will only display for two probes.

Follow the above procedure to set up the required node choices and Y axis options for the other result groups, as in Fig. 5.1-5. Note that the **Multiple Display** option has been selected. Then **Do it!**

The requested displays are shown in Fig. 5.1-6.

## 5.2   EDITING YOUR Y AXIS

You have now selected the results you want displayed, and have chosen the **Single** or **Multiple Plots** option. On selecting **Do it !** MINNIE will present the graphs using default scales which may not be the most appropriate. Furthermore, even if you were able to predetermine the detailed graph presentation you might still wish to make changes when you see the actual results of the simulation. Under its **Edit** facility MINNIE allows you considerable freedom for adjusting the picture on the screen (and the consequent hard copy you take away) to maximize the benefits obtained, and thus in some situations you may avoid the need to run further simulations.

Carrying on from the preceding section, set up your **Results** menu to display only the two current gains, as in Fig. 5.2-1.

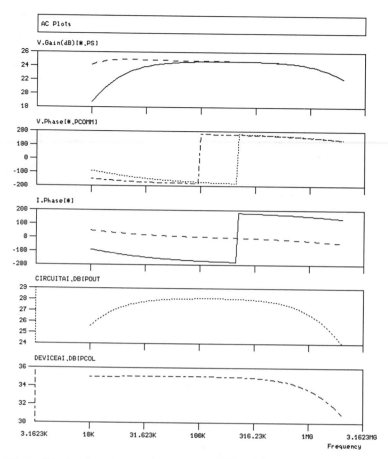

**Fig. 5.1-6** Display for the Results menu of Fig. 5.1-5

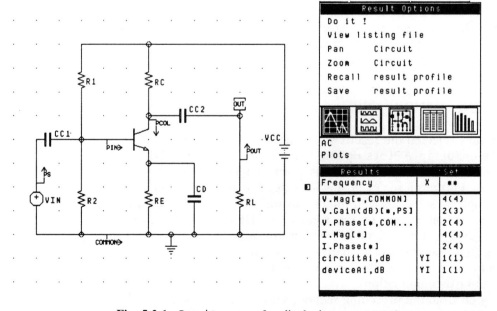

**Fig. 5.2-1** Results menu for displaying current gains

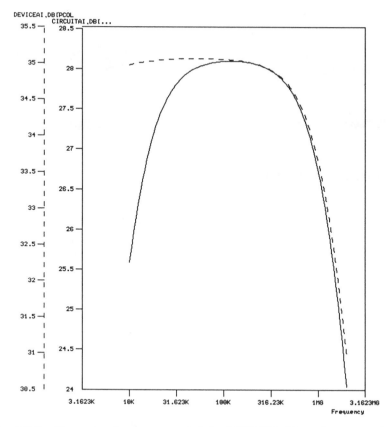

**Fig. 5.2-2** Current gains as presented by MINNIE. Note that even the high frequency slopes cannot be compared because the 0.5 dB intervals on the Y axis are different.

Then `Do it!` and you get the display of Fig. 5.2-2. This display appears to be quite adequate until you realize that you cannot make real comparisons between the two current gains: as they are plotted to different scales you would have to take readings off the graphs and draw fresh ones to get a clearer picture. Note that in this case you *cannot* ask MINNIE to plot them to a common Y axis `(YC)` because they appear on separate lines in the `Results` menu.

To resolve this problem you can use the `Editing` facility. Go to the top right-hand menu, under `Graph Options`, and select `Edit Graph`. The menu of Fig. 5.2-3(a) appears, showing the `Axis Variables` you can edit. Assuming you are happy with the frequency scaling, leave it and select `CIRCUITAI,DB[POUT`.

The `CIRCUITAI,DB[POUT` menu, as in Fig. 5.2-3(b), appears showing the `Y Axis Characteristics` for the circuit current gain.

Looking back at Fig. 5.2-2 you can see that a common Y axis would have to cover the range 24 dB to 35.5 dB (or 36 dB). Return to Fig. 5.2-3(b), and set the `Upper Bound` and `Lower Bound` to `36` and `24` respectively. Set `Smooth Curve` to `YES`, and you now have Fig. 5.2-4(a).

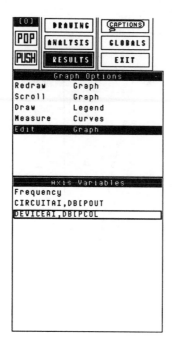
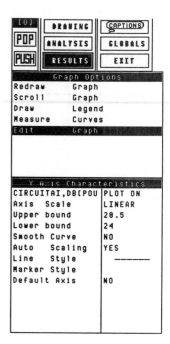

**Fig. 5.2-3** (a) Axis Variables menu (b) Y Axis Characteristics set by MINNIE for Circuit Ai

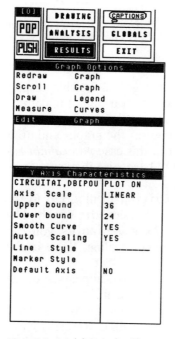
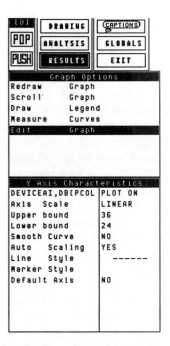

**Fig. 5.2-4** (a) Y Axis Characteristics for circuit Ai after editing (b) Y Axis Characteristics for device Ai after editing

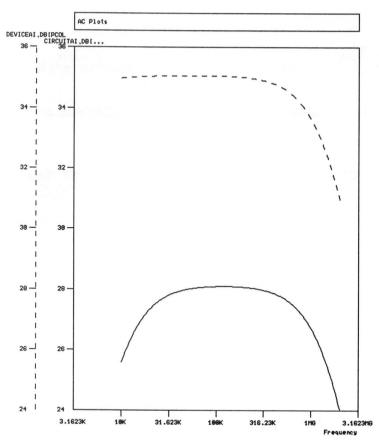

**Fig. 5.2-5** Current gains after editing the Y axis

Take the cursor to the `Y Axis Characteristics` and cancel it to get back to Fig. 5.2-3(a). This time select `DEVICEAI,DB[PCOL` and repeat the above procedure to set its characteristics, as shown in Fig. 5.2-4(b).

When ready move cursor up to `Graph Options` and select `Redraw`. The graphs are redrawn according to your specification, Fig. 5.2-5. It is now much easier to make comparisons between the two graphs.

## 5.3 MEASURING YOUR RESULTS

It is useful at times to have numerical results from the simulation run. Though it is possible to arrange to have some types of results presented in tabular form, for general purposes it is normally more convenient to have the graphical displays and to make appropriate 'measurements' where necessary. Of course MINNIE does not have to measure anything – either the results you want have been calculated and are simply waiting to be selected, or else they will be determined by mathematical interpolation between calculated values.

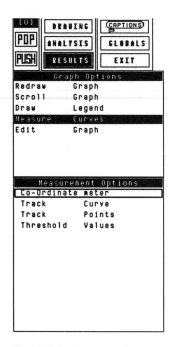

**Fig. 5.3-1** Measure Curves options

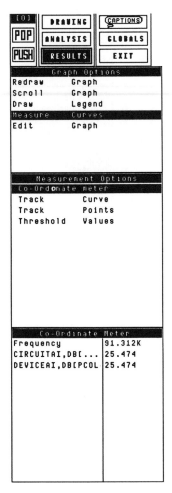

**Fig. 5.3-2** Co-Ordinate
meter: cursor position

Referring back to the edited graphs Fig. 5.2-5, you could be interested in measuring the maximum values of the current gains, the high frequency 'roll off' or slope and the bandwidth determining break frequencies.

Take the cursor to the Graph Options menu, select Measure Curves and you get the Measurements Option menu, as in Fig. 5.3-1. You can now examine the four options to see what they offer you.

1. **Co-Ordinate Meter** Select this option, take the cursor to the graph area, and press **M** (the middle mouse button). In the bottom of the right-hand menu you will find the coordinates of the cursor's position, as in Fig. 5.3-2. You have two Y axis scales (even though you have adjusted them to be equal) so you get two Y readings. Obviously this reading is meaningless unless the cursor has been placed on a significant point.

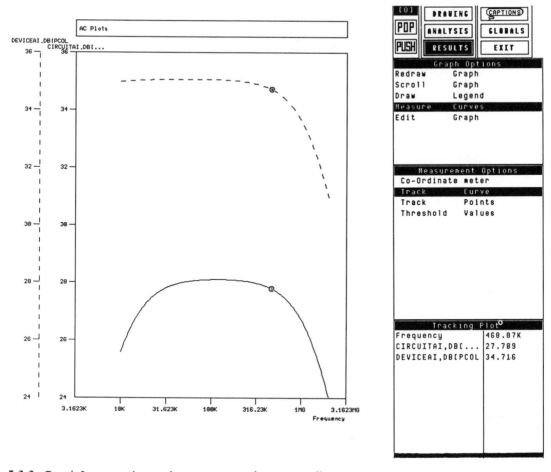

**Fig. 5.3-3** Track Curve option: points on curve and corresponding measurements

A screen dump does not show the cursor, so this has little value for hard copy.

**Measure:** What are the maximum values of the two current gains? Over what frequency ranges do they occur?

2. Track Curve Select this option, and take the cursor to the graph area. Press **M**, and circles appear on both curves, at the frequency (X axis point) corresponding to the cursor's position. The values of this frequency and the corresponding current gains appear in the bottom right-hand box under Tracking Plots, in Fig. 5.3-3.

**Measure:** Use this option to get data for calculating the slope at high frequencies. Measure the gains at two frequencies where the curves look to be tending, asymptotically, to a straight line and use the results to determine, approximately, the slope of this line.

$$\text{Slope} = (20\log A_1 - 20\log A_2)/(\log f_1 - \log f_2) \ \text{dB/decade}$$
$$= ([A_1]_{dB} - [A_2]_{dB}) \ / \ \log(f_1/f_2) \qquad \text{dB/decade}$$

(Remember that the X axis represents log(frequency) even though the frequency is written explicitly, and that

$$\log(f_1/f_2) = 1$$

means $f_1 = 10f_2$).

Also work out the corresponding dB change per octave (an **octave** is a doubling of frequency).

**Exercise:** The scales in Fig. 5.3-1 are deceptive – the vertical axis range is small, exaggerating the change of gain with frequency and hiding the curvature of the graphs in this region. To clarify this point, re-edit the Y axis of the graphs to cover the 0 dB to 36 dB range and see if the slope is anywhere near its asymptotic value.

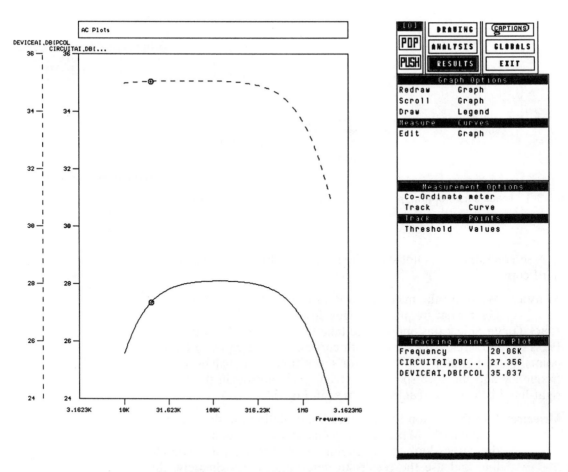

**Fig. 5.3-4**  Track Points menu: points on curve and corresponding measurements

3. Track Points Select this option, and take the cursor to the graph area. The cursor is now an **arrow** inside a circle.

Press **L** (the left mouse button) and the arrow changes direction.

Press **M** and again circles appear on both curves, at the frequency corresponding to the cursor's position. Again the values of this frequency and of the corresponding current gains appear in the bottom right-hand box, this time called Tracking Points on Plot, as in Fig. 5.3-4.

Inside each circle is a tiny arrow pointing in the same direction as the arrow in the cursor.

Press **M** a second time and the circles move along the curves, in the direction of the arrows, to the next point.

At each subsequent press of **M** the circles advance to the next point along the line. Thus if you have asked to have the calculations performed at 100 points it will take some time to travel the length of the curves.

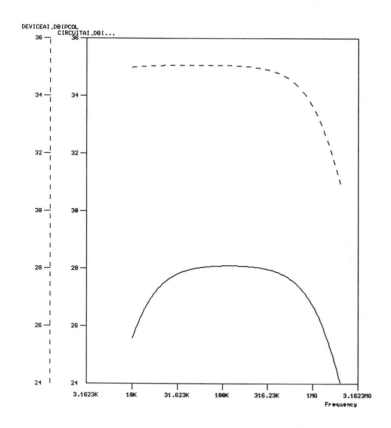

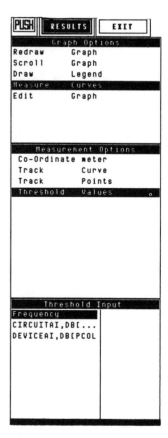

**Fig. 5.3-5** Threshold Values menu: you must select your variable(s) and enter appropriate values

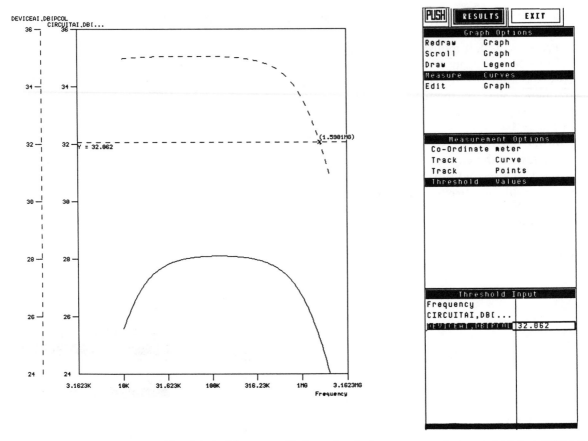

**Fig. 5.3-6** The upper limit to the device current gain bandwidth is 1.598 MHz

**Measure:** Find the largest values for each gain, and the ranges of frequencies over which they remain constant. Check against previous results.

4. **Threshold Values** Select this option and you get the menu of Fig. 5.3-5. MINNIE will draw 'threshold' lines at any particular value of any variable in the graph. You must choose which variable and what value, and then tell MINNIE.

To determine the **break frequencies**?

(a) **Device current gain.** You have its maximum value. Deduct 3 dB from this value. Select **DEVICEAI,DB[...** and type in your calculated value, as in Fig. 5.3-6. Cancel the **number box** and a line appears on the graph corresponding to this value, and at its intersection with the device current gain curve the frequency is shown (the **DEVICEAI,DB[...** box remains selected until you choose another option).

(b) **Circuit current gain.** Repeat the above procedure to determine the circuit's bandwidth.

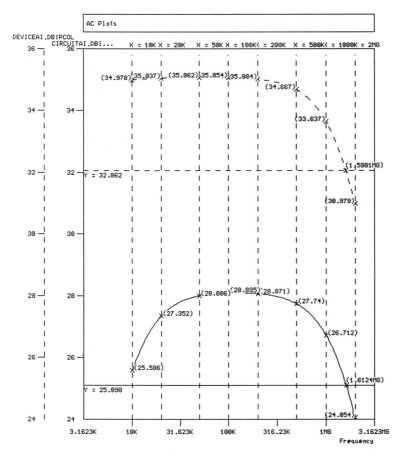

**Fig. 5.3-7** Current gain graph showing upper −3 dB points (frequency lines added to improve display)

To draw vertical lines at regular frequency intervals?

(a) Select Frequency and type in 2 MEG. Cancel the number box and a vertical line appears on the graph at this frequency (the Frequency box remains selected until you choose another option).

(b) Select the number box and type in 1 MEG. Cancel and a 1 Mhz line appears.

(c) Repeat for 500 kHz, 200 kHz, 100 kHz, 50 kHz, 20 kHz and 10 kHz. Your screen should now look as shown in Fig. 5.3-7.

## 5.4  SCALE INTERVALS – EDIT YOUR X AXIS

Select Redraw to clear the screen. You are now back with the edited graphs of Figs. 5.2-5 and 5.4-1.

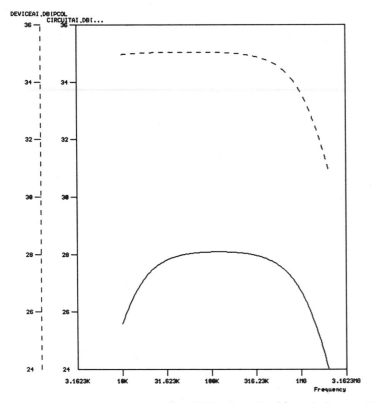
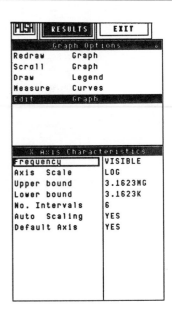

**Fig. 5.4-1** Auto Scaling choices and X Axis Characteristics menu

Notice that the display does not make full use of the available horizontal picture frame. This is because MINNIE, working in Auto Scaling mode, has decided to use 3.1623 kHz to 3.1623 MHz, a workable but non-optimal frequency range when your results only cover 10 kHz to 2 MHz. ($\log^{-1}0.5 = 3.1623$ is the half-way point between 1 and 10 on a log scale.)

A further non-optimal choice is the use of six evenly-spaced intervals on the frequency axis. You might think that 10, 15 or 20 would be better.

1. Select Edit and again you have the menu of Fig. 5.2-3(a).
2. Select Frequency and you now have the graphs and menu of Fig. 5.4-1.
3. Change Auto Scaling to NO, (press M on Auto Scaling *or* on YES)
4. Set the frequency bounds to 2.0 MEG and 10 k as appropriate. (Note that MINNIE will write MG instead of MEG in this case.)
5. Set the number of intervals to 10. You cannot change the number of intervals while Auto Scaling is ON.
6. Select Redraw, and you now have the graphs of Fig. 5.4-2.

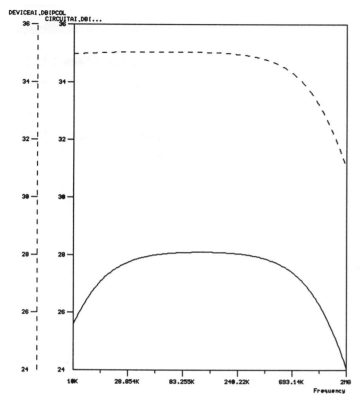

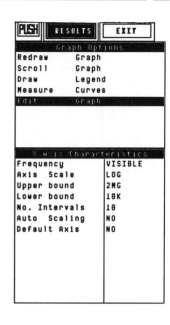

**Fig. 5.4-2**    Improved graph presentation

## 5.5    SCROLL

**Exercise:** Using the procedures outlined above, reduce the frequency
bounds of the current gain graphs to a restricted area, to view
the break frequency region in more detail (say 1.4 MHz to
1.8 MHz).

Then use the Scroll facility to see the rest of the waveform through
this modified window (note the new cursor shape ⇔):

1. place the cursor in or near the graph area;
2. drag the cursor (hold down middle mouse key **M**) *sideways*;
3. release **M**, and a new display appears.

Note that the frequency scale alters appropriately, and that the ratio of
the highest to lowest frequency displayed, $f_H/f_L$ remains constant.

## 5.6    DRAW LEGEND

This facility allows you to place anywhere in the drawing area a box
containing the names of each quantity displayed, together with its line

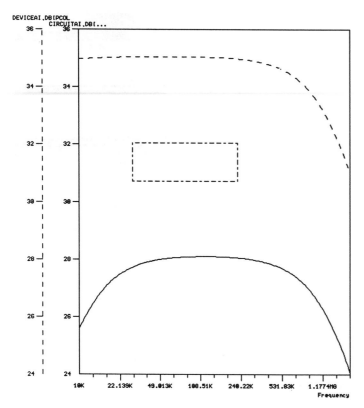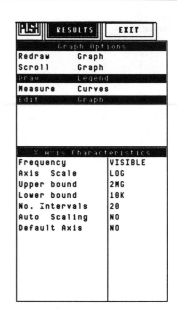

**Fig. 5.6-1** Positioning Legend box

style and marker type (if used). This information appears to be that which is already presented along the top of the graph area and on the Y axis – so its use is mainly aesthetical and would be limited to improving the presentation of hard copy.

You are still using Graph Options.

1. Go back to Fig. 5.4-2 (i.e. Edit the X axis back to its 10 kHz – 2 MHz state, and Redraw the graph).
2. Select Draw Legend, and a box (dashed lines) appears in the top right corner of the graph area.
3. Move the cursor to drawing area (i.e. anywhere outside the right-hand menu area), then press **M**, and the box moves to its new position, with bottom left corner on the cursor, as in Fig. 5.6-1.
4. Move the cursor to a new position, press **M**, and the box follows, etc. Drag **M** for fine control.
5. Place the box where you want MINNIE to present graph information.
6. Cancel Draw Legend and MINNIE produces the legend, as shown in Fig. 5.6-2.

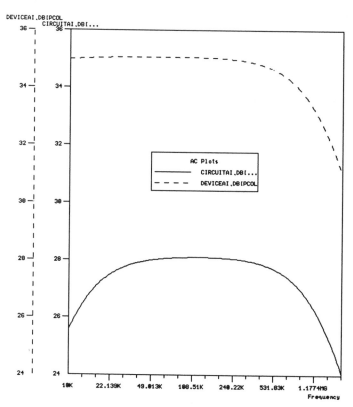

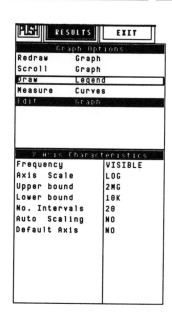

**Fig. 5.6-2** Legend in box, duplicating information already displayed

## 5.7 EXERCISE: THE SERIES *RLC*
CIRCUIT – VOLTAGE DRIVE CASE

### 5.7.1 Analysis

1. Write down an expression for the current *I* in the circuit shown in Fig. 5.7-1. Determine an expression for the radian frequency $\omega_O$ at which this current is in phase with the source voltage.
2. What is the circuit impedance *Z* at this frequency? Show that this is its minimum value. Write down an expression for the maximum current $I_{MAX}$.

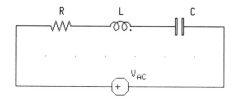

**Fig. 5.7-1** Series *RLC* circuit driven by a voltage source

3. Derive the expression

$$I = \frac{I_{\text{MAX}}}{1 + jQ_O\left[\dfrac{\omega}{\omega_O} - \dfrac{\omega_O}{\omega}\right]} \tag{5.7-1}$$

and show that for frequencies close to resonance it may be approximated by

$$I \approx \frac{I_{\text{MAX}}}{1 + jQ_O[2\delta/(1 + \delta)]} \tag{5.7-2}$$

where

$$\delta = (\omega - \omega_O)/\omega_O \tag{5.7-3}$$

4. Power is only dissipated in the resistor. Hence at every frequency $\omega$ the circuit's power dissipation is given by $P_{\text{CCT}} = I^2R$.

   The circuit's power dissipation will maximize at $\omega_O$, $P_{\text{MAX}} = (I_{\text{MAX}})^2 R$.

   As $R$ is a constant, $P_{\text{CCT}}$ will be half its maximum value when $I^2 = \frac{1}{2}(I_{\text{MAX}})^2$, or

$$I_{\text{HALF POWER}} = I_{\text{MAX}}/\sqrt{2} = 0.7071\, I_{\text{MAX}} \tag{5.7-4}$$

*Derive* expressions for the two frequencies $\omega_{\text{HIGH}}$ and $\omega_{\text{LOW}}$ at which the power dissipation is half the maximum value. Then show that

$$\frac{\omega_O}{\omega_{\text{HIGH}} - \omega_{\text{LOW}}} = Q_O = \frac{\omega_O}{\text{Bandwidth}} \tag{5.7-5}$$

*Definitions and names*
**Bandwidth** is the frequency range between the two half power frequencies.
**Quality factor** $Q_0$ is the reciprocal of the normalized bandwidth. It is the term normally used for specifying the performance of a tuned circuit.

   The quality factor $Q$ is also encountered in filter theory, where it performs the same function and is discussed in greater detail.

### 5.7.2 Design

1. Use standard component values – (consult appropriate catalogues to see what is available).
2. Design a series *RLC* circuit tuned to near 1 MHz, having a 20 kHz bandwidth. A 250 µH air-cored inductor is to be used. The measured series resistance of the inductor at 1 MHz (due more to skin effects rather than to the dc value) is 13 Ω. The signal's source impedance is known to be 5 Ω.
3. Predict the tuning frequency and the half-power frequencies of your actual circuit.
4. Predict the peak voltage and current responses in each component (treat the total resistance as a single component).

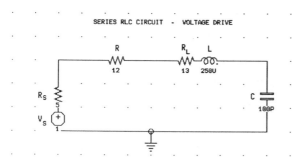

**Fig. 5.7-2**  Series *RLC* circuit

5. Predict the general shape of the phase shifts of the voltages and currents in the circuit, and their values at the circuit's resonant frequency.

### 5.7.3  Simulate

1. Set up your simulation. Note that because of the very sharp tuning it is desirable to look only at a restricted frequency range – 980 kHz to 1020 kHz is probably adequate.
2. Examine the voltages – magnitude and phase – across the capacitor, the inductance (excluding its resistance) and across the total resistance. Also look at the magnitude and phase of the current.
3. Using the measurement facilities provided:

   (a) Determine the maximum values of each response, and the frequencies at which they occur (do not expect these to be the same for all responses).
   (b) Determine the bandwidth of the circuit from the current response (as discussed above).
   (c) Determine the frequencies at which each voltage response is equal to 0.7071 times its maximum value. Note that for the capacitor and inductor voltages these are not the half power frequencies, and so do not set the circuit bandwidth.
   (d) Determine the frequencies at which the phase shifts (with respect to the source voltage) are

      (i)   $-90°$ for the voltage across the capacitor,
      (ii)  $+90°$ for the voltage across the inductance (again exclude the resistance of the inductor),
      (iii)   $0°$ for the current and for the voltage across the circuit resistance.

   and compare with the tuning frequency.

4. Finally does your predicted performance agree with the results of the simulation?

Specimen answers shown in Figs. 5.7-2, 5.7-3 and 5.7-4.

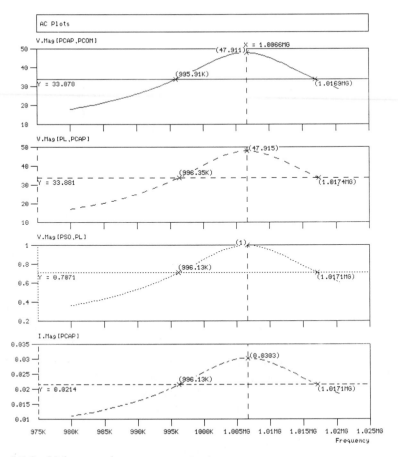

**Fig. 5.7-3** Voltage and current magnitude responses

## 5.8 EXERCISE: THE PARALLEL TUNED INDUCTOR – CURRENT DRIVE CASE

Real inductors are made using real conductors, and consequently have resistance as well as inductance. The value of this resistance is not constant, increasing with frequency due to **skin effects**.

This resistance is distributed throughout the winding (as is the inductance), but for most purposes it may be considered as a lumped resistance in series with the inductance.

Consequently when a capacitor is connected parallel to an inductor the resulting circuit will contain $R$, $L$ and $C$ but will not be a true parallel $RLC$ circuit.

Parallel tuned inductors are widely used in electronic circuits, often as the collector loads of common emitter or common base amplifying stages in radio or TV sets. Due to the high output impedances of these stages they can be considered to be acting as current sources, so the tuned

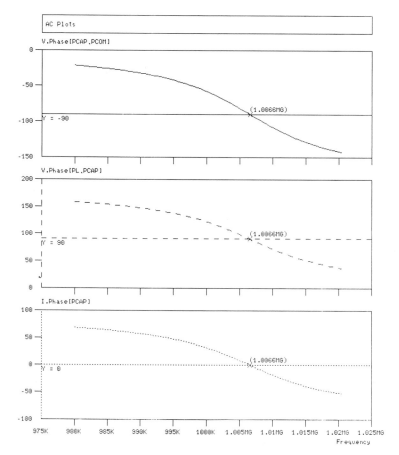

**Fig. 5.7-4**  Voltage and current phase shifts

inductor can then be represented, for the purposes of analysis, as shown in Fig. 5.8-1.

### 5.8.1  Analysis

1. Determine the frequency at which the impedance of the ideal parallel circuit of Fig. 5.8-2(b) is purely real. Sketch its variation as a function of the normalised frequency $\omega/\omega_O$. Sketch the consequent voltage response to an applied sinusoidal current of constant amplitude, as a function of $\omega/\omega_O$.

   Note: this is a good situation for applying the principles of duality. The current driven ideal parallel $RLC$ circuit is the dual of the voltage driven series $RLC$ circuit discussed previously.

2. Define bandwidth ($BW$). Show that for the circuit of Fig. 5.8-2(b) the bandwidth may be written as

$$\text{Bandwidth} = \frac{1}{CR} = \frac{\omega_O}{Q_{PO}} \tag{5.8-1}$$

where $Q_{PO}$ is the **Quality Factor** of the parallel $RLC$ circuit at $\omega_O$.

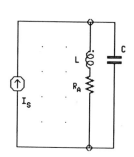

**Fig. 5.8-1**  Tuned inductor driven by current source; $R_A$ is the resistive component of the inductor *plus* any additional series resistance

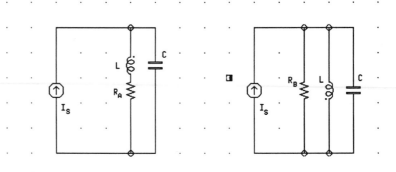

**Fig. 5.8-2** (a) Tuned inductor (b) Equivalent parallel circuit (at $\omega_O$)

3. Show that the impedances of the circuits in Fig. 5.8-2 at $\omega_O$ are equal if

$$R_B = \frac{(\omega_O L)^2}{R_A} \tag{5.8-2}$$

provided we can assume that

$$R_B >>> R_A \tag{5.8-3}$$

(thus $R_A + R_B \approx R_B$).

### 5.8.2 Design

The output of a radio VHF tuner is a 10.7 MHz carrier, frequency modulated. Its source impedance is 50 Ω. The maximum signal amplitude is 10 mV when driving a 50 Ω load. The broadcasting standard in the UK uses wide band FM, with a peak frequency deviation from the nominal carrier of ±75 kHz, so the required bandwidth is 150 kHz.

The tuner is followed by the **intermediate frequency** (IF) amplifier. The input stage of this amplifier is a common base stage, with a 0.5 mA collector current (to provide the correct input impedance). The voltage gain of this stage may be approximated by the expression

$$A_V \approx (q/kT) I_C Z_L \approx 40 I_C Z_L \tag{5.8-4}$$

(assuming a 25°C junction temperature).

The collector load of this stage is an inductor parallel tuned to 10.7 MHz. Determine the values of the inductance, capacitance and resistance if the stage voltage gain is to be about 100 at the resonant frequency.

Numerical answers, analysis profile and possible displays are shown in Figs. 5.8-3, 5.8-4, 5.8-5 and 5.8-6.

For simulation purposes the current drive was taken as 150 μA peak. This corresponds to a 7.5 mV input signal at a nominal $A_V \approx 100$. The actual value is not relevant provided it is less than the 10 mV maximum input.

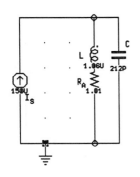

**Fig. 5.8-3** Tuned inductor: $L = 1.06\,\mu H$ (1.046 is more accurate), $C = 212\,pF$, $R_A = 1.01\,\Omega$ (0.989 Ω)

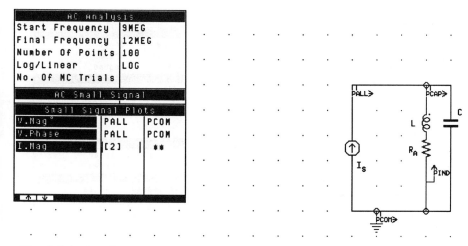

**Fig. 5.8-4** Possible analysis profile

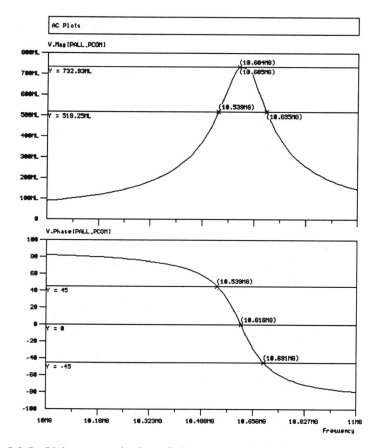

**Fig. 5.8-5** Voltage magnitude and phase across the inductor

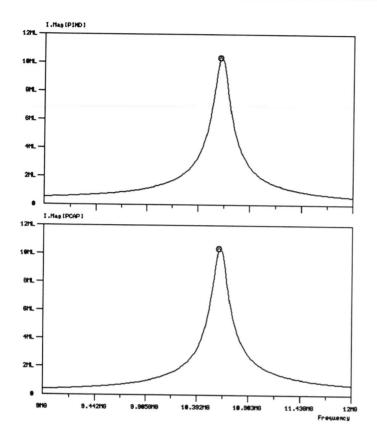
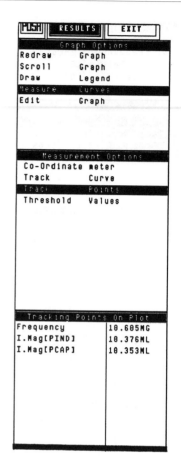

**Fig. 5.8-6**   Current magnitudes

As well as voltage phase and magnitude a request is made for the currents in $L$ and $C$. Note from Fig. 5.8-4 the restricted frequency range – the expected bandwidth is 150 kHz, so a 2 MHz range should be more than adequate. This simulation takes about $2\frac{1}{2}$ minutes on the UMIST Apollo network.

Due to the inaccuracy of the values used in the simulation the resonant frequency is slightly less than 10.7 MHz (the inaccuracy introduced by using equations derived for the equivalent parallel circuit is much smaller). The half power frequencies are shown, and the bandwidth is measured as 156 kHz. When interpreting this last reading bear in mind that the simulation has been performed at only 100 points in a 2 MHz frequency range. Consequently the *average* spacing between successive points is about 20 kHz, and MINNIE cannot provide exact measurements at points in between.

The discrepancy between the two peaks seen in Fig. 5.8-6 is due to MINNIE not performing a simulation at the true resonant frequency. The values shown are for the nearest simulation point.

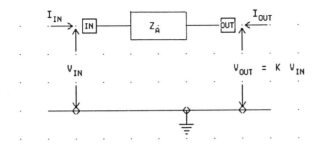

**Fig. 5.9-1** The impedance $Z_A$ links input and output terminals

## 5.9 EXERCISE: THE MILLER EFFECT – CAPACITANCE MULTIPLICATION

### 5.9.1 Discussion

The input impedance of an amplifier can always be represented as an impedance to ground consisting of a resistance and a parallel reactance. The reactance will, except in a very few special situations, be capacitive. The effect of this reactance depends on its magnitude relative to the other impedances associated with the amplifier's input. Two situations are of major interest:

1. The input signal is a voltage. The input impedance $Z_{IN}$ should be very much larger than the source impedance $R_S$ (assumed resistive) so that the full signal (the source voltage) can appear across the input. The effect of the input capacitance $C_{IN}$ is to reduce $Z_{IN}$, acting as a potential divider with $R_S$, and introducing a break frequency to the transfer function at

$$\omega_A \approx 1/(R_S C_{IN}) \tag{5.9-1}$$

2. The input signal is a current. The input impedance should be very much smaller than the source impedance so that the full signal (the

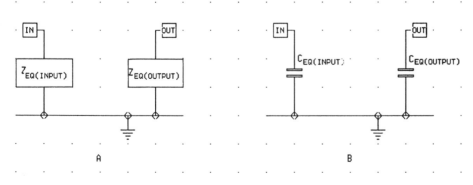

**Fig. 5.9-2** (a) To simplify analysis you can replace $Z_A$ by the two $Z_{EQ}$; (b) From (a) – if $Z_A$ is a capacitance you can replace it by the two $C_{EQ}$

source current) can enter the useful part of the amplifier (represented by the input resistance $R_{IN}$). The effect of the capacitance $C_{IN}$ is to provide an alternative, non useful, path for the current from the source. It introduces a break frequency to the (different) transfer function at

$$\omega_B \approx 1/(R_{IN} C_{IN}) \tag{5.9-2}$$

From the above it can be seen that it is desirable to minimize $C_{IN}$ for any amplifier intended to be used at higher frequencies. Unfortunately the Miller effect works against this objective.

*Miller effect*
Assume that at the input of a circuit there is a signal voltage $V_{IN}$. At the output, after appropriate processing, the signal emerges as a voltage $V_{OUT} = kV_{IN}$, as in Fig. 5.9-1.

If an impedance $Z_A$ exists between input and output as shown, then analysis shows that it may be replaced, for further analysis, by two equivalent capacitances, one across the input, the other at the output, as shown in Fig. 5.9-2(a)

These equivalent impedances are given by:

$$Z_{EQ(INPUT)} = Z_A/(1 - k) \tag{5.9-3}$$

$$Z_{EQ(OUTPUT)} = Z_A/(1 - 1/k) \tag{5.9-4}$$

Hence, if a capacitance $C_A$ exists between input and output terminals it can be represented by equivalents at the input and output of the circuit as shown in Fig. 5.9-2(b). They are given by

$$C_{EQ(INPUT)} = C_A(1 - k) \tag{5.9-5}$$

$$C_{EQ(OUTPUT)} = C_A(1 - 1/k) \tag{5.9-6}$$

The Miller capacitance is a serious problem in amplifying stages. It often sets the upper limit to the bandwidth of the common emitter amplifier, especially in high voltage gain situations. Capacitance between

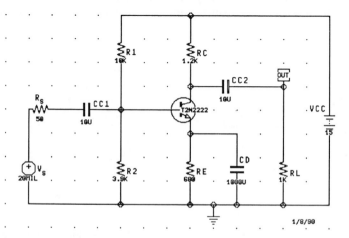

**Fig. 5.9-3**

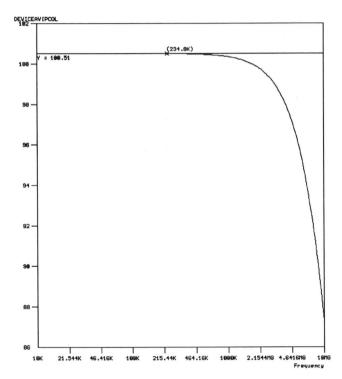

**Fig. 5.9-4**   The transistor's voltage gain is 100.51 in the midband region

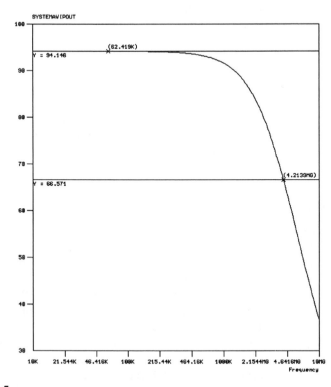

**Fig. 5.9-5**

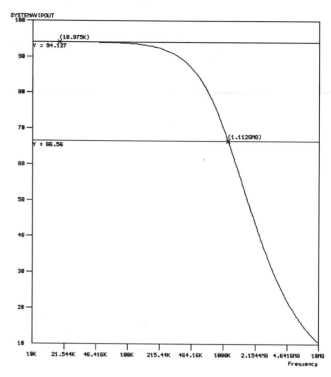

SYSTEMAV(POUT

**Fig. 5.9-6** System voltage gain with 20 pF base-collector strays. $A_{\text{VS(MB)}} \approx -94$, $f_{\text{H}} \approx 1.1\,\text{MHz}$

base and collector, $C_{\text{bc}}$, is inherent in bipolars, high frequency devices being designed to minimize it. For devices intended to be used in TV tuners and intermediate frequency (IF) amplifiers $C_{\text{bc}}$ can be as low as 0.35 pF, but values in the 5 pF – 10 pF – 15 pF range are more typical for small signal transistors. Thus, if a common emitter stage has $A_{\text{V}} = -100$ (don't forget the polarity inversion!) its equivalent input capacitance may be several hundred pF.

### 5.9.2 Simulation

Set up the common emitter circuit shown in Fig. 5.9-3. Note the source impedance $R_{\text{S}} = 50\,\Omega$ and the improved input and output coupling capacitors and emitter decoupling capacitor. The transistor is a `2N2222` from the `Discrete Components` library.

Set up an analysis profile to determine the voltages at the load, at the collector, at the base and at the source in order to enable MINNIE to calculate device and system voltage gains. Only `AC Analysis` is necessary as you do not require the DC conditions (obtained in other exercises/ tutorials). Use a 10 kHz to 10 MHz frequency range, and ask for simulations at between 100 and 200 frequency points.

The device voltage gain will be used to determine the **Miller Equivalent Capacitance** for added base-collector 'strays'. The system gain will be

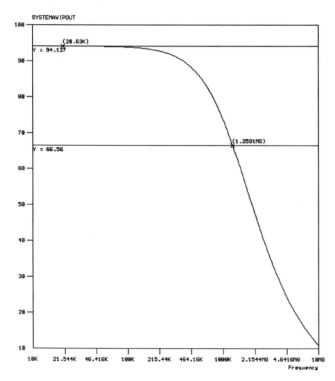

**Fig. 5.9-7** System voltage gain with $C_{EQ(INPUT)} = 2030\,pF$ between base and ground; $A_{VS(MB)} \approx -94$, $f_H \approx 1.26\,MHz$

used to compare the effects of these strays and of their Miller equivalent capacitances in order to confirm the validity of the theoretical analysis.

Device and system voltage gains are shown in Figs. 5.9-4 and 5.9-5, respectively.

The system's midband voltage gain $A_{VS(MB)} = V_{OUT}/V_S$ is approximately $-94$ (remember the polarity inversion – MINNIE appears to ignore this point!). The upper limit $f_H$ of the bandwidth, set by $A_{VS} = 0.707\,A_{VS(MB)} \approx 66.5$ is $f_H \approx 4.2\,MHz$.

Now modify the circuit to include $C_{STRAYS} = 20\,pF$ between base and collector, and repeat the simulation. The new system gain and bandwidth are shown in Fig. 5.9-6.

Now remove $C_{STRAYS}$ from the circuit, replacing them with an equivalent capacitance at the input as given by Eq. 5.9-5 ($k = A_{VD(MB)} = -100.5$). Repeat the simulation. The system gain and bandwidth are shown in Fig. 5.9-7.

Compare Figs. 5.9-7 and 5.9-6, and note that they are very similar, sufficiently so to confirm the validity of Eq. 5.9-5 (and consequently Eq. 5.9-3). There does exist a small discrepancy, which is probably due to the omission of $C_{EQ(OUTPUT)}$ from the last simulation.

*Exercise*

Repeat the last simulation, adding $C_{EQ(OUTPUT)}$ between collector and ground. Compare your results with the above.

# 6 Multivalued resistors

## 6.1 INTRODUCTION

The designer will often have to select component values in situations where the optimum choice is not initially clear. Often he will clarify his options by further analysis, but situations will remain in which he would prefer to use variable components, adjusting their values and observing the consequences experimentally. This is a laborious task and the results may be inconclusive, requiring further circuit modifications, etc. Consequently it is desirable to be able to vary component values within a MINNIE simulation run.

It should be noted that a complete set of calculations must be performed each time a single component's value is altered. Hence the processing time will increase in line with the number of possible combinations of values. Thus if a single component is given four values, processing time is multiplied by 4, whereas if two components have four values each the processing time is multiplied by 16.

Consequently this facility should always be used with care.

1. **Think carefully** about which results you **really** need; don't waste time waiting for unnecessary output.
2. If you are looking for precision always start with a coarse set of values, seeking to narrow down the range of possibilities to explore.

   Thus if you wish to optimize system performance when two variables are changed within specified ranges, and would like to examine at least 12 values of each variable, a single analysis run would require 144 complete system solutions. However, if you first run the simulation using only 4 coarsely spaced values of each variable, then by examining the results you would be able to select a much reduced range for final examination. Using 4 values (not 3) in this range for each variable in the final run would give you similar resolution to the single run case, but the total number of complete simulations would be only $4^2 + 4^2 = 32$.

Though the procedures outlined in this chapter are illustrated with resistor values they are directly applicable to other passive components and, as shown in Chapter 9, may also be applied to voltage (and current) sources.

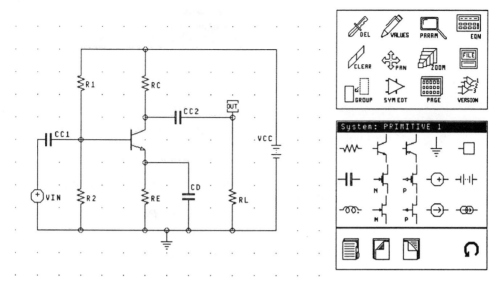

**Fig. 6.2-1** Circuit diagram, and right-hand menu showing the calculator symbol (**EQN**) and the magnifying glass symbol (**PARAM**).

## 6.2 TUTORIAL: INVESTIGATING THE COMMON EMITTER STAGE

In this tutorial you start with the common emitter amplifier, shown in Figs. 3.4-1, and 6.2-1, as set up in Fig. 4.4-5. You can now examine how its performance changes with variations in $R_E$ and $R_C$. Remember that the voltage gain of a common emitter stage can be written as (using hybrid parameters).

$$A_V \approx \frac{h_{fe} Z_L'}{h_{ie}} \approx 40 I_C Z_L'$$

where $Z_L' = R_C$ parallel with $Z_L$ and 25°C junction temperature is assumed.

Clearly $R_E$ controls $I_C$, while $R_C$ is part of $Z_L'$, so both resistors will

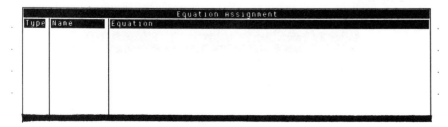

**Fig. 6.2-2** Equation Assignment Menu

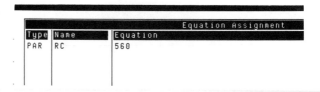

**Fig. 6.2-3**   MINNIE is informed that a parameter called $R_C$ will be defined, having a minimum value 560 (of appropriate units not yet specified). MINNIE does not yet know what $R_C$ is!

affect the voltage gain. You can also expect bandwidth changes as time constants (R * C) are altered.

The values used so far for $R_C$ and $R_E$ are $1.2\,k\Omega$ and $680\,\Omega$ respectively. For this tutorial you could use

$$560\,\Omega < R_C < 2.2\,k\Omega \quad \text{and} \quad 390\,\Omega < R_E < 1\,k\Omega$$

*Using the calculator*

Select the calculator, near the top of the right-hand menu, with **EQN** written under it, as shown in Fig. 6.2-1, and you will get the **Equation Assignment** menu of Fig. 6.2-2. It has three columns headed **Type**, **Name** and **Equation**.

Move the cursor to form a box under **Type**, and press **M** on it until **PAR** appears (the alternatives are **EQN**, **MODEL** and blank space).

Move the cursor sideways under **Name**, press **M** to select the box (highlighted) and type in the name you will assign to the component. The presence of a *LABEL* name has no significance (its effect is purely visual), so the name you use here is not related and can be quite different. However, to avoid later confusions you could reuse the label names or something similar ($R_C$ or $R_{COL}$, etc.).

Move the cursor sideways under **Equation**. Select the box and type in the lower limit of the range (**560** $\Omega$ for **RC**) as in Fig. 6.2-3.

Now move the cursor back to the left column, and on the next line press **M** again to find **PAR**. Proceed as above for $R_E$, using $390\,\Omega$ as its minimum value, to obtain the effect shown in Fig. 6.2-4.

The menu on the right has some options (**Open Line**, **Delete Line** and **Select Template**) which are relatively self evident. If you have time try them out.

| Type | Name | Equation |
|------|------|----------|
| PAR | RC | 560 |
| PAR | RE | 390 |

Equation Assignment

**Fig. 6.2-4**   Equation assignment complete

```
                              Resistor
Resistance (nominal)
Instance name                                              1
1st order temperature compensation coefficient[0]
2nd order temperature compensation coefficient[0]
Resistance for AC analysis
Resistor tolerance (between 0.0 and 1.0)       [0]
Resistance designable                          [NO]
```

**Fig. 6.2-5**  Menu for attaching parameter information to the selected resistor

Cancel **Equation Assignment** and you return to the initial menu, as in Fig. 6.2-1.

*Using the magnifying glass*
Select the magnifying glass, which is near the top of right-hand menu, with **PARAM** written under it. Then move the cursor to $R_C$, and select it so that the menu in Fig. 6.2-5 appears.

At present you are only interested in **Resistance (nominal)** and **Resistance for AC Analysis**. When dealing with fixed value resistors this menu is not relevant. It acquires importance in special situations, such as when the AC resistance differs from the DC (or nominal value).

In the present situation you can use this menu to tell MINNIE that the nominal and the AC values of the selected resistor are those of the parameter called $R_C$ (still to be defined), as shown in Fig. 6.2-6.

Press **M** on the heading **Resistor** to cancel the menu and, selecting $R_E$, repeat the above procedure.

Cancel the menu again, and this time press **M** on the magnifying glass also, to deselect it too. It then reverts to normal.

*Analysis*
You need the **Analysis Options** main menu shown in Fig. 6.2-7. Depending on what you did the last time you ran this circuit analysis, MINNIE could place you instead in one of the secondary menus (**DC Analysis**, **AC Analysis**, etc.). If so, refer back to section 3.4 and get the main menu back.

You have already looked at **AC Analysis** and **DC Analysis**, and your circuit should be set up for the appropriate analysis. If not, follow previous procedures and set it up now.

```
                              Resistor
Resistance (nominal)                                       RC
Instance name                                              1
1st order temperature compensation coefficient[0]
2nd order temperature compensation coefficient[0]
Resistance for AC analysis                                 RC
Resistor tolerance (between 0.0 and 1.0)       [0]
Resistance designable                          [NO]
```

**Fig. 6.2-6**  The selected resistor will take the attributes of the parameter $R_C$.

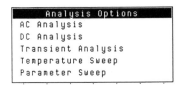

```
      Analysis Options
AC Analysis
DC Analysis
Transient Analysis
Temperature Sweep
Parameter Sweep
```

**Fig. 6.2-7** **Analysis Options** main menu (Figs. 2.1-3, 3.4-2)

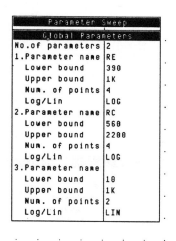

```
┌─────────────────────────┐
│    Parameter Sweep      │
│    Global Parameters    │
│ No.of parameters │ 1     │
│ 1.Parameter name │       │
│   Lower bound    │ 10    │
│   Upper bound    │ 1K    │
│   Num. of points │ 10    │
│   Log/Lin        │ LIN   │
│ 2.Parameter name │       │
│   Lower bound    │ 10    │
│   Upper bound    │ 1K    │
│   Num. of points │ 5     │
│   Log/Lin        │ LIN   │
│ 3.Parameter name │       │
│   Lower bound    │ 10    │
│   Upper bound    │ 1K    │
│   Num. of points │ 2     │
│   Log/Lin        │ LIN   │
└─────────────────────────┘
```

**Fig. 6.2-8** Parameter Sweep menu for resistors. The default values may not suit your circuit.

Assuming the analysis choices are satisfactory, select **Parameter Sweep** and the **Parameter Sweep** menu of Fig. 6.2-8 appears. (Of the remaining options, **Transient Analysis** will be looked at later.)

You have two parameters which need defining: $R_C$ and $R_E$. Their upper and lower bounds are known. The **Log/Lin** entry allows you to decide whether you want to have linear or logarithmic scaling used to determine the spacing between the 4 values to be used for each resistor. These values will be the upper and lower bounds plus two intermediate values. But remember that there is no zero on a log scale.

Figure 6.2-9, shows the entries used to obtain the results presented later.

Note that **Global Parameters** has appeared in the right-hand menus under the **Selected Analyses**.

When you are ready, select **RUN(int)**. However, first be aware of the time this analysis will take, since the menu requests $(4 \times 4) = 16$ complete simulations. On the UMIST Apollo network this simulation took just under 8 minutes, so:

1. make sure that you do not ask for unnecessary work;
2. try to schedule your work for slack periods on your network; and
3. make sure that you do have sufficient time to wait for your results to appear.

*DC results*

As usual MINNIE assumes that you wish to look immediately at the **AC** results, as in Fig. 6.2-10. Following the procedure of section 3.4, cancel **AC** and select **DC** to reach the situation shown in Fig. 6.2-11, and note that **Sweep of [RE]** and **Sweep of [RC]** have appeared in both menus.

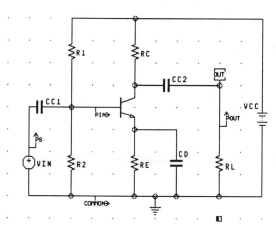

```
┌─────────────────────────┐
│    Parameter Sweep      │
│    Global Parameters    │
│ No.of parameters │ 2     │
│ 1.Parameter name │ RE    │
│   Lower bound    │ 390   │
│   Upper bound    │ 1K    │
│   Num. of points │ 4     │
│   Log/Lin        │ LOG   │
│ 2.Parameter name │ RC    │
│   Lower bound    │ 560   │
│   Upper bound    │ 2200  │
│   Num. of points │ 4     │
│   Log/Lin        │ LOG   │
│ 3.Parameter name │       │
│   Lower bound    │ 10    │
│   Upper bound    │ 1K    │
│   Num. of points │ 2     │
│   Log/Lin        │ LIN   │
└─────────────────────────┘
```

**Fig. 6.2-9** Global parameters for $R_E$ and $R_C$ (Log spacing requested)

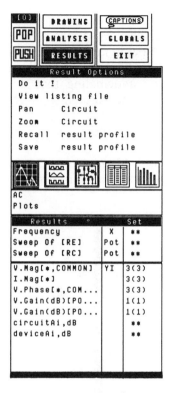

**Fig. 6.2-10** AC Results menu

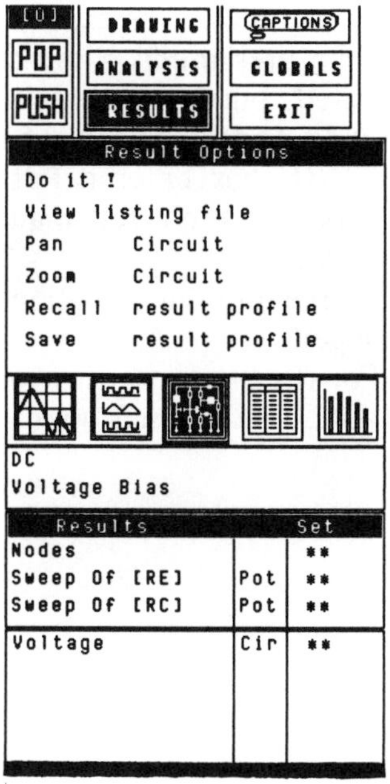

**Fig. 6.2-11** DC Results menu

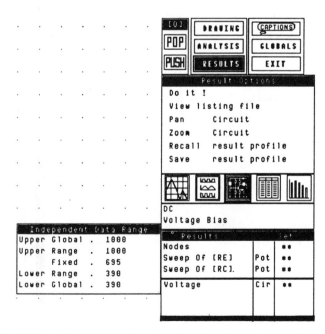

**Fig. 6.2-12** DC Results menu, showing also the Independent Data Range for $R_E$.

In Fig. 6.2-11, as expected, MINNIE anticipates that the DC voltages will be presented on the circuit diagram (other display options can be selected, but in this case they are pointless). New items on the menu include Nodes, Sweep of [RC] and Sweep of [RE]. Next to them MINNIE has entered Pot (for potentiometer), anticipating that this will be the preferred manner of presentation of the variability of $R_E$ and $R_C$.

In the present situation the blank space next to Nodes cannot be changed.

For the Sweep entries we can alternate Pot with Fixed. Select Sweep Of [RE] and a small menu, Independent Data Range, appears. In this

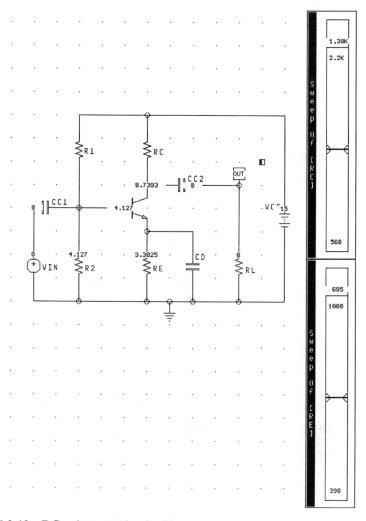

**Fig. 6.2-13**  DC values on circuit. The nominal values of $R_E$ and $R_C$ are 695 Ω and 1.38 kΩ, respectively. The real values, following from the discussion in the text, are 730.6 Ω and 1.394 kΩ.

menu you will find the range of values and the fixed values MINNIE is using, as shown in Fig. 6.2-12.

The `Pot` option is suitable for now. If you have time, do investigate the `Fix` option.

Now select `Do it!` and the results should appear as shown in Fig. 6.2-13.

At the bottom of the right-hand menu (*not* shown in Fig. 6.2-13) you see that the `Boxes` option for graphic representation of circuit voltages, referred to in section 3.4 and in Fig. 3.4-12, is again available.

By the right-hand side of the circuit you see a schematic representation of two slide potentiometers, on which you can use the cursor to vary the values of $R_E$ and $R_C$. At the ends of the potentiometers are the limits to the range of variation. Immediately above the top of each `pot` is a small extension in which MINNIE places the currently selected value.

Note that, as you move the cursor up and down *inside* one of the slider areas the indicated value changes, so that you know what you are selecting. However, the selection is *not* complete until you press **M**.

| Sweep Of [ RC] | Sweep Of [ RE] | Nodes | Voltage |
|---|---|---|---|
| 560 | 390 | 1 | 4.0434 |
| 560 | 390 | 2 | 4.0434 |
| 560 | 390 | 3 | 15 |
| 560 | 390 | 4 | 3.1325 |
| 560 | 390 | 5 | 10.535 |
| 560 | 390 | 6 | 0 |
| 560 | 390 | 7 | 0 |
| 560 | 390 | 8 | 0 |
| 560 | 390 | 9 | 0 |
| 560 | 533.8 | 1 | 4.097 |
| 560 | 533.8 | 2 | 4.097 |
| 560 | 533.8 | 3 | 15 |
| 560 | 533.8 | 4 | 3.2385 |
| 560 | 533.8 | 5 | 11.625 |
| 560 | 533.8 | 6 | 0 |
| 560 | 533.8 | 7 | 0 |
| 560 | 533.8 | 8 | 0 |
| 560 | 533.8 | 9 | 0 |
| 560 | 730.6 | 1 | 4.1321 |
| 560 | 730.6 | 2 | 4.1321 |
| 560 | 730.6 | 3 | 15 |
| 560 | 730.6 | 4 | 3.3123 |
| 560 | 730.6 | 5 | 12.476 |
| 560 | 730.6 | 6 | 0 |
| 560 | 730.6 | 7 | 0 |
| 560 | 730.6 | 8 | 0 |
| 560 | 730.6 | 9 | 0 |
| 560 | 1000 | 1 | 4.1554 |
| 560 | 1000 | 2 | 4.1554 |
| 560 | 1000 | 3 | 15 |

**Fig. 6.2-14** Tabular presentation of circuit voltages; there are $4 \times 4 \times 9 = 144$ entries.

When you do MINNIE will position two small markers to indicate the selected place and this selected value will *nominally* be used for determining which results are displayed.

Observe the following points in your circuit.

1. Stability of the base voltage: as you change $R_E$ the emitter current changes. The consequent change in base current affects the base voltage. This circuit is strongly biased, $(I_{R1} \gg I_B)$ so $V_B$ does not change very much.

2. The base collector voltage: it should remain reverse biased throughout the excursions of the collector waveform. For discrete components you should have not less than about 0.5 V reverse bias in the worst case (when the signal on the collector is at its negative peak). We are using a 20 mV amplitude input signal, so with a voltage gain less than 30 the amplitude of the output signal would be less than 600 mV, and consequently the circuit should work with a minimum 1.1 V collector-base quiescent voltage.

   MINNIE appears to be more fussy. When using the npn device from **Primitives 1** the voltage gain becomes an attenuation with low $V_{CB}$ and high $I_E$. Better performance should be obtainable with device from the **Discrete Components** menu.

**TABULAR** output is an alternative way of presenting the DC voltages. It has the advantage of being more condensed, though the user can still be faced with a data extraction problem. The procedure is quite simple – just select the **Table** option, then select **Do it!** Figure 6.2-14 shows the top end of the fairly lengthy table produced for this circuit.

*Some arithmetic*

Do remember that you have only asked for four values, distributed on a logarithmic basis. What does this mean?

Consider $R_C$, for which the specified range is 560 Ω to 2200 Ω. Four values $A\ B\ C\ D$ means that there are three intervals $A–B$, $B–C$, and $C–D$. You have asked MINNIE to space them at equal intervals on a *Log* scale. Hence as $A = 560\,\Omega$ and $D = 2200\,\Omega$

$$\log(B/A) = \log(C/B) = \log(D/C) = 1/3\ \log(D/A) = 0.19808$$
$$B = A \times 10^{0.19808} = 883.6\,\Omega; \quad C = A \times 10^{(2 \times 0.19808)} = 1394.3\,\Omega$$

Clearly then, as you move the cursor along its potentiometer $R_C$ can only take on one of these four values. Though for each slider position MINNIE gives you a nominal value of $R_C$ (as indicated above the potentiometer), the value actually used to obtain the results you see is the *real* one *closest* to the *apparent* one on a linear basis: even though we have specified Log scale, the nominal value of $R_C$ at which MINNIE changes from $A$ to $B$ (from 560 Ω to 883.6 Ω) is at (560 + 883.6)/2 = 721 Ω.

*Exercise*
Determine analytically the values of $R_E$ actually used. Determine the nominal values at which MINNIE changes from one to the other. Confirm your results by observing the on-screen behaviour. (Answers are at the end of this book.)

*AC Results*
First cancel DC and select AC so that Fig. 6.2-10 reappears.

Under Results we find Frequency, Sweep of [RE] and Sweep of [RC]. Each one has four graph options: X, Pot, Fam and Fix.

X:   X axis. Frequency, $R_E$ are $R_C$ are multivalued variables, so MINNIE allows you to use any *one* as the independent variable (to be plotted along the X axis). (Note that one MUST be the X axis).

Pot:   Potentiometer. This is the display mode we have discussed under DC. One or two of these three quantities may be presented in this form (the third has to be the X axis).

Fix:   Fixed value. Again this was referred to under DC. The same availability and restrictions apply as for Pot.

Fam:   Family. In this presentation mode the complete family of results of one of these variables is presented for each selection point of the other two. One of these two must be the X axis, the other may be Pot or Fix. This is a very useful facility for comparisons and optimizations.

To summarize, the options are:

> only one  X,   but it cannot be omitted;
> only one  Fam;
> up to two Pot;
> up to two Fix.

The results shown here were obtained using graph options shown in Fig. 6.2-15.

The system voltage gains, as specified in section 3.4 (Fig. 3.4-6) are displayed in Fig. 6.2-16 for one value of $R_E$.

In Fig. 6.2-16, $R_E$ is again represented by a slider potentiometer, and as we move the slider we again go through its four real values discussed earlier. For each of these $R_E$ values MINNIE presents simultaneously graphs for all four values of $R_C$.

$R_C$ also has a slider potentiometer, and as we move the slider we also go through its four real values. However, as the corresponding four curves are already displayed, the effect this time is simply to highlight the corresponding curve. In this way the curves can be easily identified. The real value of $R_C$ appears on the screen below the graph, as Family Valuator. (Note how these values agree with the previous calculations.)

What happens if you specify log scale and set the low value to zero (as with a potentiometer)?

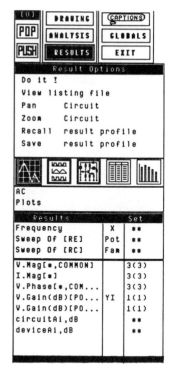

**Fig. 6.2-15** Results Set used to display the System Voltage Gain ($= V_{out}/V_{in}$) for this circuit.

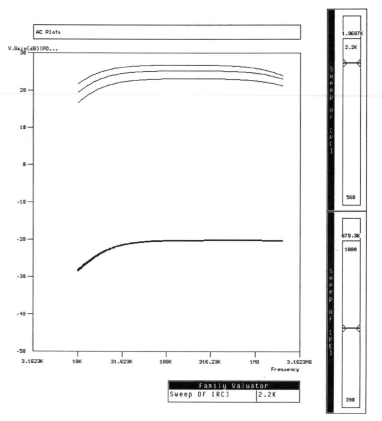

**Fig. 6.2-16** Family of curves of System Voltage Gain for nominal $R_E$ = '680' $\Omega$. The actual simulation uses $R_E = 632.2\,\Omega$. The actual values of $R_C$ are, from top to bottom: $1.394\,\text{k}\Omega$, $883.6\,\Omega$, $560\,\Omega$, $2.2\,\text{k}\Omega$. The Family Valuator box indicates that the $2.2\,\text{k}\Omega$ curve is enhanced.

MINNIE uses its lowest internal value, $1 \times 10^{-32}$, in the equations. Then, using the procedure described earlier it works out the corresponding intermediate values to send to HSpice in its analysis request. HSpice may not be able to handle these values if they are too low – it then sets them to its own lower limit at $1 \times 10^{-5}$.

Thus if you specify a potentiometer as having values in the range 0 to $2\,k\Omega$, and ask for 10 values spaced on a log basis, MINNIE will set the following values in its analysis request:

$$10.00 \times 10^{-33} \quad 83.62 \times 10^{-27} \quad 69.93 \times 10^{-26} \quad 58.48 \times 10^{-22}$$
$$48.90 \times 10^{-18} \quad 40.90 \times 10^{-14} \quad 34.20 \times 10^{-10} \quad 28.60 \times 10^{-6}$$
$$23.92 \times 10^{-2} \quad 20.00 \times 10^{+2}$$

and HSpice will perform the first eight simulations with $1 \times 10^{-5}$!

However, if you set the lower limit for the potentiometer at $1\,\Omega$, MINNIE will use the more realistic sequence

$$1 \quad 5.414 \quad 12.59 \quad 29.31 \quad 68.21 \quad 158.7 \quad 369.3 \quad 859.5 \quad 2000$$

# Circuit waveforms and frequency response: Nyquist plot

7

## 7.1 INTRODUCTION

This is one of the most important facilities available on MINNIE, as it makes it possible to simulate the use of the Oscilloscope to view any waveshape, including transients. It is for this reason that to look at nice, stable sine waves you use what, for lack of a better name, MINNIE calls the `Transient Analysis` option.

To look at waveforms we must first define the characteristics of the stimulus (input waveform), even when it is a sinusoid and we have already specified an AC signal source for `AC Analysis`. Hence the procedure starts when we are setting up the circuit in `DRAWING` mode.

## 7.2 TUTORIAL: COMMON EMITTER AMPLIFIER WITH SINUSOIDAL VOLTAGE DRIVE

### 7.2.1 Setting up your circuit

Set up or retrieve from file the common emitter amplifier (circuit only) used in section 3.4, shown in Fig. 7.2-1. The analysis profiles used pre-

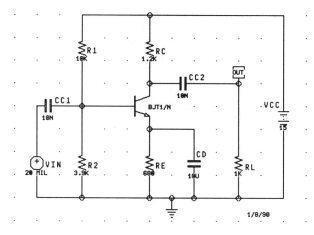

**Fig. 7.2-1** Common emitter circuit, as used in section 3.4

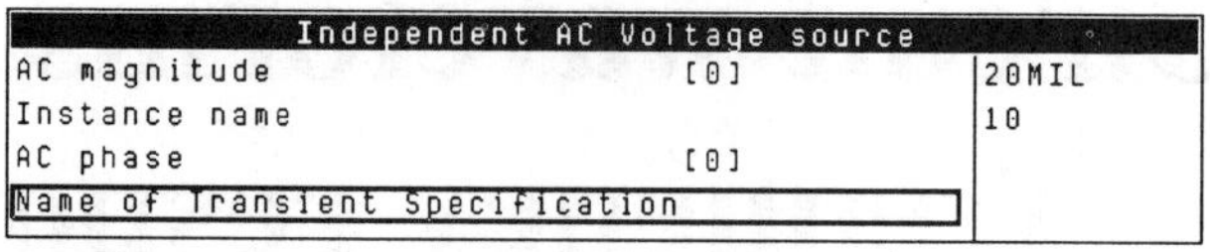

```
┌─────────────────────────────────────────────────────────┐
│          Independent AC Voltage source                    │
│ AC magnitude                        [0]        │ 20MIL    │
│ Instance name                                  │ 10       │
│ AC phase                            [0]        │          │
│ Name of Transient Specification                │          │
└─────────────────────────────────────────────────────────┘
```

**Fig. 7.2-2**  Independent AC Voltage Source menu.

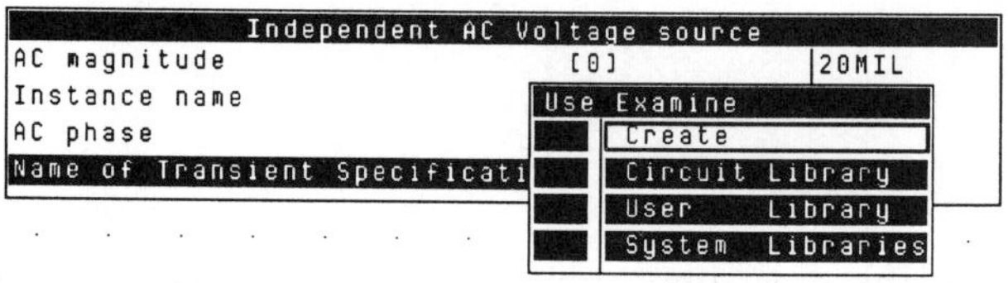

```
┌─────────────────────────────────────────────────────────┐
│          Independent AC Voltage source                    │
│ AC magnitude                        [0]        │ 20MIL    │
│ Instance name                      ┌──────────────────────┐
│ AC phase                           │ Use Examine          │
│ Name of Transient Specificati      │  Create              │
│                                    │  Circuit Library      │
│                                    │  User    Library      │
│                                    │  System  Libraries    │
└────────────────────────────────────┴──────────────────────┘
```

**Fig. 7.2-3**

viously are not necessary and would increase simulation time (especially the profile for the potentiometers $R_E$ and $R_C$). It is assumed that the DC voltages have been examined and are correct.

To look at waveforms (as on an oscilloscope) it is necessary to have an appropriate source. In **DRAWING** mode you have introduced an **AC voltage source** and have given it a magnitude using the **VALUES** facility. MINNIE will use this magnitude for its **AC Analysis** option (implicitly assuming a sinusoidal waveform), but will not use it for sketching waveforms (even sinusoids). Instead, MINNIE asks you to define the input waveform, providing you with a wide variety of possible inputs.

### Independent AC Voltage Source

In **DRAWING** mode select **PARAM** (the magnifying lens) as for devices and potentiometers and then select the **AC voltage source** ($V_{IN}$) already in your circuit. You will be presented with the menu shown in Fig. 7.2-2. Note that the **20 MIL** was the **AC magnitude** peak voltage specified under **VALUES**.

You can set magnitude and phase (the default AC magnitude is that specified under **VALUES**). You can also choose to use an existing **Transient Specification** or to create a new one.

### Name of Transient Specification

Move the cursor to **Name of Transient Specification** and select it. You will now be presented with a new menu, Fig. 7.2-3.

(If you have an *existing specification* available you need only select the corresponding blank space in the right column, type the name (it will then appear in the usual slot in the component value area on the right, above the numbers), and press **M** to enter it in the menu.)

You can choose to examine the libraries or create new specifications. Your new specifications will appear in the **Circuit Library**, with any others previously defined for this circuit. The other libraries are beyond the scope of this book (and are probably empty).

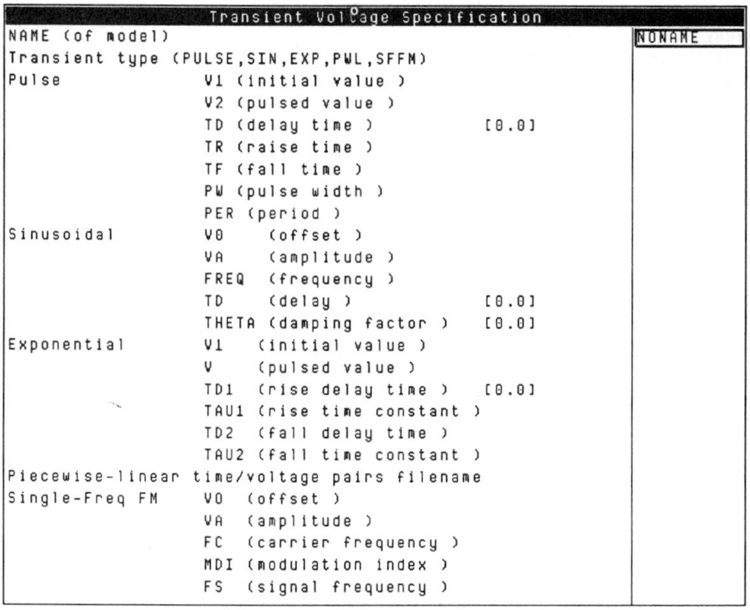

```
                    Transient Voltage Specification
NAME (of model)                                              NONAME
Transient type (PULSE,SIN,EXP,PWL,SFFM)
Pulse              V1 (initial value )
                   V2 (pulsed value )
                   TD (delay time )           [0.0]
                   TR (raise time )
                   TF (fall time )
                   PW (pulse width )
                   PER (period )
Sinusoidal         V0    (offset )
                   VA    (amplitude )
                   FREQ (frequency )
                   TD    (delay )             [0.0]
                   THETA (damping factor )    [0.0]
Exponential        V1    (initial value )
                   V     (pulsed value )
                   TD1  (rise delay time )    [0.0]
                   TAU1 (rise time constant )
                   TD2  (fall delay time )
                   TAU2 (fall time constant )
Piecewise-linear  time/voltage pairs filename
Single-Freq FM     V0    (offset )
                   VA    (amplitude )
                   FC   (carrier frequency )
                   MDI  (modulation index )
                   FS   (signal frequency )
```

**Fig. 7.2-4** Transient Voltage Specification menu.

*Create a New* Transient Voltage Specification

MINNIE has facilities for specifying parameters for certain commonly used waveforms (pulse, sinusoid, exponential, etc.). These facilities may be Examined or Used under the heading Create. Move the cursor to Create and select Use. You will now get the Transient Voltage Specification menu shown in Fig. 7.2-4.

Give your waveform a name to be used for identification purposes: you may eventually have a stock of sinusoids, so the name used, SIN001 as in Fig. 7.2-5, allows for later versions.

Indicate the type of waveform: SIN is obvious. Then fill in appropriate parameters for your sinusoid in the correct places. Note that MINNIE will introduce default values for only two of the possible parameters, so it is *necessary* to specify the rest, as in Fig. 7.2-5. When ready, cancel the menu by pressing M on the menu heading. (By now you may have realized that this is a standard way of cancelling most menus.)

You are now with the menu of Fig. 7.2-6, the same as Fig. 7.2-2 but now including your new waveform name next to Name of Transient Specification. If you have not created a new waveform specification this slot remains empty until you enter a name of an existing waveform (or create a new one).

Cancel this menu, and then cancel the PARAM (magnifying lens) box. This portion of the DRAWING procedure is now complete. You can either complete any other drawing activity, or proceed immediately with the next stage of setting up your waveform. (Remember that you can move freely between ANALYSIS, DRAWING and RESULTS.)

```
┌──────────────────────────────────────────────────────────┬─────────┐
│          Transient Voltage Specification                  │         │
│NAME (of model)                                             │SIN001   │
│Transient type (PULSE,SIN,EXP,PWL,SFFM)                     │SIN      │
│Pulse              V1 (initial value )                      │         │
│                   V2 (pulsed value )                       │         │
│                   TD (delay time )          [0.0]          │         │
│                   TR (raise time )                         │         │
│                   TF (fall time )                          │         │
│                   PW (pulse width )                        │         │
│                   PER (period )                            │         │
│Sinusoidal         V0    (offset )                          │0        │
│                   VA    (amplitude )                       │20 MIL   │
│                   FREQ  (frequency )                       │100 K    │
│                   TD    (delay )            [0.0]          │         │
│                   THETA (damping factor )   [0.0]          │         │
│Exponential        V1    (initial value )                   │         │
│                   V     (pulsed value )                    │         │
│                   TD1   (rise delay time )  [0.0]          │         │
│                   TAU1 (rise time constant )               │         │
│                   TD2   (fall delay time )                 │         │
│                   TAU2 (fall time constant )               │         │
│Piecewise-linear time/voltage pairs filename                │         │
│Single-Freq FM     V0    (offset )                          │         │
│                   VA    (amplitude )                       │         │
│                   FC    (carrier frequency )               │         │
│                   MDI (modulation index )                  │         │
│                   FS    (signal frequency )                │         │
└──────────────────────────────────────────────────────────┴─────────┘
```

**Fig. 7.2-5** `Transient Voltage Specification` set up for a 100 kHz, 20 mV amplitude Sinusoid. No DC offset, time delay or damping factor.

```
┌────────────────────────────────────────────────┬────────┐
│         Independent AC Voltage source           │        │
│AC magnitude                       [0]            │20MIL   │
│Instance name                                     │10      │
│AC phase                           [0]            │        │
│Name of Transient Specification                   │SIN001  │
└────────────────────────────────────────────────┴────────┘
```

**Fig. 7.2-6** The newly specified waveform appears in the box next to `Transient Specification`.

### 7.2.2 Defining your waveform requirements

Select `ANALYSIS` mode. MINNIE may assume you want `AC Analysis`, so cancel menus until you are in the top level menu, `Analysis Options`, as in Fig. 7.2-7(a).

Select `Transient Analysis`, and you should now have the menu shown in Fig. 7.2-7(b). Check the entries to see if they are adequate. Make any necessary changes. In particular, make sure that you will get a full cycle of your 100 kHz waveform.

Now move the cursor down to select `Time Plot`. This action brings up a `Transfer Plots` menu, shown in Fig. 7.2-8(a). Select its heading to bring up the subsidiary menu `Available Plots`, shown in Fig. 7.2-8(b).

As we are dealing with a voltage waveform select `Volt.OutVar`. This will then appear in the `Transfer Plots` menu. Use the procedures described previously to define measuring probe positions, such as those in Fig. 7.2-9.

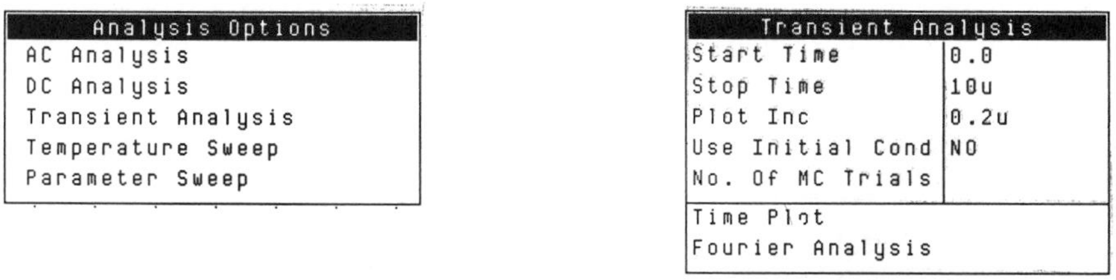

```
┌──────────────────────────┐     ┌──────────────────────────────┐
│    Analysis Options      │     │     Transient Analysis       │
│ AC Analysis              │     │ Start Time      │0.0         │
│ DC Analysis              │     │ Stop Time       │10u         │
│ Transient Analysis       │     │ Plot Inc        │0.2u        │
│ Temperature Sweep        │     │ Use Initial Cond│NO          │
│ Parameter Sweep          │     │ No. Of MC Trials│            │
└──────────────────────────┘     ├──────────────────────────────┤
                                 │ Time Plot                    │
                                 │ Fourier Analysis             │
                                 └──────────────────────────────┘
```

**Fig. 7.2-7** Menu selection sequence in **ANALYSIS** mode. (a) Top level menu – select Transient Analysis. (b) Transient Analysis menu – check over data, then press M on Time Plot.

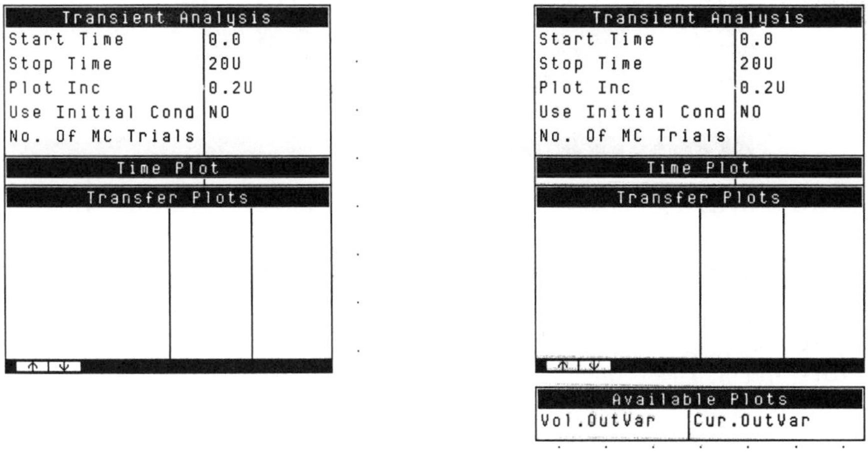

```
┌──────────────────────────┐     ┌──────────────────────────┐
│   Transient Analysis     │     │   Transient Analysis     │
│ Start Time      │0.0     │     │ Start Time      │0.0     │
│ Stop Time       │20U     │     │ Stop Time       │20U     │
│ Plot Inc        │0.2U    │     │ Plot Inc        │0.2U    │
│ Use Initial Cond│NO      │     │ Use Initial Cond│NO      │
│ No. Of MC Trials│        │     │ No. Of MC Trials│        │
├──────────────────────────┤     ├──────────────────────────┤
│       Time Plot          │     │       Time Plot          │
├──────────────────────────┤     ├──────────────────────────┤
│     Transfer Plots       │     │     Transfer Plots       │
│                          │     │                          │
│                          │     │                          │
│                          │     │                          │
│                          │     │                          │
│                          │     │                          │
│ ↑ │ ↓                    │     │ ↑ │ ↓                    │
└──────────────────────────┘     ├──────────────────────────┤
                                 │     Available Plots      │
                                 │ Vol.OutVar │ Cur.OutVar  │
                                 └──────────────────────────┘
```

**Fig. 7.2-8** Menu selection sequence (continuation) in **ANALYSIS** mode. (a) Time Plot menu. Press M on Transfer Plots to bring up the subsidiary Available Plots menu. (b) Transfer Plots/Available Plots combined menu. Select Volt.OutVar (or Cur.OutVar if appropriate).

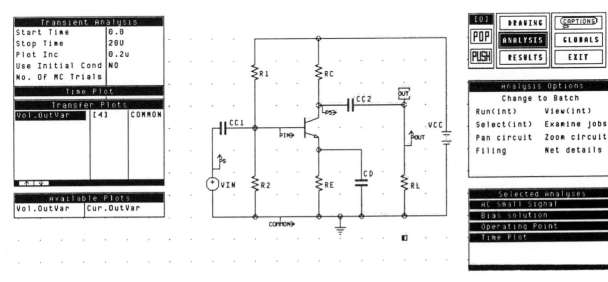

**Fig. 7.2-9** Waveforms to be examined at source (**PS**), base (**PIN**), collector (**P5**) and at the load (**POUT**).

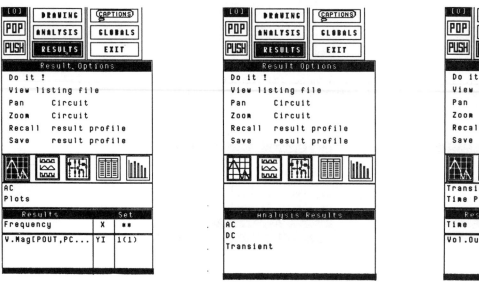

**Fig. 7.2-10** Menu sequence for selecting waveform displays (a) AC Results – Plots option; (b) Analysis Results – top menu; (c) Transient menu – Time Plots option. This is the menu you want for waveform and transient displays.

If you wish, set up or modify other analysis options, then select Run(int) to start the analysis, and wait for MINNIE to finish. Remember that you will have to enter an identifier (circuit name) if you have not done so already for this set of circuits.

When ready MINNIE will automatically go into RESULTS mode.

### 7.2.3 Displaying your waveforms

MINNIE may automatically put you into the AC display mode, sub-section Plots, as in Fig. 7.2-10(a) (suitable for displaying frequency characteristics). Cancel AC and you now have the top level menu, as in Fig. 7.2-10(b). Select Transient, and you should now have the Transient menu, as in Fig. 7.2-10(c).

Move the cursor to the middle column next to Vol.OutVar[*,... and press M to establish the Y-axis (common or independent). Then select Do it!

MINNIE presents your waveforms, as shown in Fig. 7.2-11. Note that the waveforms include the DC levels.

### 7.2.4 Waveform problem!

Examination of the Fig. 7.2-11 waveforms reveals that the output voltage is drifting downwards over the first two cycles. This is an unexpected

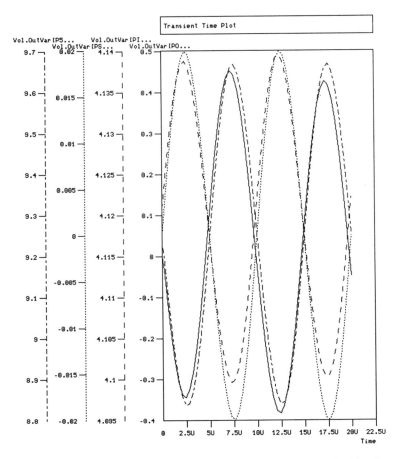

**Fig. 7.2-11**  First two cycles of the waveforms. Voltages identified by first two letters of probe name. Look carefully at the output voltage (PO...) and the base voltage (PIN...). See how the peak levels change from first to second cycle.

result, as the capacitor $C_{C2}$ should remove the DC bias voltage and true sinusoids have no DC components. The reason for this anomaly lies in the manner in which the analysis is performed. The calculations assume that the output waveform is at $0\,\mathrm{V}$ at $t = 0$ as shown, and this assumption is incorrect.

Looking carefully we see that at this frequency the output voltage appears to lead the collector voltage by a small phase angle.

*Exercise*
Confirm analytically that this is correct, and show that for $C_{C2} = 10\,\mathrm{nF}$ and $R_{L} = 1\,\mathrm{k\Omega}$ this phase angle is $9.04°$ at $100\,\mathrm{kHz}$.

It should be clear that a similar situation arises at the base, so the base voltage leads the source by a corresponding small phase angle. Assuming that there are no phase shifts within the active device (apart from the

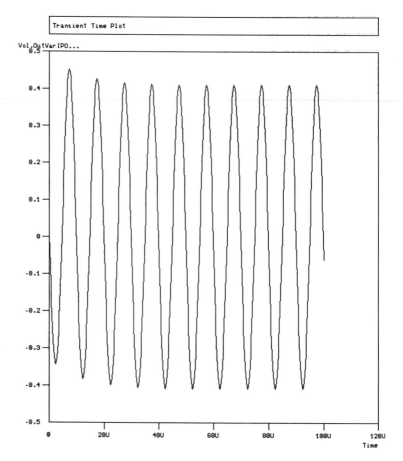

**Fig. 7.2-12** The first ten cycles of the output voltage. The downward drift is negligible after three cycles.

built-in polarity inversion), we see that the load voltage must lead the inverted source voltage.

Consequently, as the rising source voltage does start at $0\,V$ at $t = 0$, the load voltage should have a *negative* magnitude at $t = 0$.

The nature of the calculation process is such that in this case the effects of this erroneous assumption vanish in about three or four cycles, as in Fig. 7.2-12. Consequently it is desirable to leave the first few cycles, and examine later ones instead.

Return to Analysis Mode and modify the start and stop times in the Transient Analysis menu. Results for the fourth cycle are shown in Figs. 7.2-13, 7.2-14 and 7.2-15.

It is clear that the coupling capacitors are too small for satisfactory operation below $100\,kHz$, so they should be changed!

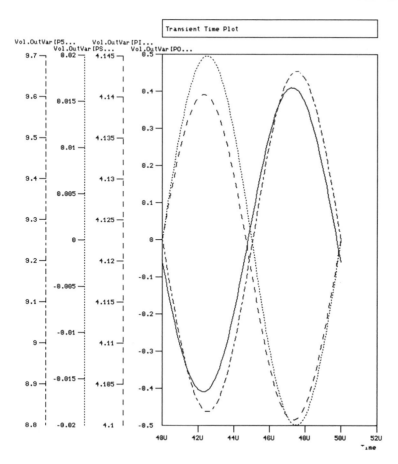

**Fig. 7.2-13**   Fifth cycle of the four waveforms. Single plot, independent Y axis option. This presentation allows close scrutiny of each waveform but can be confusing. The loss of horizontal space can be corrected using Edit options.

## 7.3   EXERCISE: A WIDE BAND BIPOLAR AMPLIFIER

This example is based on a combined tutorial/laboratory exercise designed for final year undergraduates in the Department of Electrical Engineering and Electronics at UMIST. The questions and equations assume familiarity with the *h*-parameter equivalent circuits, but it is a straightforward job to transfer to other equivalent circuits. The overall results remain valid.

It is not necessary to work through the analysis in order to perform the simulation, but it would help in the understanding of this and other high frequency circuits.

Versions of this circuit are designed and built by all our students, usually achieving bandwidths near 20 MHz (limited in the laboratory by CRO probe capacitance – the circuits are capable of near 40 MHz).

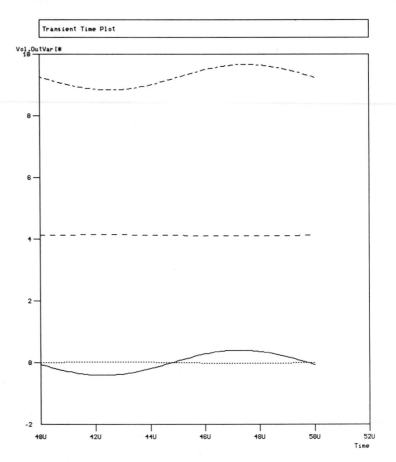

**Fig. 7.2-14** Same waveforms as Fig. 7.2-13. Single plot, common Y axis option. This presentation is very useful for assessing the suitability of biasing arrangements. It is clear that much larger signals can be applied before the collector voltage drives the device into its saturation mode.

Note that the device used is the **BF199**, not available in the HSpice library.

In this analysis and simulation, use the circuit of Fig. 7.3-1 with the following component values and device types:

$$R_S = 50\,\Omega \quad R_T = 56\,\Omega \quad R_2 = 5.6\,k\Omega \quad R_1 = 4.7\,k\Omega$$
$$R_Z = 680\,\Omega \quad R_{E1} = 470\,\Omega \quad R_C = 1.2\,k\Omega \quad R_{F1} = 4.7\,k\Omega$$
$$R_{F2} = 6.8\,k\Omega \quad R_{E2} = 4.7\,k\Omega$$

Load $= 1\,k\Omega$, resistive

$R_{OFFSET}$ = preset resistor, variable in the 0 to $2\,k\Omega$ range

$$C_{IN} = 1\,\mu F \quad C_Z = C_F = 10\,\mu F$$

Stray capacitances: assume $0.2\,pF$ for all inter-electrode stray capacitances

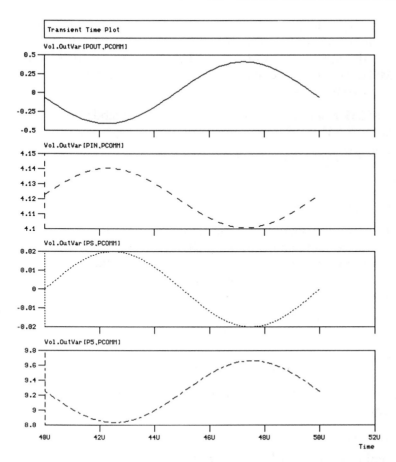

**Fig. 7.2-15** Same waveforms as Fig. 7.2-13. Multiple plot, independent Y axis option. This presentation also allows close scrutiny. Clearer presentation, but less easy to examine phase and timing relationships.

$T_1$, $T_2$, $T_3$, $T_4$: all are **2N2222** from the discrete components transistor library

Absolute maximum ratings:

$$
\begin{aligned}
P_{\text{tot}} &= 500\,\text{mW} \\
I_{\text{C}} &= 800\,\text{mA} \\
V_{\text{CEO}} &= 30\,\text{V} \\
V_{\text{CBO}} &= 60\,\text{V} \\
T_{\text{J}} &= 200\,°\text{C}
\end{aligned}
$$

Typical values:

$$
\begin{aligned}
h_{\text{fe}}: \text{at } 1\,\text{ma} \quad & 50 < h_{\text{fe}} < 300 \\
\text{at } 10\,\text{ma} \quad & 75 < h_{\text{fe}} < 375 \\
f_{\text{T}}: \text{at } 20\,\text{ma} \quad & f_{\text{T}} > 250\,\text{MHz} \\
& C_{\text{bc}} < 8\,\text{pF}
\end{aligned}
$$

Note that $f_T$ is dependent on current level. As the currents in this circuit (intended for the **BF199**) are less than 20 mA, and are rather low for the **2N222**, the actual values of $f_T$ are likely to be substantially lower than 250 MHz. (If you have time repeat with a higher frequency device, $f_T > 550$ MHz at 5 mA.)

Z = **1N5339** from the discrete components zener diode library. Nominal voltage is 5.6 V.

$V_S = 40$ mV peak   $V_{CC} = 7$ V   $V_{EE} = -12$ V

### 7.3.1  Analysis

1. Describe the operation of the circuit in Fig. 7.3-1.
2. Draw the mid-band equivalent circuit for Fig. 7.3-1.
3. Show that for $h_{fe} \approx h_{FE}$ and $h_{fe} \gg 1$ the mid-band voltage gain $A_V' = A_{V1} \times A_{V2}$ can be approximated by

$$A_V' = \frac{V_{C2}}{V_{IN}} \approx 40 R_C I_{EQ} \qquad (7.3\text{-}1)$$

where

$$I_{EQ} = (I_{C1} \times I_{C2})/(I_{C1} + I_{C2}).$$

4. Show that for the above conditions the voltage gain of the input emitter follower $T_1$ is given by

$$A_{V1} = I_{C1}/(I_{C1} + I_{C2}) \qquad (7.3\text{-}2)$$

and hence determine its value for $I_{C1} = I_{C2}$.

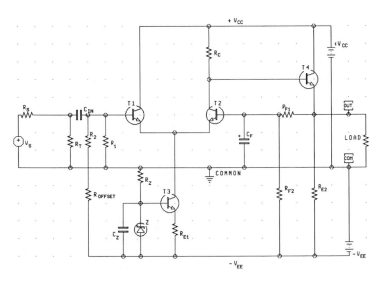

**Fig. 7.3-1**  Wide-band amplifier

In view of the often made (and correct) assertion that the voltage gain of an emitter follower is normally just less than 1 (0.98 – 0.99 – 0.995 etc.) explain this result. Check out the value for $T_4$.

5. Draw the high frequency equivalent circuit, neglecting $r_{bb'}$.
6. Discuss the effects of circuit voltage gain on:

    (a) the collector-base capacitance of $T_1$ and $T_2$; and
    (b) the emitter-base capacitance of $T_4$.

7. Based on your discussions/conclusions from (5.) and (6.) above, develop a modified high frequency equivalent circuit for use in analysis. All capacitances should be grouped into four equivalents, $C_A$, $C_B$, $C_C$ and $C_D$. Write down general expressions for these capacitances.

8. Show that the internal (device) capacitance $C_{b'e}$ ($= C_{ob}$) is given by

$$C_{b'e} \approx 40 I_C \omega_T \qquad (7.3\text{-}3)$$

where $\omega_T$ is the output short circuit unity current gain frequency (transition frequency) of the transistor.

*Note:* $C_{b'e}$ and $C_{b'c}$ are used for internal device capacitances. $C_{be}$, $C_{bc}$ and $C_{ec}$ are used for external (packaging and stray) capacitances.

The current $i_{b'}$ is the component of the device base current which flows through the resistive component $r_{b'e}$ of the device input parameter $h_{ie}$.

9. Show that the ratio $V_{OUT}/i_{b'4}$ has a break frequency at

$$\omega_D = |1/(C_D R_{EQ})| \qquad (7.3\text{-}4)$$

where $R_{EQ}$ is the parallel combination of $R_{F1}$, $R_{E2}$ and the load resistance, and

$$C_D = (1 - 1/A_{V4})(C_{be4} + C_{b'e4}) + \text{CRO probe capacitance}.$$

Comment on the break frequencies for the ratios $i_{LOAD}/i_{b'4}$ and $i_{RE2}/i_{b'4}$.

Determine the DC current $I_{C4}$. Assuming 15 pF for the probe capacitance estimate the break frequency $f_D$.

10. Show that for the same conditions as above the current ratio $i_{b'4}/i_{b'2}$ has a break frequency at

$$\omega_C = |1/(C_C R'_C)| \qquad (7.3\text{-}5)$$

where

$$R'_C = (R_C \times h_{fe} R_{EQ})/(R_C + h_{fe} R_{EQ})$$

and

$$C_C = C_{bc2} + C_{b'c2} + C_{bc4} + C_{b'c4} + (1 - A_{V4})(C_{be4} + C_{b'e4}).$$

Determine $I_{C2}$. Estimate the break frequency $f_C$.

11. Show that the current ratio $i_{b'2}/i_{b'1}$ has a break frequency at

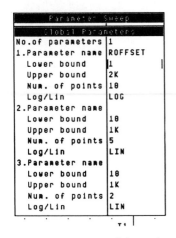

Parameter Sweep
Global Parameters
No.of parameters |1
1.Parameter name |ROFFSET
Lower bound |1
Upper bound |2K
Num. of points |18
Log/Lin |LOG
2.Parameter name
Lower bound |18
Upper bound |1K
Num. of points |5
Log/Lin |LIN
3.Parameter name
Lower bound |18
Upper bound |1K
Num. of points |2
Log/Lin |LIN

**Fig. 7.3-2** Possible setting of Global Parameters for $R_{\text{OFFSET}}$

$$\omega_B = |h_{\text{fe2}}/(C_B \times h_{\text{ie2}})| \approx |40 I_C/C_B| \qquad (7.3\text{-}6)$$

where

$$C_B = (C_{\text{be2}} + C_{\text{b'e2}}) - (C_{\text{be1}} + C_{\text{b'e1}}) + (C_{\text{bc3}} + C_{\text{b'c3}})$$

Then, using the approximation for $C_{\text{b'e}}$ obtained in (8.) above, and assuming the external (strays, etc.) capacitances $C_{\text{be}}$ are equal, estimate the break frequency $f_B$ for $I_{C1} = I_{C2}$.

12. The signal's source impedance is $50\,\Omega$. It reaches the amplifier through a $1\,\text{m}$ length of $50\,\Omega$ coaxial cable ($100\,\text{pF}$ per metre). The $56\,\Omega$ resistance $R_T$ is used to terminate this cable.

   Show that the ratio $i_{\text{b'1}}/v_S$ has a break frequency at

$$\omega_A = |1/(C_A \times R_S')| \qquad (7.3\text{-}7)$$

where $R_S'$ is the *equivalent* source resistance.

### 7.3.2 Simulation

Set up the circuit of Fig. 7.3-1 using the component values given. Then set up the DC conditions. The preset resistor needs to be adjusted to a

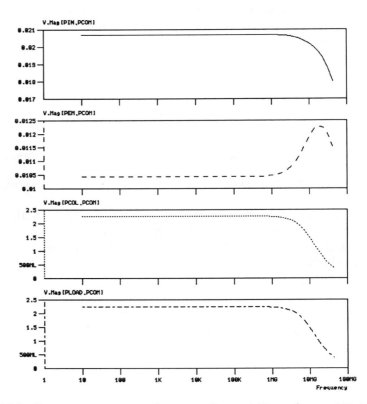

**Fig. 7.3-3** Frequency responses, from top: base of $T_1$, emitters of $T_1$ and $T_2$, collector of $T_2$ and emitter of $T_4$

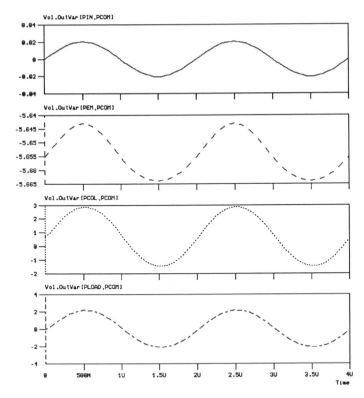

**Fig. 7.3-4** Waveforms for $f = 500\,\mathrm{kHz}$

value which sets the **DC** output voltage at or near 0 V. To do this, first obtain the circuit's **DC** voltages for several settings of $R_{\mathrm{OFFSET}}$. Follow the procedure outlined in Chapter 6 to set up $R_{\mathrm{OFFSET}}$ as a variable resistor in the range 1 Ω to 2000 Ω, using 10 points on a log scale, Fig. 7.3-2. (read the discussion at the end of Chapter 6).

Run the **DC** simulation and from the results select the value of $R_{\mathrm{OFFSET}}$ for which the **DC** output voltage is closest to 0 V. Keep the error to less than 10 mV, running additional simulations if necessary.

For the **AC** simulation, remove the variable $R_{\mathrm{OFFSET}}$, replacing it by a fixed resistor of the value obtained above. Note that as this is intended to be an adjustable resistor (a circuit preset), *Preferred Values* of resistance are not relevant.

Set up an appropriate **Analysis Profile**, start the simulation and display your results. Possible output displays are shown in Figs. 7.3-3 and 7.3-4.

Compare the results of the simulation with those predicted by your analysis. Comment on any differences.

If you have the time, build this circuit using **BF199** bipolars and any suitable Zener diode (5.6 V nominal), test it and compare with analytical and simulation results. Careful circuit layout is necessary!

Compare with results obtained from a simulation using a higher frequency device ($f_{\mathrm{T}} > 500\,\mathrm{MHz}$).

## 7.4 EXERCISE: CLASS AB (*PUSH-PULL*) BIPOLAR AMPLIFIER

A requirement exists for an output stage able to drive a $50\,\Omega$ resistive load (such as a properly terminated $50\,\Omega$ coaxial transmission line) with a sinusoidal current variable in both magnitude and frequency. The maximum current is estimated at $180\,\text{mA}$ rms, and the frequency range extends from $100\,\text{Hz}$ to $1\,\text{MHz}$. The signal's source impedance is a nominal $300\,\Omega$.

For this circuit the following bipolar devices may be used:

| Device: | | 2N2219A | 2N3637 | |
|---|---|---|---|---|
| Type/Material: | | npn/Si | pnp/Si | |
| Absolute maximum ratings: | $P_T$ | $800\,\text{mW}^*$ | $1\,\text{W}^*$ | (* in free air at 25°C) |
| | $I_C$ | $800\,\text{mA}$ | $1\,\text{A}$ | |
| | $V_{CEO}$ | $50\,\text{V}$ | $175\,\text{V}$ | |
| | $V_{BEO}$ | $6\,\text{V}$ | $5\,\text{V}$ | |
| | $T_J$ | 175°C | 200°C | |
| $h_{FE}$ (minimum) | | 100 | 100 | |
| at: | | $150\,\text{mA}$ | $50\,\text{mA}$ | |

$h_{fe}$: the incremental current gain $h_{fe}$ ($\beta$) is not immediately available. Assume $h_{fe} > 100$.

| | | | |
|---|---|---|---|
| $f_T$ | $300\,\text{MHz}$ | $200\,\text{MHz}$ | |
| $\theta_{\text{AMBIENT-JUNCTION}}$ | $0.1°\text{C/mW}^{**}$ | $0.1°\text{C/mW}^{**}$ | (** with T05 heatsink) |

Note that these devices are not designed to form a complementary pair – they simply are the nearest equivalents in the HSpice library to the ZTX653/ZTX753 pair used by the UMIST undergraduates for their versions of this circuit.

Also note that their $V_{BEO}$ values are low and could cause difficulties in the laboratory.

### 7.4.1 Design

Design a suitable two transistor output stage. Keep it simple, but make due allowance for the following points.

1. Though the complete amplifier, of which this is only the output stage, will have a feedback loop to stabilize performance and reduce distortion, it is still desirable to minimize the distortion introduced by your circuit.
2. The problem of thermal runaway should not be overlooked.
3. Device and component ratings must not be overlooked. Preferred values of components should be used.

### 7.4.2 Report

Your report should contain a well-presented discussion of your design choices. Circuit diagrams should be clear and drawn to acceptable stan-

dards. You should present clear, unambiguous, predictions of performance with special reference to:

1. the biasing conditions (no signal!);
2. maximum and quiescent device power dissipation, the corresponding
   values of $T_J$ (assume 25°C ambient temperature), and the resultant
   values of the quiescent current; and
3. the circuit efficiency at maximum load current (include effects of
   biasing chain currents).

You should present a clear statement of the test procedures required
to assess the circuit's performance: biasing conditions, waveforms,
frequency range at rated output, slew rate, etc.

*Question*
Assuming that the power for your output stage comes from two un-
regulated sources (transformer, bridge rectifiers, smoothing capacitor)
calculate the minimum value of this smoothing capacitor which will
guarantee a maximum ripple voltage (peak to peak), at maximum load
current, less than 5% of the nominal supply voltage.

Your local mains supply is variable in the 220 V rms to 240 V rms
range. Discuss how your design could be modified to allow for the effects
of both ripple and supply variations. How is the efficiency affected?

*Simulation*
Include in your report the results of a complete simulation of your
circuit under relevant operating conditions. Compare the results with

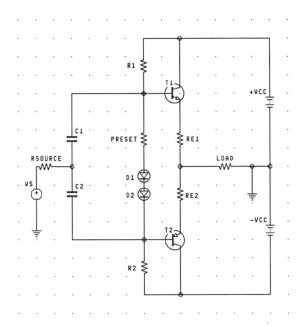

**Fig. 7.4-1** Simple Push-Pull output stage.

your predictions and, if possible, with the values obtained experimentally (use the ZTX devices referred to above).

### 7.4.3 Answers

Like all real design problems there is no single solution. The preferred circuit outline is shown in Fig. 7.4-1.

**D1** and **D2** are introduced to reduce cross-over distortion; they provide more stable voltage drops than resistors would, but as the assumed voltages across them and across the base-emitter junctions are unlikely to be correct the preset is introduced and adjusted to obtain the design quiescent (no signal) current.

The resistors $R_E$ are used to limit the effects of the junction temperature rise. The voltages across them are added directly to $V_{BE}$ when determining the base voltages to be set by the diodes and the preset.

Possible component values and supply voltages are shown in Fig. 7.4-2. Note that at maximum current levels the base-emitter voltages can exceed 1 V. The base-collector minimum reverse bias is set at about 2 V.

The peak device currents $I_M$ are approximately 255 mA. In this design the quiescent current $I_Q$ is set at approximately 20 mA (8% of $I_M$), yielding a quiescent power dissipation of approximately 340 mW and $T_j \approx 59°C$.

The device power dissipations are $\approx 466$ mW each at rated output, corresponding to $T_j \approx 71.5°C$. Hence we can estimate, at $-2$ mV/°C, a base-emitter voltage reduction of $\approx 25$ mV. This is an increase across

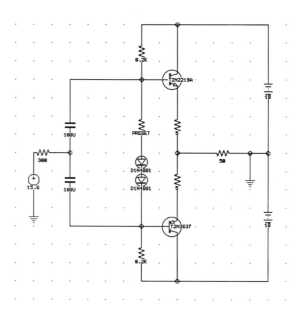

**Fig. 7.4-2** Possible solution

the $5\,\Omega$ resistors $R_E$ and does not cause more than a $5\,mA$ (25%) change in $I_Q$.

The device minimum input impedances can be estimated as

$$Z_{\text{IN(DEVICE)}} = h_{\text{fe}}\, R'_L \approx 5.5\,k\Omega$$

leading to

$$Z_{\text{IN(CIRCUIT)}} \approx 2.35\,k\Omega.$$

This value is not very large. The source voltage is adversely affected, and to obtain the required output it is necessary to have $V_S \approx 15.8\,V$ (assuming a device voltage gain $A_V = 1$).

Smoothing Capacitor: $900\,\mu F$ for each supply line.

### 7.4.4  Simulation

*Quiescent conditions*

As in the laboratory, it is first necessary to determine the correct value of the preset resistor. Its objective is to set the quiescent emitter/collector currents $I_Q$ to their design value, $20\,mA$.

No attempt should be made, neither in the laboratory nor on the simulator, to assess signal performance until the correct, *designed*, DC bias conditions have been successfully established.

Using the techniques described in Chapter 6, set up the preset resistor to take values in the $0\,\Omega$ to $500\,\Omega$ range (remember that log scales do not have 0, so start from 1 or use a Linear scale).

At this stage your analysis profile should *only* contain `Operating Point` (from `DC Analysis`) and `Global Parameters` (from `Parameter`

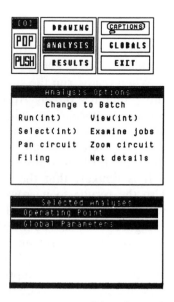

**Fig. 7.4-3** (a) `Parameter Sweep, Global Parameters` menu (b) `Selected Analyses` for determining correct value of preset resistor

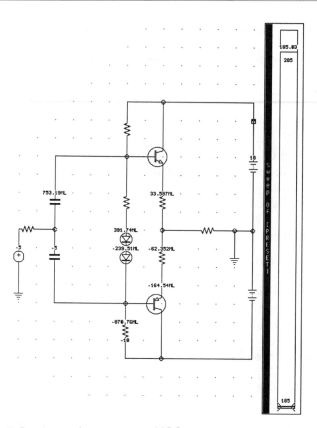

**Fig. 7.4-4**   DC voltages for Preset = 185 Ω

Sweep), Fig. 7.4-3. If you include other items they will all be calculated for each value of Preset, resulting in excessive processing time.

When ready, run the simulation. For four Preset values it takes about three minutes on an Apollo DN3000. Display your results to select the most appropriate value for Preset. $I_Q$ can be calculated from the voltages across the resistors $R_{E1}$ and $R_{E2}$. Due to mismatch between devices (even nominally complementary devices) $I_Q$ is unlikely to be the same for both transistors, so some compromise will be necessary.

It is unlikely that the first run will yield an optimum value for $I_Q$. Use the results to narrow down the range of variation of Preset and repeat this simulation until you are satisfied.

Figure 7.4-4 shows the DC voltages (Bias Conditions) obtained after three runs. It can be seen that Preset = 185 Ω yields usable values. Note that the DC voltage across the load is −62.35 mV. This is less than 0.2% of the supply voltages and indicates that the two transistors are better matched than might be expected (of course MINNIE and HSpice will assume perfect resistance values unless otherwise specified).

*Sinusoidal response*

When satisfied return to **DRAWING** mode and replace **Preset** by a fixed resistor. Remove the **EQN** and **PARAM** settings from the appropriate menus. If you have not already done so, set up a suitable sinusoid definition for your source. For the results shown here a 100 kHz, 15.6 V peak sinusoid having a 5 V **DC offset** was used.

Enter **ANALYSIS** mode. Remove the values set under **Parameter Sweep**, **Global Parameters**. Remove **Global Parameters** from the menu on the right of the screen, Fig. 7.4-3(b).

Set up an appropriate analysis profile, run the simulation, and display your results.

Possible displays are shown in Figs. 7.4-5, 7.4-6, 7.4-7 and 7.4-8. The probes were set as follows:

| | |
|---|---|
| PIN | input of circuit, between **C1** and **C2**. |
| PEM1, PEM2 | emitters of **T1**, **T2**. |
| PLOAD | between **LOAD** and **RE1**, **RE2**. |
| PCOM | common (ground, reference level) |

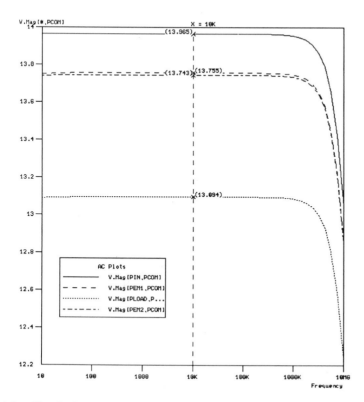

**Fig. 7.4-5** Circuit signal voltage magnitudes as functions of frequency, for constant source voltage $V_S = 15.6$ V peak

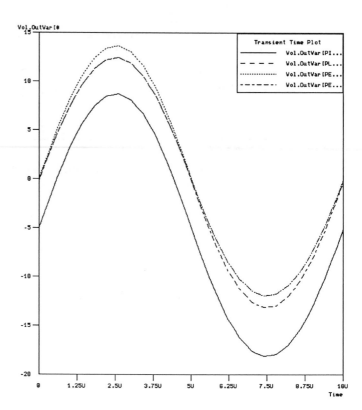

**Fig. 7.4-6** Circuit voltage waveforms at 100 kHz, for a 15.6 V peak source sinusoid

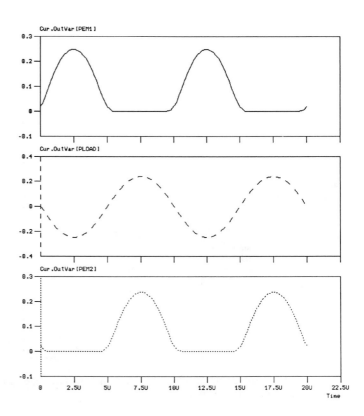

**Fig. 7.4-7** Current waveforms

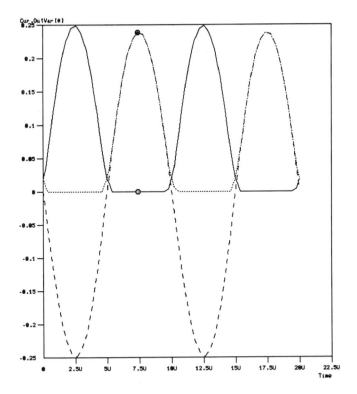

**Fig. 7.4-8**   Current waveforms of Fig. 7.4-7 using common Y axis

### 7.4.5   Further work

1. Use the **FOURIER** facility described in section 8.3 to determine the harmonic content of the load current.
2. Determine the response to a 100 kHz square wave.

Note the effect of the capacitive component of the input impedance $Z_{IN}$ on the value of the input voltage. Calculate the **Device Voltage Gain** and the **Circuit Voltage Gain** (with respect to circuit input voltage – the 300 Ω resistance is part of the source) and compare with your predictions.

Explain why:

1. during the top half of the sinusoid the emitter voltage of the pnp transistor is the same as that across the load; and
2. during the bottom half of the sinusoid the emitter voltage of the npn transistor is the same as that across the load.

Also explain what happens to the −5 V **DC** offset voltage present in the source.

In Fig. 7.4-7 MINNIE presents both current waveforms with the same polarity. Explain why this is correct.

Note that the peak magnitudes of the currents are not identical. Explain why this is so, and whether it will affect the symmetry of the waveform applied to the load.

### 7.5 EXERCISE: OPERATIONAL AMPLIFIERS – SIMPLE BAND-PASS ACTIVE FILTER

#### 7.5.1 Discussion

The circuit in Fig. 7.5-1 is a well-known second-order active filter known as the **Sallen and Key band-pass network**. It can be shown that its transfer function is given by

$$H(s) = \frac{V_{OUT}(s)}{V_{IN}(s)}$$

$$= \frac{ks/R_1C_1}{s^2 + \left[\dfrac{1}{R_1C_1} + \dfrac{1}{R_3C_2} + \dfrac{1}{R_3C_1} + \dfrac{1-k}{R_2C_1}\right]s + \dfrac{R_1 + R_2}{R_1R_2R_3C_1C_2}} \quad (7.5\text{-}1)$$

where $k$ is the voltage gain of the non-inverting op-amp and is set by

$$k = (R_A + R_B)/R_A \quad (7.5\text{-}2)$$

Equation 7.5-1 may be written as

$$H(s) = K\frac{(\omega_P/Q_P)\,s}{s^2 + (\omega_P/Q_P)s + \omega_P^2} \quad (7.5\text{-}3)$$

where

$\omega_P$ = the mid-band frequency (frequency of maximum response, resonant frequency); $\omega_P = (\omega_H\omega_L)^{\frac{1}{2}}$;

$Q_P = \omega_P/(\omega_H - \omega_L)$, the 'quality factor', the reciprocal of the normalized

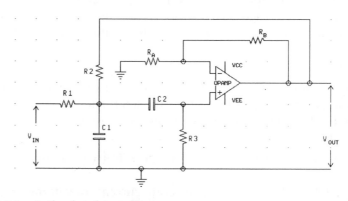

**Fig. 7.5-1** Active band-pass filter

bandwidth as defined by the half power frequencies $\omega_H$ and $\omega_L$; and

$K$ = the filter's transfer function at $\omega = \omega_P$.

The values of $\omega_P$, $Q_P$ and $K$ are easy to obtain from the above equations. A simple realization of this filter can be obtained by setting $R_1 = R_2 = R_3$ and $C_1 = C_2$, leading to

$$\omega_P = \sqrt{2}/RC \quad Q_P = \sqrt{2}/(4 - k) \quad K = k/(4 - k) \quad\quad (7.5\text{-}4)$$

Note that for a given bandwidth and mid-band frequency the values of $Q_P$, $k$ and $K$ are fixed. Consequently adjustment to the overall system transfer function must be achieved by other means.

### 7.5.2 Design

Design an active filter based on the above circuit, having a 250 Hz midband frequency and $Q_P = 10$. Use preferred values of capacitors and inductors (consult catalogues if necessary). Determine K. Simulate your design and compare results against specification.

A possible solution is $R = 10\,\text{k}\Omega$, $C = 90\,\text{nF}$, $R_A = 5.6\,\text{k}\Omega$ and $R_B = 16\,\text{k}\Omega$ (say $15\,\text{k}\Omega + 1\,\text{k}\Omega$).

### 7.5.3 Simulation

1. Set up the circuit as shown in Fig. 7.5-2. The **OP AMP** is taken from the **Discrete Components** page.
2. Select the **PARAM** facility, move the magnifying glass cursor to the op-amp and select it. The **DCL OPAMP** menu of Fig. 7.5-3 appears.
3. Select **Model name** and the list of library op-amps appears, as in Fig. 7.5-4. Use the arrows at the bottom to scroll the list.
4. Select the **ALM741** op-amp (the well-known 741).
5. Set up a suitable analysis profile, as in Fig. 7.5-5.

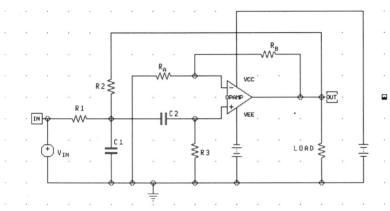

**Fig. 7.5-2** Circuit for simulation

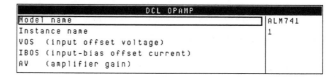

**Fig. 7.5-3** Discrete Components Library op-amp menu

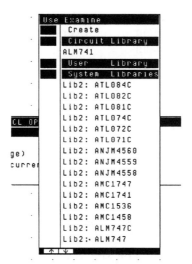

**Fig. 7.5-4** List of library op-amps

**Fig. 7.5-5** Analysis Profile

6. Display your results, and confirm by measurement the mid-band frequency $f_P$, the half power bandwidth $f_H - f_L$, and quality factor $Q_P$, (see Fig. 7.5-6). Confirm the value of $K$.

## 7.6 EXERCISE: OPERATIONAL AMPLIFIERS – THE WIEN BRIDGE OSCILLATOR

### 7.6.1 The Wien Bridge

This well-known passive $RC$ band stop circuit is shown in Fig. 7.6-1.

*Analysis*
1. Show that the $R_1 C_1 R_2 C_2$ (Wien network) branch of this circuit is a band-pass filter having the following characteristics:
   (a) the output voltage maximizes at

$$\omega_O = 1/(R_1 R_2 C_1 C_2)^{\frac{1}{2}};$$

(7.6-1)

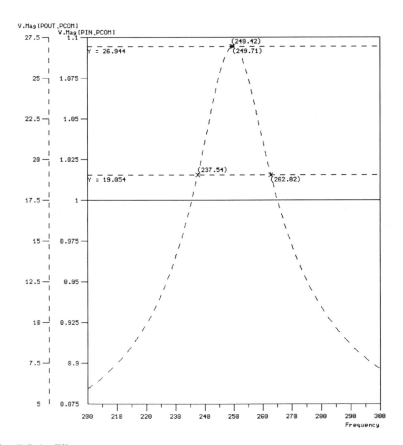

**Fig. 7.5-6** Filter response

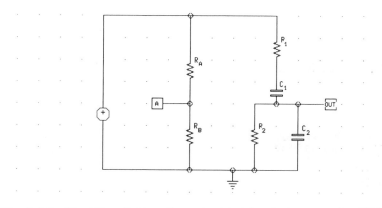

**Fig. 7.6-1** The Wien Bridge; the output is taken between nodes **OUT** and **A**

(b) the output voltage at $\omega_O$ is given by

$$V_O = V_S/(1 + R_1/R_2 + C_2/C_1) \tag{7.6-2}$$

where $V_S$ is the applied voltage; and

(c) the phase shift at $\omega_O$ is zero.

2. (a) Determine the corresponding expressions for $R_1 = R_2$ and $C_1 = C_2$.

(b) Show that this circuit now has a quality factor $Q_O = \frac{1}{3}$.

3. $R_A = 2R_B$ is the normal design choice for the Wien Bridge. The bridge output voltage is taken between the nodes labelled **OUT** and **A**.

Show that the bridge is a band-stop circuit and write down the equations for:

(a) the frequency at which the output voltage minimizes;
(b) the output voltage at this frequency; and
(c) the corresponding phase shift.

*Design*

Select components for a Wien Bridge with $f_O = 10\,\text{kHz}$. Use preferred value components (consult catalogues as necessary). The circuit is to form the load/feedback network of an operational amplifier, so the currents should not be large. Resistance magnitudes between a few hundred ohms and a few tens of kilo-ohms should be adequate. Electrolytic capacitors *must* be avoided.

A possible solution is:

$$R_1 = R_2 = 10\,\text{k}\Omega,$$
$$C_1 = C_2 = 1.59\,\text{nF}\ (1000\,\text{pF} + 470\,\text{pF} + 120\,\text{pF}),$$
$$R_A = 10\,\text{k}\Omega,$$
$$R_B = 20\,\text{k}\Omega\ (10\,\text{k}\Omega + 10\,\text{k}\Omega).$$

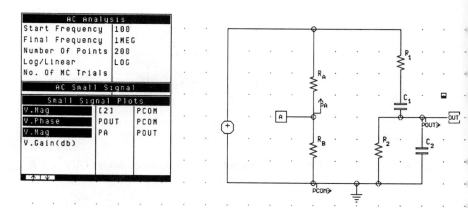

**Fig. 7.6-2** Possible analysis profile for Wien Bridge simulation; probe positions as indicated

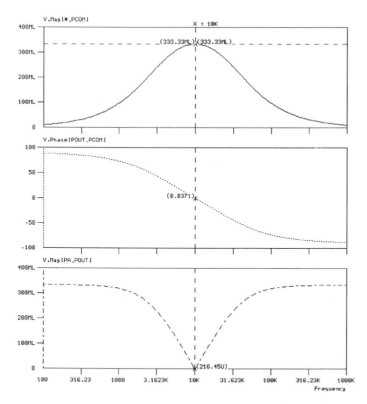

**Fig. 7.6-3** Performance of the Wien Bridge ($V_{SOURCE} = 1\,V$)

*Simulation*

Perform a simulation of your circuit and display your results. Possible analysis profile and results are shown in Figs. 7.6-2 and 7.6-3. It is not necessary to cover such a wide frequency range, but it does show the full phase shift characteristic. Note that the large number of points is necessary if you wish to determine $f_O$ accurately. To cut down simulation time reduce the number of points *and* the frequency range together.

Note that though the results shown were obtained using the component values given above, they are valid for all sets of values which satisfy the design equations (provided the same voltage is applied).

Use the **Measure** facility to determine the voltage magnitudes and phase shift at $f_O$, and to confirm the value of $Q_O$. See how the voltage between the input non-inverting terminal and the **OUT** node minimizes at $f_O$.

### 7.6.2 Loop Gain and Nyquist Plot

*Simulation*

Set up the circuit shown in Fig. 7.6-4, using your component values and an **ALM741** op-amp from the **Discrete Components** page. Set the supply voltages to between ±12 and ±18 V.

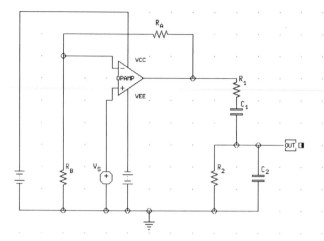

**Fig. 7.6-4** Circuit for determining the Loop Gain of the Wien Bridge Oscillator

Note that the performance of this initial circuit is not quite adequate to sustain oscillations, so a small modification will be necessary (to marginally increase the loop gain).

Set up an appropriate **Analysis** profile. There are two points with which you should be concerned.

1. Op-amp gain and phase shift: for correct operation the voltage gain at the selected frequency $f_O$ should be accurately set to $A_V = 3$ as determined by the (negative) feedback network $R_A - R_B$. Furthermore its phase shift should be 0. Consequently you should examine the op-amp output voltage magnitude and phase.

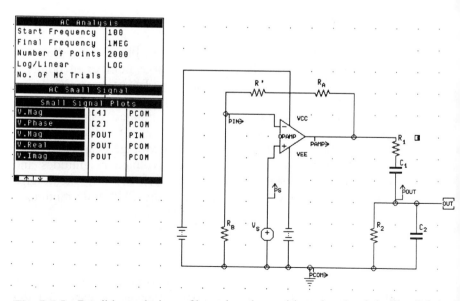

**Fig. 7.6-5** Possible analysis profile and probe positions for circuit in Fig. 7.6-4; note the added resistance $R' = 0.1\% R_A$

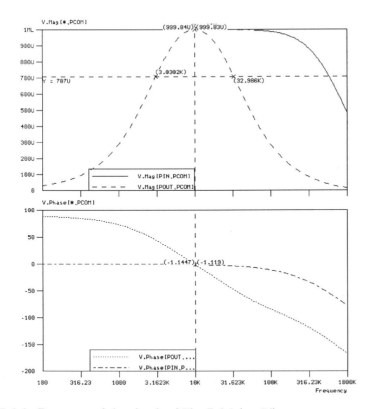

**Fig. 7.6-6**   Response of the circuit of Fig. 7.6-4 (no $R'$)

2. To determine the loop gain and obtain the Nyquist plot for an oscillator, it is necessary to break the (regenerative) feedback loop and determine the real and $j$ terms of the ratio of the feedback voltage to the input voltage.

In Fig. 7.6-4 the voltage to be fed back (when the loop is closed) is that on the **OUT** node, while the input voltage is $V_S$ applied to its non-inverting terminal.

A possible Analysis profile is shown in Fig. 7.6-5, together with the slight circuit modification – $R'$ – referred to above. Results (obtained using the component values of part A above and with $R' = 0.1\% R_A = 20\,\Omega$) are shown in Figs. 7.6-6, 7.6-7, 7.6-8, 7.6-9, 7.6-10 and 7.6-11.

The reason for the increase in the loop gain can be seen in Fig. 7.6-6. It shows that for $V_S = 1\,\text{mV}$ the voltage magnitude at the **OUT** node never quite reaches $1\,\text{mV}$, so the loop gain is always less than 1. The shortfall is of the order of $0.16$–$0.17\,\mu\text{V}$, or $0.016\%$–$0.017\%$, and is more than compensated for by the added resistance, as can be seen in Fig. 7.6-7.

In Fig. 7.6-6 the loop gain peaks, at $10\,\text{kHz}$, at $0.99983$–$0.99984$, just short of the minimum $1.0+$ required to sustain oscillations. The bandwidth, $2956\,\text{kHz}$, is slightly less than the $3333\,\text{kHz}$ expected from

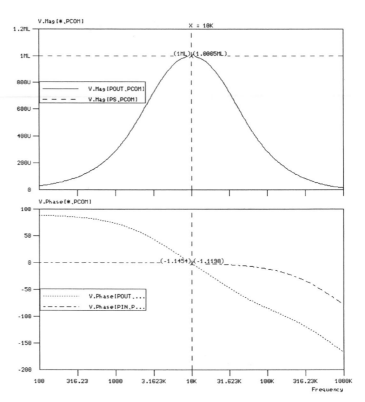

**Fig. 7.6-7** Response of the circuit of Fig. 7.6-5 (with $R'$)

$Q_O = \frac{1}{3}$. This discrepancy may be explained by observing that the voltage at **PIN** (and consequently at the op-amp's output) has started to fall at about 30 kHz.

It can be seen that at 10 kHz the phase shift is $-1.119°$ at the inverting input (and op-amp output) and $-1.1447°$ at the **OUT** node. Clearly most of the error is attributable to the non-ideal high frequency performance of the op-amp (compare with Fig. 7.6-3 for the Wien Bridge alone).

It must also be remembered that the analysis was performed at 2000 points in the 100 Hz–1 MHz frequency range. On a log scale this implies a constant ratio of 1.0046158 between any two consecutive frequency points, corresponding to a 46.16 Hz increment at 10 kHz. This lack of resolution could account for a small part of the bandwidth and $Q_O$ discrepancies. (With 200 points the frequency interval increases to 458 Hz, so to reduce simulation time cut down on the frequency range as well as on the number of simulation points. Note that 200 points between 6 kHz and 15 kHz would yield 45.9 Hz increments at 10 kHz).

In Fig. 7.6-7 the applied voltage is 1 mV, that at node **OUT** is 1.0005 mV at 10 kHz. Consequently the loop gain exceeds 1 at this frequency. The effect on the phase shifts is marginal.

Note from Fig. 7.6-8 that the peaks of the $j$ component occur virtually at the half-power frequencies, at which the phase shifts are $\pm45°$ and the

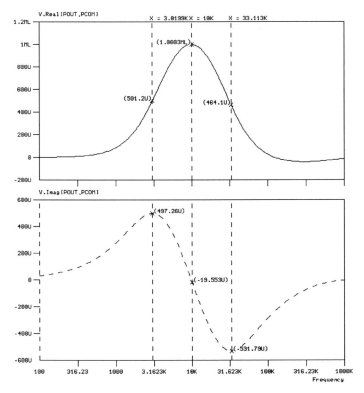

**Fig. 7.6-8** Real and *j* parts of the voltage at **OUT** node

real and *j* magnitudes are nearly equal. Again there are discrepancies probably due to the limited frequency resolution.

The Nyquist plot is shown in Fig. 7.6-9. To obtain the loop gain the output voltages must be divided by the input magnitude (1 mV). Plotting the real part (**NORMX**) along the X axis and the *j* part (**NORMY**) on the Y axis yields a circle which is clearly seen to enclose the point 1 + *j*0. Furthermore though MINNIE does not show frequency on this plot we can establish, from examination of Fig. 7.6-7, that the movement of the locus of the loop gain with increasing frequency proceeds in a *clockwise* direction as it encircles 1 + *j*0. Consequently the system should oscillate.

### 7.6.3 The Wien Bridge oscillator

*Discussion*

In theory a feedback oscillator cannot start up by itself, it requires some form of external stimulus which it can then build up and keep going. In a real situation this external stimulus is provided by the noise (due to thermal excitation of electrons, device 1/*f* noise, inductive and capacitive interference from other sources, etc.) which is always present in all conductors.

A simple way to simulate the presence of noise is to place a small

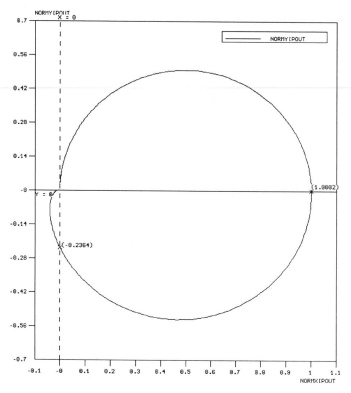

**Fig. 7.6-9** Nyquist plot for the open loop circuit

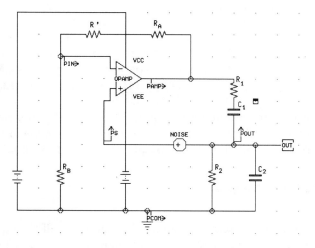

**Fig. 7.6-10** Wien Bridge Oscillator: a $1\,\mu V$ source simulates the presence of noise

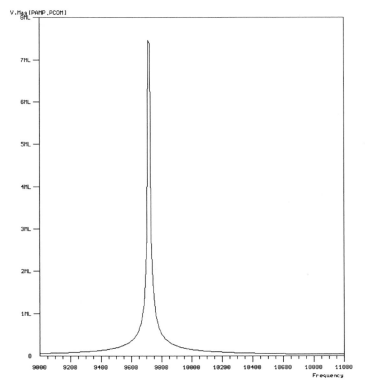

**Fig. 7.6-11**   Results of preliminary simulation

voltage source in the system, such as the one labelled **NOISE** in Fig. 7.6-10. A small value should theoretically be adequate, so its amplitude might be set at $1\,\mu V$.

The **selectivity** of the circuit with regenerative feedback will be very much sharper than for the open loop case. Consequently it is desirable to use much better frequency resolution.

The results obtained in section 7.6-2 above (the phase shifts in particular) indicate that the actual frequency of oscillation $f_O$ will not be exactly $10\,kHz$, so it is desirable to first determine its actual value. For this purpose a low resolution simulation, covering the $9\,kHz$ to $11\,kHz$ range in 200 points is adequate. A second simulation in the vicinity of $f_O$ will provide finer detail.

*First simulation*

Set up the circuit as shown in Fig. 7.6-10, with **NOISE** set to $1\,\mu V$. Run the simulation and display the results, as in Fig. 7.6-11.

It is clear that the circuit's $f_O$ lies in the $9.7\,kHz$ region. It is also noticeable that the response does not go to infinity (as theory predicts), but this may be due to the relatively low ($10\,Hz$) resolution on the frequency axis.

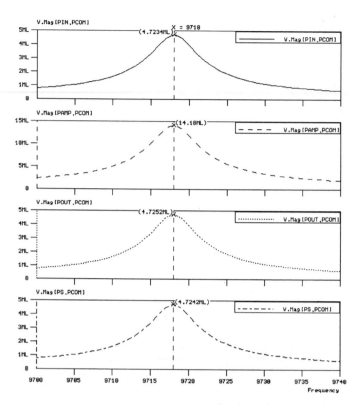

**Fig. 7.6-12**  Voltage magnitudes between 9700 and 9740 Hz

*Second simulation*
A second simulation will narrow the value of $f_O$ to somewhere between 9700 Hz and 9740 Hz.

Note that MINNIE/HSpice do not like the number of points to exceed the number of Hz in the specified frequency range. If you ask for 200 points in a 40 Hz range your top limit will be ignored and the analysis will assume a frequency range up to 10 MHz!

The maximum response on the op-amp's output is just under 7.5 mV, almost 7500 times greater than the NOISE stimulus, but still finite.

*Final simulation*
A final simulation would request analysis at 1 Hz intervals in the vicinity of resonance. Typical results are shown in Fig. 7.6-12.

As the analysis was performed at 1 Hz intervals it is clear that the response maximizes at 9718 Hz ± 0.5 Hz. From the shape of the responses near $f_O$ it is also clear that they remain finite in the fractional frequencies at which no analysis is performed.

This result shows up a limitation in the performance of this simulation package – in a laboratory situation this circuit would oscillate.

# Linear circuits: square waves and step functions

# 8

## 8.1 SQUARE WAVES, PULSE TRAINS AND STEP FUNCTIONS

The basic waveshape is that of the **pulse train**. The other two are derived by appropriate selection of parameters. Consequently MINNIE deals with them together under the common heading `PULSE`.

The nominal shape is shown in Fig. 8.1-1. MINNIE uses the following quantities to define the pulse train produced by an `AC Voltage source`. (For current pulses the format is similar).

**V1**    initial value of voltage (either polarity).

**V2**    second (pulsed) value of voltage (either polarity).

**TD**    delay time, at voltage level **V1**, between the start time $t = 0$ and the *first* transition from **V1** to **V2**. The default value is set to 0.

**TR**    rise (or raise) time: the duration of the **V1** to **V2** transition.

**TF**    fall time: the duration of the **V2** to **V1** transition.

**PW**    pulse width: the duration of the **V2** level during each repetition of the waveshape (it excludes rise and fall times).

**PER**   period: in a *repetitive* waveform it is the time between consecutive occurrences of the same part of the waveshape.

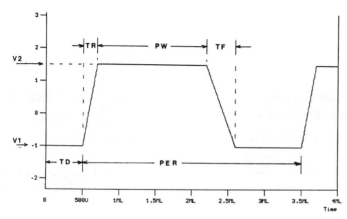

**Fig. 8.1-1**   Basic pulsed waveshape definitions

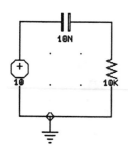

**Fig. 8.2-1** Differentiating circuit. $\tau = RC = 0.1\,\text{ms}$

period = 1/(repetition rate)

(For sinusoids: repetition rate = frequency)

Note that idealized waveshapes are assumed at the source: voltage levels **V1** and **V2** are held constant, and the transitions have constant slopes.

## 8.2 TUTORIAL: SQUARE WAVE RESPONSE OF THE SIMPLE DIFFERENTIATING CIRCUIT

Draw the circuit of Fig. 8.2-1. It is often referred to as a **high pass** or as a **differentiating** circuit according to context, and use the **VALUES** facility to set $R = 10\,\text{k}\Omega$ and $C = 10\,\text{nF}$. This gives a $0.1\,\text{ms}$ time constant $\tau$.

The ac voltage source will be defined, using the **PARAM** facility, as required. The procedure for setting up a **square wave** follows the same outline (and uses the same menus) as that for setting up a sinusoid – see section 7.2.1.

In **DRAWING** mode, select the **PARAM** (magnifying glass) facility. Move the cursor (now shaped like a magnifying glass) to the voltage source, and press **M** to select the voltage source. The **Independent AC Voltage Source** menu of Fig. 8.2-2 appears, but with the right-hand column empty.

Move the cursor to **Name of Transient Specification** (left-hand column), and select it by (pressing the middle mouse button **M**). The **Library** menu, shown in Fig. 8.2-3, appears (but without **SQ1** under

| Independent AC Voltage source | | |
|---|---|---|
| AC magnitude | [0] | 10 |
| Instance name | | 3 |
| AC phase | [0] | |
| Name of Transient Specification | | SQ1 |

**Fig. 8.2-2** Independent AC Voltage Source menu

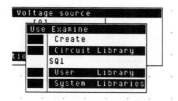
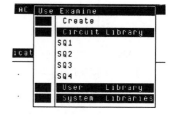

**Fig. 8.2-3** Library menu (a) after the square wave SQ1 has been created (b) after more square waves have been created

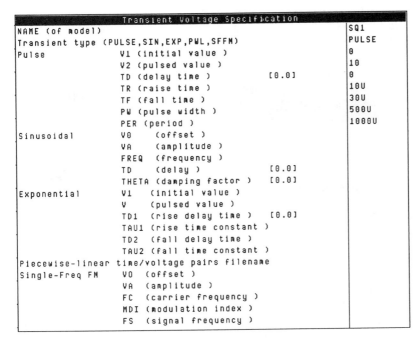

**Fig. 8.2-4** Transient Voltage Specification menu

Circuit Library – you have not created it yet). At present there are no entries, so all you can do is create a new waveshape[1].

Move the cursor to **Create** and press **M** to select it. The **Transient Voltage Specification** menu of Fig. 8.2-4 appears but with its right-hand column empty (save for a default name).

Insert the names and values shown in Fig. 8.2-4 by adopting the following procedure for each:

1. place the cursor in the right-hand column next to the appropriate parameter;
2. select (press middle mouse button **M**) and the corresponding box becomes enhanced;
3. type the required value;
4. deselect (press **M** again) and the value is accepted.

When ready deselect this menu (by pressing **M** on its heading), returning to Fig. 8.2-2.

The defined waveform is filed, with the name you gave it, in this circuit's library. Consequently you can reuse it with future variations of this circuit.

---

[1] If a waveform previously defined for *this* family of circuits (i.e. circuit variations filed under the same name) exists, it can be selected for **Use** at this stage, returning immediately to Fig. 8.2-2. Alternatively it can be selected for **Examine**, and if required, modified as outlined later.

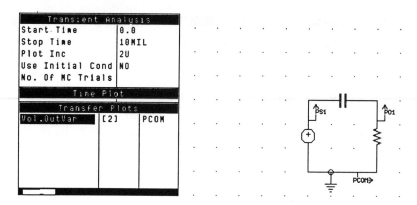

**Fig. 8.2-5**  Analysis Profile: Transient Analysis, Time Plot

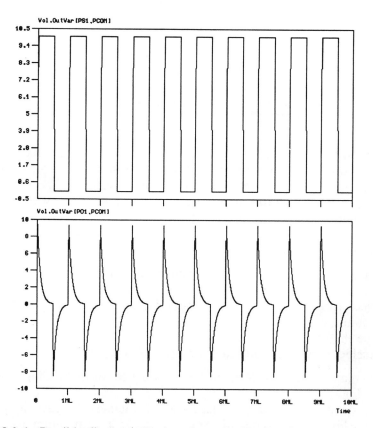

**Fig. 8.2-6**  Possible display (edited as shown in Chapter 5)

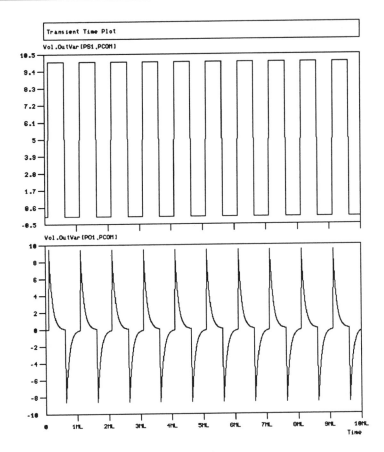

**Fig. 8.2-7**  As Fig. 8.2-6, but with $TD = 0.1$ ns

Deselect again and then cancel the **PARAM** facility. Now select Analysis mode, and Transient Analysis, and then set up the analysis profile shown in Fig. 8.2-5 (following the procedures outlined for AC Analysis, AC Small Signal in section 2.1). Then, when you are ready select Run (int).

When the analysis is complete (about nine minutes on the UMIST Apollos) MINNIE will automatically go into **RESULTS** mode. Set up an appropriate display, such as Fig. 8.2-6.

### 8.2.1  Simple exercises

1. Repeat with the delay time set to 0.1 ns. See Fig. 8.2-7 for display.
2. Set up a **step function** as follows:

| | | | |
|---|---|---|---|
| V1 | 0 | TR | 1 ns |
| V2 | 5 V | TF | 1 ns (actual value not important) |
| TD | 0.1 ms | PW | 2 ms (PW $\gg$ time constant $\tau$) |
| PER | 2.1 ms (PER $>$ (PW + TR + TF)) | | |

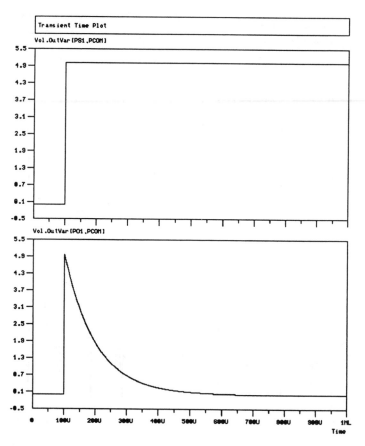

**Fig. 8.2-8** Differentiating circuit's response to step input

The analysis need only cover 10 or 15 time constants – say 1.5 ms.

Set up an appropriate analysis profile, simulate, and display your results.

See Fig. 8.2-8 for a display of results.

### 8.3 TUTORIAL: THE COMMON EMITTER WITH SQUARE WAVE INPUT – WAVEFORMS AND THEIR HARMONIC CONTENTS

Set up the circuit of Fig. 8.3-1 using the following components:

$$
\begin{array}{lll}
\text{R1} = & 10\,\text{k}\Omega & \text{R2} = 3.9\,\text{k}\Omega & \text{RC} = 1.2\,\text{k}\Omega \\
\text{RE} = & 600\,\Omega & \text{RL} = 1.0\,\text{k}\Omega \\
\text{CC1} = & 10\,\text{nF} & \text{CC2} = 10\,\text{nF} & \text{CD} = 10\,\mu\text{F} \\
\text{VCC} = & 15\,\text{V}
\end{array}
$$

Transistor: 2N2222 from the Discrete Components library.

Follow the procedures outlined above to set up the 10 kHz, 20 mV input square wave, as defined in Fig. 8.3-2.

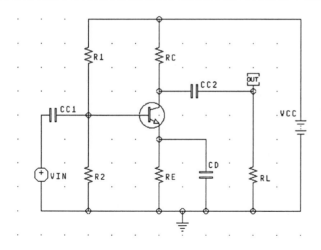

**Fig. 8.3-1**

```
               Transient Voltage Specification
NAME (of model)                                    SQ0
Transient type (PULSE,SIN,EXP,PWL,SFFM)            PULSE
Pulse              V1 (initial value )             0
                   V2 (pulsed value )              20MIL
                   TD (delay time )        [0.0]   0
                   TR (raise time )                100N
                   TF (fall time )                 100N
                   PW (pulse width )               5U
                   PER (period )                   10U
Sinusoidal         V0    (offset )
                   VA    (amplitude )
                   FREQ  (frequency )
                   TD    (delay )          [0.0]
                   THETA (damping factor ) [0.0]
Exponential        V1    (initial value )
                   V     (pulsed value )
                   TD1   (rise delay time )  [0.0]
                   TAU1 (rise time constant )
                   TD2   (fall delay time )
                   TAU2 (fall time constant )
Piecewise-linear time/voltage pairs filename
Single-Freq FM     VO  (offset )
                   VA  (amplitude )
                   FC  (carrier frequency )
                   MDI (modulation index )
                   FS  (signal frequency )
```

**Fig. 8.3-2**   Square wave. 100 kHz repetition rate

Enter **ANALYSIS** mode. From the high level menu, Fig. 8.3-3, select the appropriate Analysis Options to set up the analysis profiles referred to below.

Set up the AC Analysis, AC Small Signal profile for output, collector and base signals, as shown in Fig. 8.3-4 (the input is obviously not needed).

**Fig. 8.3-3**

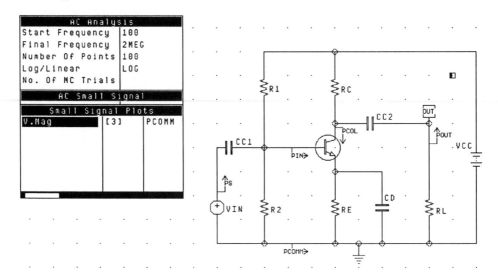

**Fig. 8.3-4**

Transient Analysis
Start Time | 0
Stop Time | 50U
Plot Inc | 1U
Use Initial Cond | NO
No. Of MC Trials
Time Plot
Fourier Analysis

**Fig. 8.3-5** `Transient Analysis` options

When you select the `Transient Analysis` option in Fig. 8.3-3 you are offered the choice of `Time Plot` or `Fourier Analysis`, as shown in Fig. 8.3-5. For this tutorial both are required.

Set up the `Transient Analysis`, `Time Plot` profile for output, collector, base and source signals, as shown in Fig. 8.3-6.

Set up the `Transient Analysis`, `Fourier Analysis` profile for output, collector, base and source signals, as shown in Fig. 8.3-7.

When ready, select `Run(int)` and let MINNIE get on with the analysis. Then display the results:

1. MINNIE will place you in the `AC` display mode, subset `Plots`. Adjust your options appropriately and select `Do it!` to present the results. Figure 8.3-8 shows a possible display after editing.
2. (a) Cancel `Graph Options` to clear the display.
   (b) Cancel `AC` to obtain the higher level menu of Fig. 8.3-9(a).
   (c) Select `Transient` to obtain the menu of Fig. 8.3-9(b).
   (d) Select the `Time Plot` to get Fig. 8.3-10(a).
   (e) Adjust your options appropriately and select `Do it!` to present the waveforms. Figures 8.3-11 and 8.3-12 show possible displays (after editing).
3. (a) Again cancel `Graph Option` to clear the display.
   (b) Cancel `Time Plot` to return to the menu of Fig. 8.3-9(b).
   (c) Select `Fourier` to get Fig. 8.3-10(b).
   (d) Adjust your options appropriately and select `Do it!` to display the harmonic content of the waveforms. Figures 8.3-13 and 8.3-14 show possible displays.

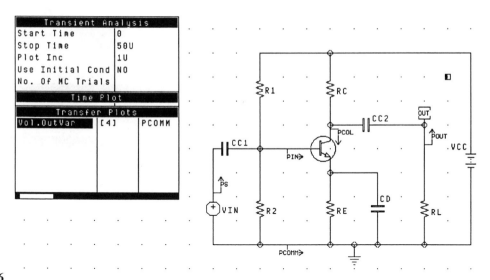

**Fig. 8.3-6**

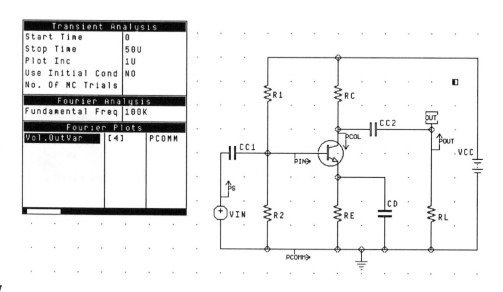

**Fig. 8.3-7**

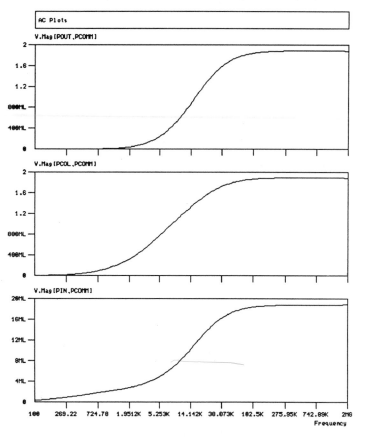
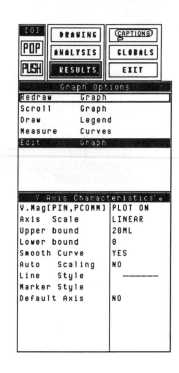

**Fig. 8.3-8** Bode Plots, 100 Hz to 2 MHz, after editing. The circuit's bandwidth clearly exceeds 2 MHz.

**Fig. 8.3-9** (a) Analysis Results main menu (b) Transient Results menu

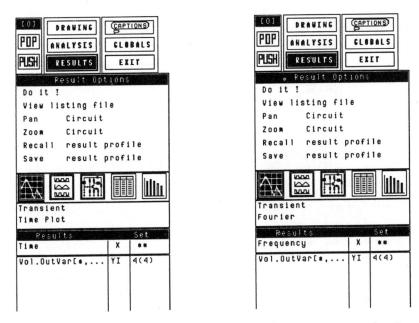

**Fig. 8.3-10** (a) Results menu for waveforms (b) Results menu for Fourier analysis

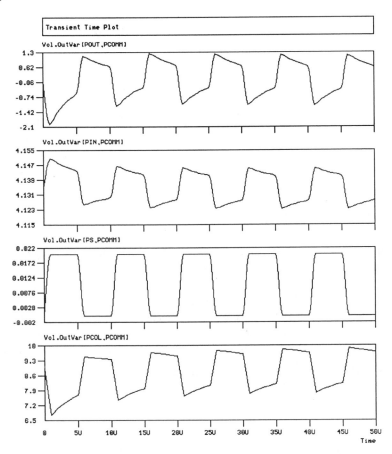

**Fig. 8.3-11** Waveforms – multiple display, independent Y axis

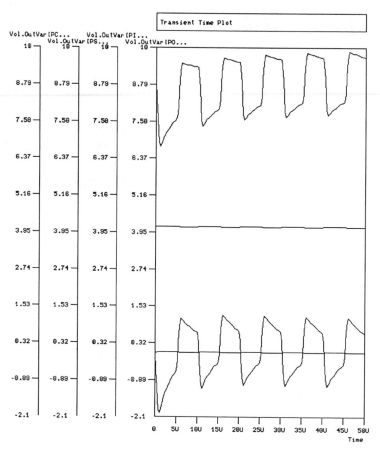

**Fig. 8.3-12** Waveforms: single display; common axis; compare with Fig. 8.3-11

## 8.4 EXERCISE: TRANSIENT RESPONSE OF A SWITCHED *RC* CIRCUIT USING INITIAL CONDITIONS

A capacitive load, equivalent to a $100\,\mu\text{F}$ capacitor, is to be repeatedly charged to $1200\,\text{V}$ from a completely discharged condition. A $1500\,\text{V}$ voltage source is available, capable of delivering currents only up to a maximum of $50\,\text{mA}$ without damage.

The circuit in Fig. 8.4-1 is designed to meet these requirements, the resistors being used to limit the current. The switches are used to control the charging rate, resistors being short-circuited when not required.

1. Describe the operation of the circuit, paying particular attention to the sequence in which the switches are operated.
2. The capacitor is to be fully charged, from $V_C = 0\,\text{V}$ to $V_C = 1.2\,\text{kV}$, in minimum time. Determine the capacitor voltage at which each switch must be operated.
3. The charging process starts at time $t_1 = 0$. Determine the times at which each switch must be operated and the total charging time.

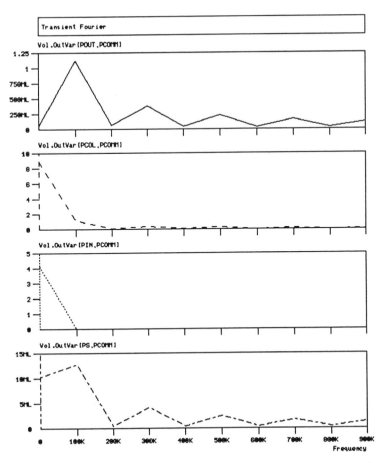

**Fig. 8.3-13** Harmonic content of the waveforms: the 0 Hz values are, of course, the DC bias values

| Frequency | Vol.OutVar [POUT,P... | Vol.OutVar [PCOL,P... | Vol.OutVar [PIN,PC... | Vol.OutVar [PS,PCOMM] |
|---|---|---|---|---|
| 0 | 56.16ML | 8.878 | 4.135 | 10.2ML |
| 100K | 1.118 | 1.15 | 11.73ML | 12.73ML |
| 200K | 69.3ML | 77.4ML | 416.1U | 397.7U |
| 300K | 380.8ML | 387.5ML | 3.971ML | 4.222ML |
| 400K | 45.66ML | 49.72ML | 385.3U | 396.6U |
| 500K | 230.1ML | 233.7ML | 2.362ML | 2.51ML |
| 600K | 34.47ML | 37.3ML | 380.5U | 394.9U |
| 700K | 158.7ML | 160.9ML | 1.666ML | 1.768ML |
| 800K | 33.97ML | 36.24ML | 374.6U | 392.5U |
| 900K | 121.7ML | 123.1ML | 1.272ML | 1.349ML |

**Fig. 8.3-14** Harmonic content of waveforms, tabular presentation

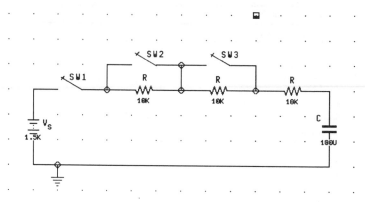

**Fig. 8.4-1** Capacitor charging circuit: $V_S = 1.5\,\text{kV}$ at $50\,\text{mA}$ max, $R = 10\,\text{k}\Omega$

| Capacitor | |
|---|---|
| Capacitance (nominal) | 100U |
| Instance name | 5 |
| 1st order temperature compensation coefficient [0] | |
| 2nd order temperature compensation coefficient [0] | |
| Initial voltage across capacitor [0] | 0 |
| Non-linear capacitor coefficients (Esc., then %) | |
| Capacitor tolerance (between 0.0 and 1.0) [0] | |
| Capacitance designable [NO] | |

**Fig. 8.4-2** PARAM menu for setting up capacitor parameters and initial conditions

### 8.4.1  Discussion

MINNIE does not have facilities for the direct simulation of switch action. (It is possible to simulate an electronic switch with bi-polars or FETs and appropriate driving circuitry, but that lies outside the scope of this work.) Consequently it is necessary to break up the problem into its separately linear parts, using the answers to one as the initial conditions for the next, in exactly the same way as you would for an analytical solution.

As the maximum current that can be delivered is $50\,\text{mA}$, the maximum voltage drop that can be allowed across each $10\,\text{k}\Omega$ resistor is $500\,\text{V}$. Consequently at $t = 0$ it is necessary to close SW1 and keep SW2 and SW3 open until the voltage $V_C$ has risen to $500\,\text{V}$. At this point it is necessary to close either SW2 or SW3 in order to re-maximize the current ($50\,\text{mA}$). When $V_C$ reaches $1000\,\text{V}$ the remaining switch must be closed.

### 8.4.2  Simulation

Set up the circuit of Fig. 8.4-1 with SW1 closed. Set all the component values as indicated, then using the PARAM facility select the capacitor. The Capacitor menu of Fig. 8.4-2 appears. Set the Initial voltage `across capacitor` to 0 V (discharged). The `Capacitance (nominal)` should be at the value set using the `VALUES` facility. If not, set it now.

Set up a `Transient Analysis` profile, as shown in Fig. 8.4-3. Note that it is desirable to have a reasonable idea of the circuit's performance in order to cut down the simulation time. The 2 ms `Plot Inc` imply 1000 sets of calculations over the 2 s simulation interval – you may wish to reduce this resolution.

It is essential that you tell MINNIE that initial conditions are to be used. Otherwise MINNIE will assume that a DC steady state already exists (with the capacitor fully charged to 1.5 kV!).

Run your simulation, but note that you may be informed that error messages were found in the HSpice output files. Press **M** to acknowledge the message, and if you wish to read the message (it might be important) select `View listing file` from the `Result Options` menu. This will bring up the `Analysis Listing File`, shown in Fig. 8.4-4. Scroll through this file to find the error message. Here, you may get the message shown in Fig. 8.4-4, which can be safely ignored.

Display your results, as in Fig. 8.4-5. Note that MINNIE has chosen to use a log scale for voltages. As there is no zero on a log scale MINNIE uses a very small number, $1 \times 10^{-35}$, instead. Use the `Edit Graph` and `Measure Curves` facilities, described in Chapter 5, to improve the

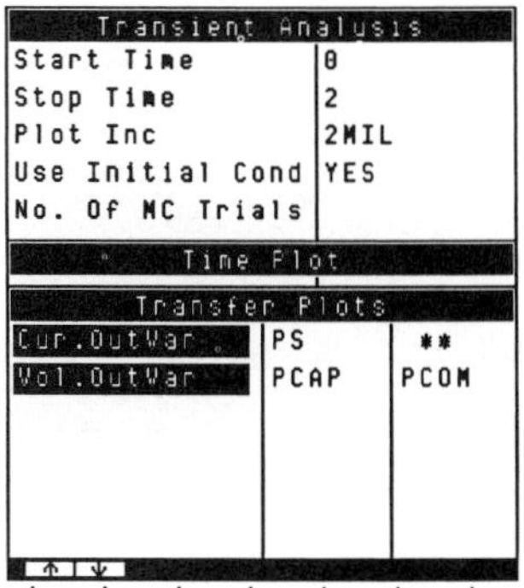

**Fig. 8.4-3** Suitable analysis profile for first charging interval

```
Analysis Listing File
*  ===============
v1 2 3 0
r1 2 3 1e+15

*  designable parameters
*  =====================
*  none

*  analysis requests
*  =================
.op all
.tran 2e-3 2 start=2e-3 uic
   .print tran i(v1) v(1)

.end

**warning** an operating point request at  time=0 and a transient uic
    results in no operating point


.title minnie v7.2.6 hspice request for transtest. 06 nov 90
******  transient analysis                tnom=  25.000 temp=  25.000
******

        time     current        voltage
                    v1             1
 2.0000000e-03 -1.500000e-01  2.296875e-06
 4.0000000e-03 -1.500000e-01  5.296875e-06
 6.0000000e-03 -1.500000e-01  8.296875e-06
 8.0000000e-03 -1.500000e-01  1.129688e-05
```

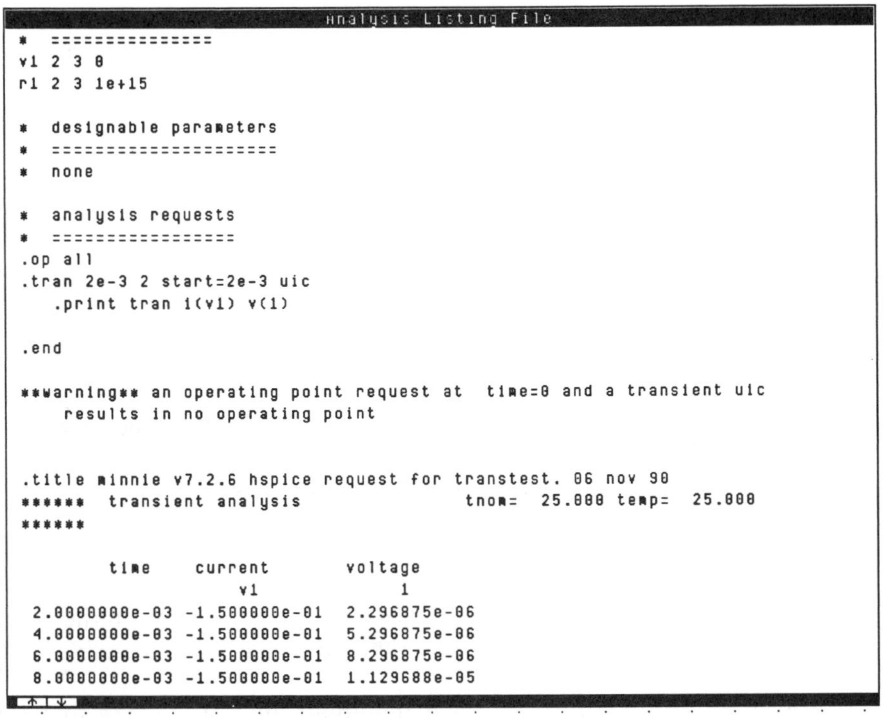

**Fig. 8.4-4** `Analysis Listing` File: the error message is a warning concerning the first point in the simulation; in this case no problems are caused

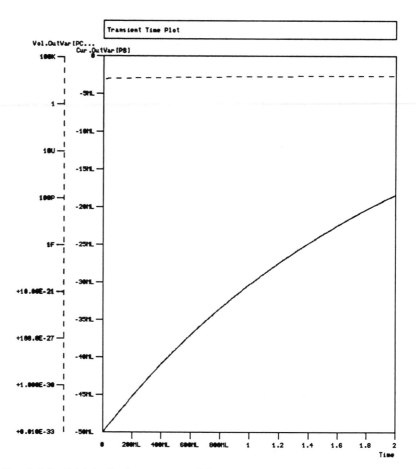

**Fig. 8.4-5** Initial display presented by MINNIE; the voltage scale requires attention

presentation of your results and to determine the time $t_2$ at which $V_C$ reaches 500 V, as in Fig. 8.4-6.

Now return to **Drawing** mode, close either **SW2** or **SW3** and reset the capacitor's initial value to 500 V. The second simulation starts where the first one ends, but its time count starts from zero.

Modify the analysis profile if necessary, run the simulation, and display your results, as in Fig. 8.4-7, measuring the time taken to reach 1000 V.

Finally repeat with all switches closed and the capacitor's initial voltage set to 1 kV, determining the time taken to reach 1.2 kV, as shown in Fig. 8.4-8.

From the above results it takes a minimum time of 3.1135 s to fully charge the capacitor. This agrees very well (to within 0.01%) with the results obtained analytically.

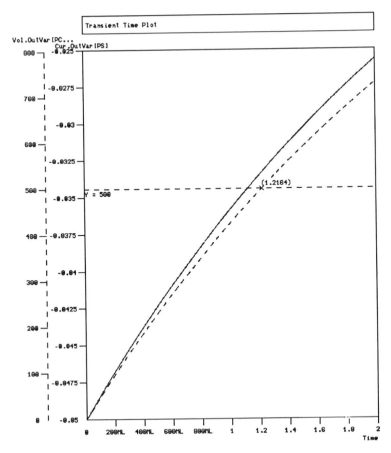

**Fig. 8.4-6** The capacitor voltage reaches 500 V in 1.2164 s

## 8.5 EXERCISE: TRANSIENT RESPONSE OF A SWITCHED *RL* CIRCUIT USING INITIAL CONDITIONS

In Fig. 8.5-1 the switch **SW2** and the inductor **L** represent a magnetic relay. ($R_C$ represents the resistance of the inductor). The operation of the relay is such that when the current in the inductor rises above 50 mA its contacts close, and they open when it falls below 20 mA.

The relay is controlled by a semiconductor switch connected to a DC voltage. This arrangement may be represented by switch **SW1** and the 7.5 V voltage source.

The circuit has been at rest for some time, so there is no current flowing in the inductor. At time $t_1 = 0$ switch **SW1** closes, and it re-opens at $t_2 = 15$ ms.

1. Explain the operation of the circuit.
2. (a) When do the reed relay contacts close?

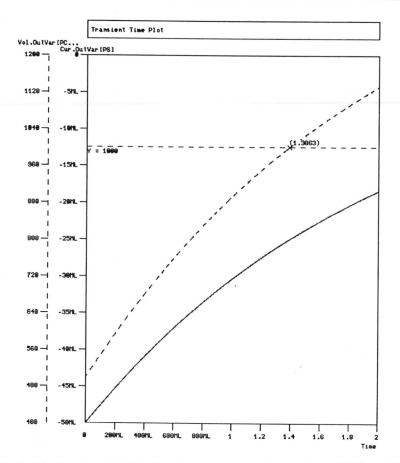

**Fig. 8.4-7** It takes 1.3863 s for the capacitor to charge from 500 V to 1000 V; the charging time so far is 2.6027

(b) When do they open?
(c) How long are they closed for?

### 8.5.1 Simulation

Set up the circuit with **SW1** closed. Use the **PARAM** facility to set **L = 1H**, and set the **Initial current through inductor** to **0**, as in Fig. 8.5-2.

Remember to remove unused conductors – MINNIE will object if you leave loose wires on your circuit.

Set up an appropriate analysis profile to cover the time (15 ms) that **SW1** remains closed. Remember to tell MINNIE that you are using initial conditions, as in Fig. 8.5-3.

Run your simulation and present your results. Use the **Edit Graph** facility to improve presentation. Use the **Measure Curves** facility to determine the time at which the reed relay contacts close and the

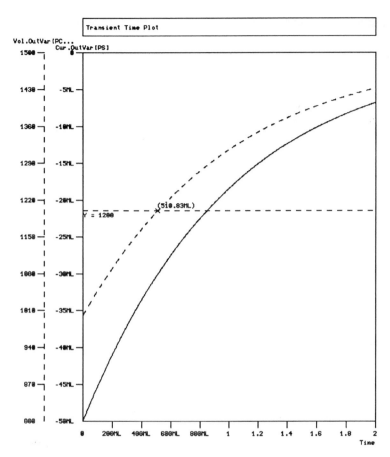

**Fig. 8.4-8**  It takes 510.83 ms for the capacitor to charge from 1000 V to 1200 V.

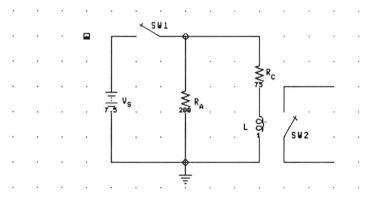

**Fig. 8.5-1**  Schematic representation of a reed relay drive circuit; $V_S = 7.5\,V$, $R_A = 200\,\Omega$, $R_C = 75\,\Omega$, L = 1 H.

| Transient Analysis | |
| --- | --- |
| Start Time | 20U |
| Stop Time | 20MIL |
| Plot Inc | 20U |
| Use Initial Cond | YES |
| No. Of MC Trials | |
| Time Plot | |
| Transfer Plots | |
| Cur.OutVar | PCOIL | ** |
| Vol.OutVar | PIND | |

**Fig. 8.5-3** Initial conditions are specified

| Inductor | | |
| --- | --- | --- |
| Inductance (nominal) | | 1 |
| Instance name | | |
| 1st order temperature compensation coefficient | [0] | |
| 2nd order temperature compensation coefficient | [0] | |
| Initial current through inductor | [0] | 0 |
| Number of turns ( * Inductance = Effective) | [1] | |
| Non-linear inductor coefficients (Esc., then %) | | |
| Inductor tolerance (between 0.0 and 1.0) | [0] | |
| Inductance designable | [NO] | |

**Fig. 8.5-2** The 1 H inductor has its initial current set to zero

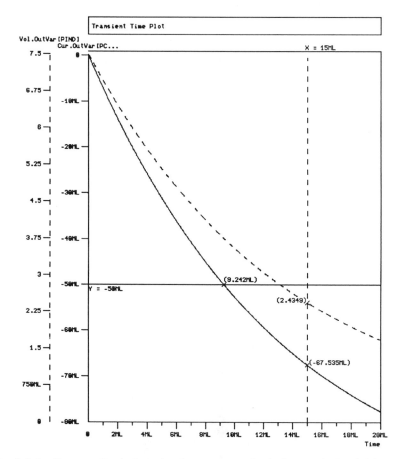

**Fig. 8.5-4** Current through and voltage across the inductor during initial 15 ms

magnitude of the current in the inductor when **SW1** opens, as in Fig. 8.5-4. This will be the initial current for the next part of the simulation.

Return to **Drawing** mode. For the second part of the simulation **SW1** is open, so it is necessary to remove it and all its related wiring. The inductor has the initial current corresponding to $t_2 = 15$ ms flowing through it. Set up this initial condition.

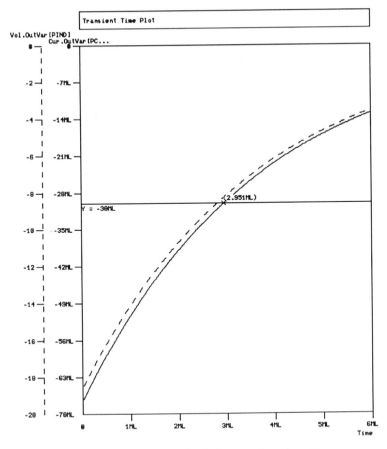

**Fig. 8.5-5** Current and voltage for the inductor after $t_2 = 15\,\text{ms}$

Set up the appropriate `Analysis Profile`, run the simulation, and display your results, as in Fig. 8.5-5.

While `SW1` is closed the current in L rises exponentially towards $100\,\text{mA}$ (with time constant $L/R_C = 1/75\,\text{s}$). At $t_A = 9.242\,\text{ms}$ it reaches $50\,\text{mA}$ and `SW2` closes. At $t_2 = 15\,\text{ms}$ the current has risen to $67.535\,\text{mA}$, as shown in Fig. 8.5-4.

In Fig. 8.5-5 the current and voltage are both decaying towards 0 (with a time constant $L/(R_C + R_A) = 1/275\,\text{s}$). The relay contacts `SW2` open when $I = 30\,\text{mA}$, at $t_B = 2.951\,\text{ms}$. Consequently the relay's contacts were closed for $8.709\,\text{ms}$. Again there is very good agreement with the figures obtained analytically.

# 9 | Non-linear circuits and waveform shaping

## 9.1  EXERCISE: DIODE CLAMP AND TRANSISTOR SQUARER

This tutorial is based on a laboratory experiment originally designed for second year undergraduates at UMIST. It is now a simulation exercise using MINNIE.

The objective is to use a high pass $RC$ circuit, together with a diode and/or a bipolar transistor, to:

1. centre a sinusoid on a given DC voltage level;
2. set a peak of the sinusoid to a given DC level;
3. derive a series of pulses of the same frequency from an input sinusoid; and
4. derive a square wave of the same frequency from an input sinusoid.

### 9.1.1  Centring a Sinusoid

In **DRAWING** mode set up the circuit shown in Fig. 9.1-1, using the following component values:

$$C = 0.1\,\mu F \quad R_L = 10\,k\Omega \quad R_S = 50\,\Omega$$

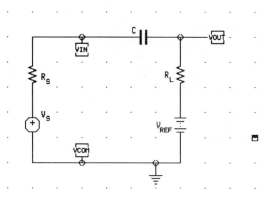

**Fig. 9.1-1**

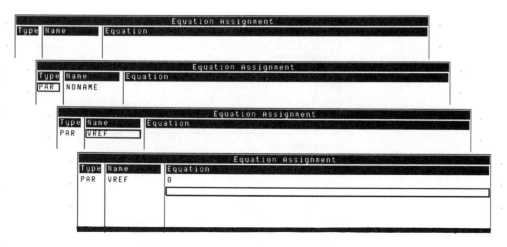

**Fig. 9.1-2** Defining $V_{REF}$ as a parameter

$V_S$ = 4V peak amplitude, 10 kHz sinusoid: use the procedure outlined in section 7.2 to set up this voltage source.

$V_{IN}$ = the actual voltage input to the circuit (the source impedance is not part of the actual circuit).

$V_R$ = variable in the 0–10 V range, to be set following the procedures outlined in Chapter 6 and detailed below.

The steps needed to set up $V_R$ are shown in Fig. 9.1-2.

1. Select **EQN** (the calculator) and you get the **Equation Assignment** menu.
2. Press **M** on the top row directly under **Type** until **PAR** appears.
3. Select **NO NAME** (under the **Name** heading).
4. Type **VREF**.

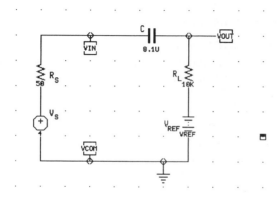

**Fig. 9.1-3** Circuit showing captions and values; note that **VREF** appears in *both* contexts

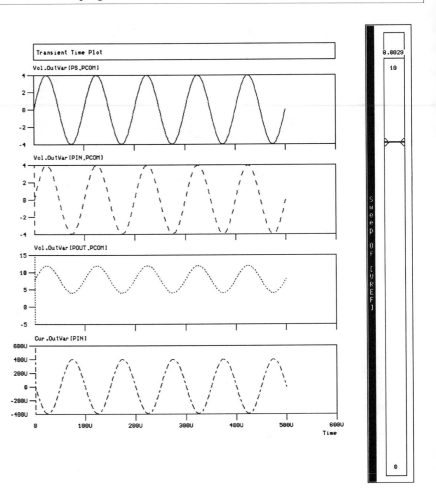

**Fig. 9.1-4**

5. Move sideways, select box under **Equation** and type in **0** (for 0 V, its minimum value).
6. Cancel **Equation Assignment**.

Then use either **VALUES** or **PARAM** to identify the variable DC voltage source as **VREF** for the analysis (names typed on circuit using **CAPTIONS** have no significance in the analysis).

Now select **ANALYSIS** mode. As you will be looking at waveforms, not frequency response, the **AC Analysis** option is not required. Leave it alone. The **DC Analysis** option is also not required.

Select instead **Transient Analysis**. Set **Start Time** and **Stop Time** to cover the first 5 cycles of your waveform. Bearing in mind that each cycle period is 100 μs, set an appropriate value for the **Plot Inc** (plot increment). Remember to set the time units – if you get them wrong you could be asking MINNIE to work all night!

Select **Time Plot**, **Transfer Plots**, and **Vol.OutVar**. Then set probes

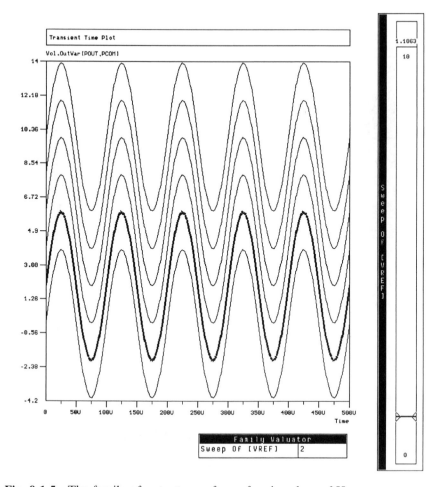

**Fig. 9.1-5** The family of output waveforms for six values of $V_{REF}$

to measure at source (only to get a picture of $V_S$), at circuit input, and at circuit output, all with respect to ground.

Select Cur.OutVar. As it is a series circuit the current is the same in all components. Select one suitable probe, and then cancel Time Plot.

Select Fourier Analysis and set Fundamental Freq to your value. Next select Fourier Plots, and then Vol.OutVar and Cur.OutVar as above. Set probes as for transient analysis, except at source (not required).

Cancel Fourier Analysis, and Transient Analysis, and you are now back at the main Analysis Options menu.

Select Parameter Sweep and fill in your Global Parameters. You have only one variable quantity, $V_{REF}$. It is to vary in the 0 to 10 V range. Limit the number of points you request or you will have a long wait for results! Six points on a linear scale will produce the following values for $V_{REF}$:

$$0 \quad 2V \quad 4V \quad 6V \quad 8V \quad 10V$$

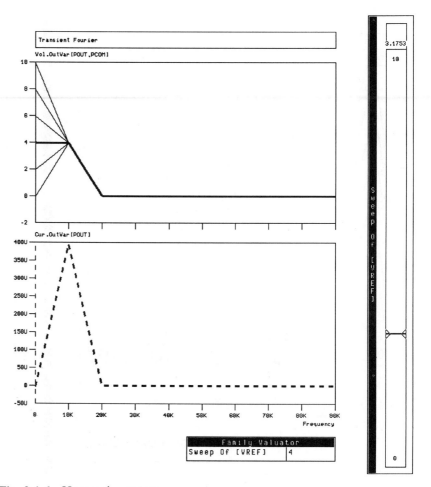

**Fig. 9.1-6** Harmonic content

When ready select Run(int) and let MINNIE get on with the analysis. (On the UMIST Apollos it will take about nine minutes.)

When ready MINNIE enters RESULTS mode. Display your results appropriately. Typical results are shown in Figs. 9.1-4, 9.1-5 and 9.1-6.

The waveforms in Fig. 9.1-4 show the following points:

1. The capacitor blocks the DC component from $V_{REF}$. As the signal is a pure sinusoid it has no DC component of its own. Consequently the waveform at the circuit input is centred on the 0 V DC level.
2. At the output the DC voltage and the signal are present simultaneously. We are dealing with a linear system so superposition principles apply and the DC voltage is added algebraically to the signal voltage. As a result the sinusoid is centred on the DC level.
3. The current flows through the capacitor. Consequently it cannot have any DC component.

Note that in Fig. 9.1-5 all waveforms for a given voltage level are identical (there is no drift in their DC components). This means that MINNIE assumes that the capacitor has charged fully to the applied DC level before the start of the simulation (this is the default assumption used by MINNIE when initial conditions are not set).

Figure 9.1-6 shows the harmonic content, and as expected the sinusoid has no harmonics. The DC values are due to $V_{REF}$.

Your report should clearly describe your results. After the initial cycles your waveform has reached a **dynamic steady state** – all non-signal fluctuations have ended. Each cycle is identical to its predecessor. Hence the charge $Q_G$ gained by the capacitor during a charging portion of a cycle MUST be exactly balanced by an identical charge $Q_L$ lost during the rest of the cycle. Then at the end of the cycle the capacitor is in EXACTLY the same condition as at the beginning.

Using these ideas show analytically that, for a perfect input sinusoid, the output must always be centred on $V_{REF}$.

### 9.1.2   Set the peak of a sinusoidal voltage to a given DC level

Modify your circuit as shown in Fig. 9.1-7. Use a diode symbol from the Discrete Components library:

1. Select the PARAM facility, as described in section 3.2.
2. Move the cursor (magnifying glass) to the diode.
3. Select the diode. The DCL Junction Diode menu appears, as in Fig. 9.1-8.
4. Select Model Name and the library menu of Fig. 9.1-9 appears.

You can use any device from this menu in your simulations, but some may not appear in the handbooks available to you. It is recommended that you use only devices for which you can obtain information.

To Examine this list of devices use the arrows at the bottom to scroll the list up or down. There is little point in 'examining' the devices themselves – no information concerning model parameters is disclosed.

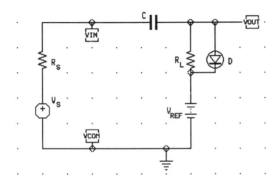

**Fig. 9.1-7**   Simple DC restoration (or level shifting) circuit

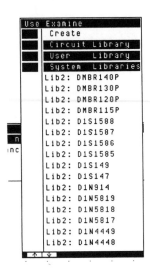

**Fig. 9.1-9** Discrete
Devices diode libraries: all
System Libraries diodes
are available to ECAD users

**Fig. 9.1-8**

5. Select one of the diodes. The **1N4004** seems adequate (note that the D in the numbers is an HSpice convention indicating Diode and is *not* part of the device name).

   To select a diode press **M** in the Use column next to the diode.

6. Cancel the library menu by selecting its heading. You are now back to the **DCL Junction Diode** menu of Fig. 9.1-8, but now with the selected diode appearing in the right column next to **Model name**.

7. Cancel the **DCL Junction Diode** menu.

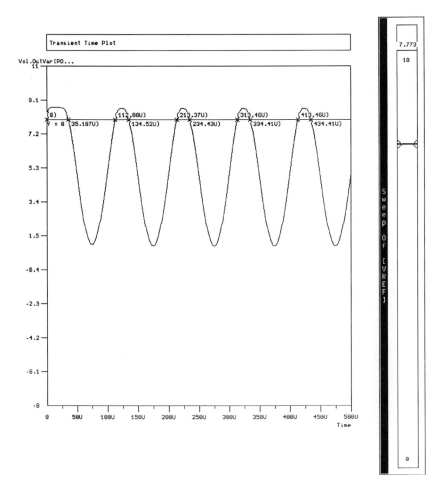

**Fig. 9.1-10** Output voltage for $V_{REF} = 8$ V

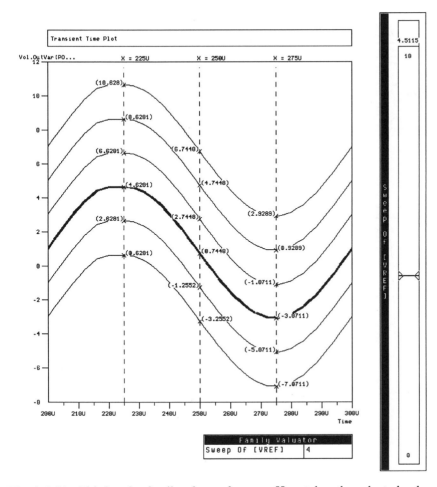

**Fig. 9.1-11**  Third cycle: family of waveforms as $V_{REF}$ takes the selected values

Select **ANALYSIS** mode. The previously defined **Analysis Profile** is still suitable except that you now require the current in the diode as well as that in the load resistor. Make appropriate modifications and then select **Run(Int)**. On the UMIST Apollos this simulation should take about $10\frac{1}{2}$ minutes.

Display your results as appropriate. Typical output is shown in Figs. 9.1-10, 9.1-11 and 9.1-12. The positive peak of the waveform is at a diode voltage drop above $V_{REF}$. Consequently the DC level of the signal can be set to any desired value by adjusting $V_{REF}$.

Note from Fig. 9.1-10 that the first cycle is noticeably different to the remaining cycles. The waveform is slightly distorted during the diode's conduction period, so its average value is no longer zero. It thus has a

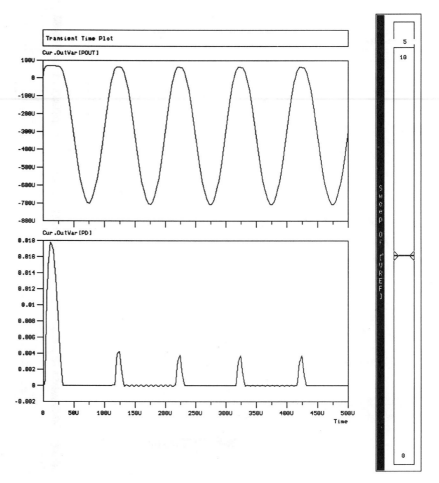

**Fig. 9.1-12**   Output voltage and diode current

DC content which affects the DC voltage across the capacitor. Most of the necessary adjustment takes place during the first cycle.

Note in Fig. 9.1-12 the current surge during the conduction period of the first cycle. This current sets up the initial small shift in capacitor voltage.

Your report should clearly describe your observations. Present appropriate waveforms. Based on the charge balancing ideas described in section 9.1.1 present a clear and accurate analysis/description of the effect the diode has on the output waveform.

Discuss the effect of replacing the Silicon diode by a Germanium diode having a $\approx 0.2\,\text{V}$ forward voltage drop.

### 9.1.3   Simple transistor pulse generator

Replace the diode by a bipolar transistor from the `Discrete Components` menu, as shown in Fig. 9.1-13. Any device could be used if information

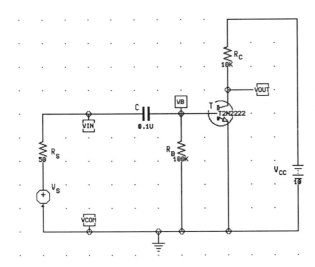

**Fig. 9.1-13**  Simple bipolar pulse generator

about its characteristics were available. For the present purpose the
**2N2222** is quite suitable. The letter T is simply the HSpice convention
for identifying devices as transistors.

The source voltage $V_S$ is now variable, in the range $0.5\,\text{V}$ to $5.0\,\text{V}$
peak. Following previous procedure select **EQN** and set up the
appropriate line in the **Equation Assignment** menu (the parameter's
**Name** could be $V_S$). Select **PARAM** and modify its sinusoid definition
so that its amplitude is now the parameter $V_S$, as in Fig. 9.1-14.

The other new components are $R_B = 100\,\text{k}\Omega$ and $R_C = 10\,\text{k}\Omega$.

Notice that the variable voltage source **V_REF** is no longer required.
To fully delete it work through the installation stages, removing it as
appropriate. Thus, after deleting it from the circuit diagram in the usual
way you should:

```
              °      Transient Voltage Specification
NAME (of model)                                          VS
Transient type (PULSE,SIN,EXP,PWL,SFFM)                  SIN
Pulse              V1 (initial value )
                   V2 (pulsed value )
                   TD (delay time )          [0.0]
                   TR (raise time )
                   TF (fall time )
                   PW (pulse width )
                   PER (period )
Sinusoidal         V0    (offset )                       0
                   VA    (amplitude )                    VS
                   FREQ  (frequency )                    10K
                   TD    (delay )             [0.0]
                   THETA (damping factor )    [0.0]
Exponential        V1    (initial value )
                   V     (pulsed value )
                   TD1   (rise delay time )   [0.0]
                   TAU1 (rise time constant )
```

**Fig. 9.1-14**  The sinusoid's amplitude is specified as the parameter $V_S$

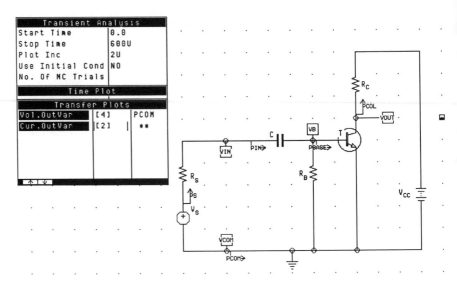

**Fig. 9.1-15** Analysis Profile for voltage and current waveforms

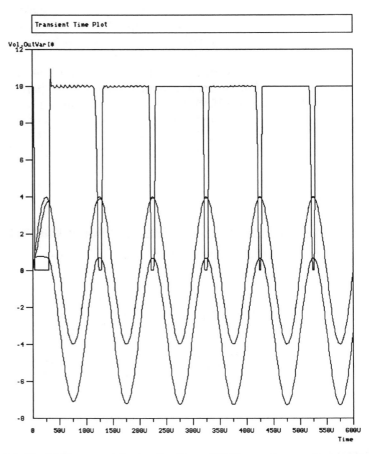

**Fig. 9.1-16** Voltage waveforms for $V_S = 4\,\mathrm{V}$ (i.e. not one of your values!); in descending order: collector, source/input (superimposed) and base voltages

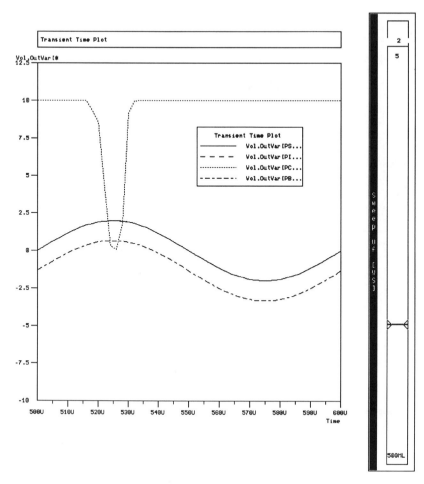

**Fig. 9.1-17** Edited version of Fig. 9.1-16, showing the sixth cycle in greater detail, for $V_S = 2\,\mathrm{V}$

1. in **DRAWING** mode select the **EQN** facility and delete the $V_{REF}$ row from the Equation Assignment Menu,
2. in **ANALYSIS** mode select Parameter Sweep and delete $V_{REF}$, and
3. still in analysis mode, cancel Global Parameters from the list of Selected Analyses in the right-hand menus.

In your report describe, with the help of clear diagrams, exactly what is happening. The base-emitter junction of the transistor is, of course, a p-n junction just like any good diode. Compare with the circuit in section 9.1.2 above.

As before, in the **ANALYSIS** mode we only require Transient Analysis and Parameter Sweep.

Under Transient Analysis set up probes for voltage waveforms at source, at the circuit's input, at the transistor's base and at its collector. Also look for Fourier Analysis of the base and collector waveforms. See Fig. 9.1-15.

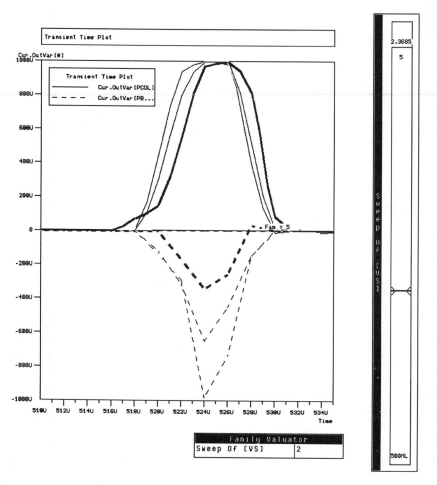

**Fig. 9.1-18** Families of graphs for collector and base currents, (again edited to display only the sixth cycle)

Under **Parameter Sweep** set the parameter $V_S$ to take 4 peak values in the 0.5 V–5 V range (on a linear scale the actual peak values will be 0.5 V, 2.0 V, 3.5 V and 5 V).

Note the choice of time interval. At 10 kHz the **Start Time** and **Stop Time** will cover the first 6 cycles of the waveform. This is necessary because the circuit will take a few cycles to reach its dynamic steady state. The **Plot Inc** is selected to provide good resolution even when only one cycle is displayed.

When ready, select **Run(Int)**. This analysis takes about 18 minutes on the UMIST Apollo network.

Display your results as appropriate. Possible graphs are shown in Figs. 9.1-16, 9.1-17 and 9.1-18.

Include in your report clear waveforms. Explain carefully what is happening, and use additional diagrams if necessary.

Examination of the waveforms shown in Fig. 9.1-16, especially

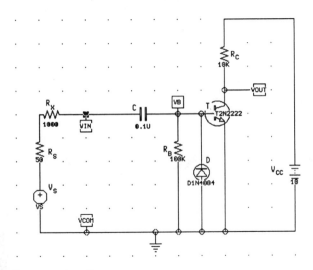

**Fig. 9.1-19**  Squarer circuit

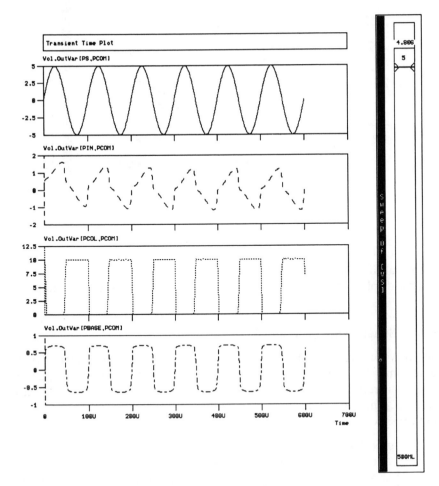

**Fig. 9.1-20**  Voltage waveforms for $V_S = 5\,\text{V}$ ($R_C = 10\,\text{k}\Omega$, $C = 0.1\,\mu\text{F}$)

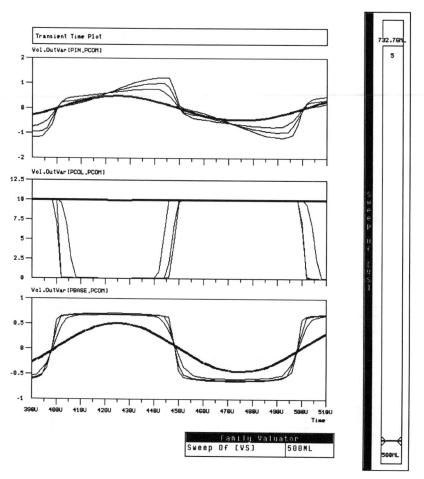

**Fig. 9.1-21**   Voltage waveforms for 5th cycle ($R_C = 10\,\text{k}\Omega$, $C = 0.1\,\mu\text{F}$)

at the collector (the top one), reveals that several cycles must pass before all the waveforms are truly repetitive.

This display can be edited to show the sixth cycle in greater detail as in Fig. 9.1-17.

### 9.1.4   Square wave generator

Set up your circuit as shown in Fig. 9.1-19. Note that the purpose of $R_B$ is to limit the surge currents charging and discharging the capacitor. These currents must flow, alternately, through the diode or the base-emitter junction. If excessive the devices would be damaged, so the $1\,\text{k}\Omega$ resistor is introduced.

1. Examine the voltages at circuit input (between $R_X$ and $C$), transistor base and collector at each value of $V_S$.

    This simulation takes about 20 minutes on the UMIST Apollo network.

Possible voltage displays are shown in Figs. 9.1-20, 9.1-21 and 9.1-22, and possible harmonic content displays are shown in Figs. 9.1-23 and 9.1-24.

2. Replace $R_C = 10\,k\Omega$ with $R_C = 1\,k\Omega$ and repeat the simulation.
3. Keeping $R_C = 1\,k\Omega$, replace $C = 0.1\,\mu F$ with $C = 0.01\,\mu F$ and repeat the simulation.

Your report should comprise a comprehensive set of waveforms using a common time scale.

Using the charge balancing ideas outlined earlier, explain the waveforms at the base and hence at the collector.

Is $R_B$ necessary? Could it have been omitted from this circuit?

Determine the *peak* charging current which would be required if the voltage across the $0.1\,\mu F$ capacitor were to follow exactly the 5 V peak input sinusoid (i.e. if $R_S = 0$, $R_X = 0$ and the diode/transistor conduction resistances are also zero).

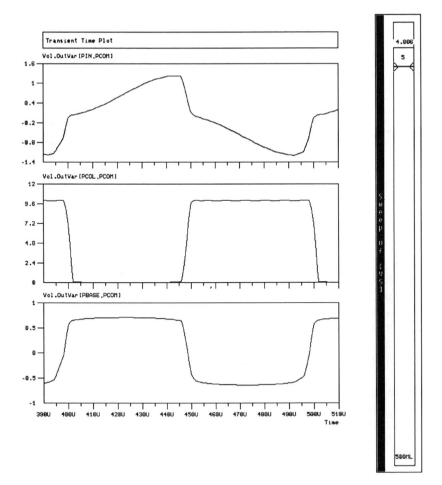

**Fig. 9.1-22**   Voltage waveforms for 5 V peak sinusoid ($R_C = 10\,k\Omega$, $C = 0.1\,\mu F$)

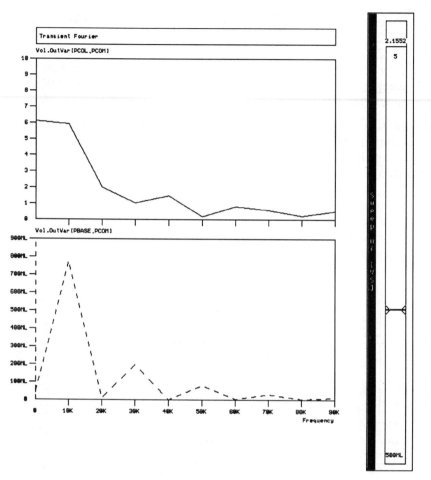

**Fig. 9.1-23** Harmonic content of voltage waveforms ($R_C = 10 \, k\Omega$, $C = 0.1 \, \mu F$)

Explain the effects of changing the collector resistance and the coupling capacitance.

Comment on the **mark–space** ratio (the **on–off** ratio) of $V_{OUT}$. Discuss how the use of a Germanium transistor and a Germanium diode could improve this ratio.

Comment on the rise and fall times of the 'square wave'. How do the voltage rates of change, $dv/dt$, of the input sinusoid affect these times?

Note the initial downwards drift in the circuit input voltage in Fig. 9.1-20. For this reason it is necessary to perform the simulation for a number of cycles, thus allowing the circuit to reach its Dynamic Steady State. Detailed measurements can then be performed on one of the later cycles, as appropriate.

The time axis in Fig. 9.1-21 has been edited to cover marginally more than the fifth cycle, in order to show clearly the start and end of

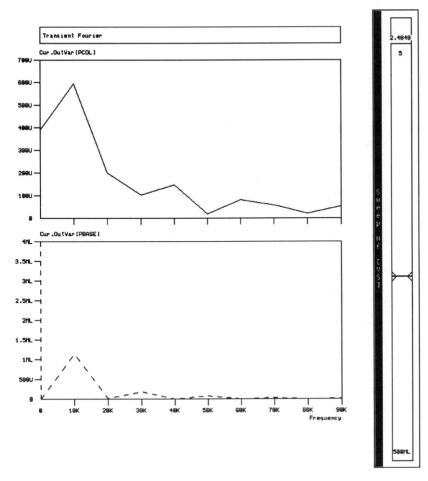

**Fig. 9.1-24** Harmonic content of current waveforms ($R_C = 10 \, \text{k}\Omega$, $C = 0.1 \, \mu\text{F}$)

the cycle. Waveforms are shown for the four values of input sinusoid amplitude, the ones corresponding to 500 mV peak amplitude being highlighted.

Note that the 500 mV input waveform is too small, so neither the diode nor the transistor is turned on.

## 9.2 EXERCISE: OPERATIONAL AMPLIFIERS – PEAK DETECTOR

*Description*

A **peak detector** is a circuit which produces an output DC voltage equal to the peak value of an input repetitive waveform. In its simplest form it is also used as a demodulator for amplitude modulated waveforms,

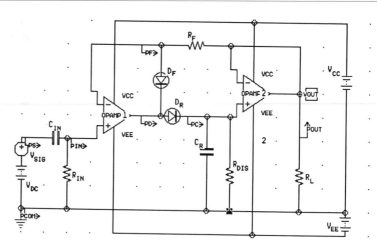

**Fig. 9.2-1** Peak detector circuit

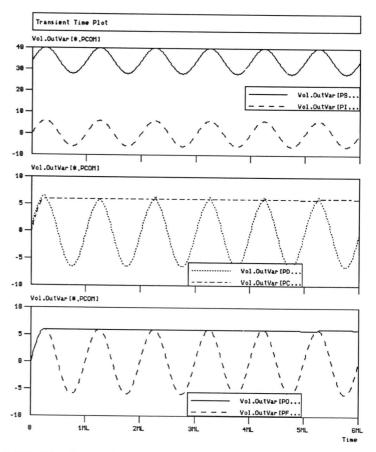

**Fig. 9.2-2** Circuit waveforms: top: source and input voltages; middle: voltages on either side of $D_R$; bottom: output voltage and voltage at $D_F - R_F$ node

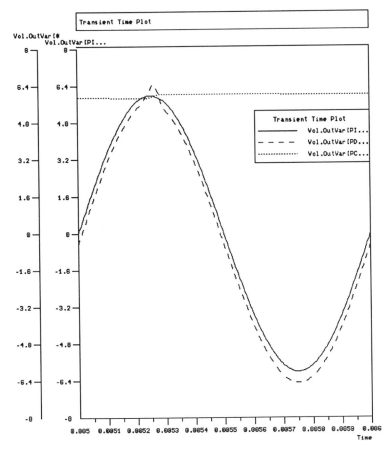

**Fig. 9.2-3** Input sinusoid (at non-inverting terminal), output of OPAMP 1, and output of OPAMP 2

and as a half-wave rectifier. The circuit used in this simulation, shown in Fig. 9.2-1, is somewhat more advanced than the basic form, having the following additional characteristics:

1. High input impedance. The input op-amp effectively buffers the source, the input impedance being set by $R_{IN}$.
2. Very low output droop. The second op-amp buffers the reservoir capacitor $C_R$, enabling the circuit to drive relatively low impedances without affecting the accuracy of the DC output.
3. Relatively wide bandwidth for a peak detector using op-amps.
4. Protection of the input op-amp against excessive differential input voltages.

*Discussion*
Referring to Fig. 9.2-1, describe the operation of the circuit, giving particular attention to the function of diode $D_F$ and the effects of the

'feedback' resistor $R_F$. Sketch the waveforms you expect at each point in the circuit, with all relevant DC voltage levels.

A small capacitor, say $10\,\text{pF}-100\,\text{pF}$, may be placed parallel to $D_F$. Explain, by reference to its effect on **OPAMP 1**, how it affects the frequency response of the circuit, enabling it to operate (with suitable op-amps) up to $500\,\text{kHz}$ (or more), though at reduced accuracy.

*Simulation*

Set up the circuit of Fig. 9.2-1 using the following components:

> Op-amps: **AMC1536**
> Diodes: **1N4004**
> $C_{IN} = 1\,\mu\text{F}$        $C_R = 0.1\,\mu\text{F}$
> $R_{IN} = 100\,\text{k}\Omega$    $R_{DIS} = 1\,\text{M}\Omega$      $R_L = 10\,\text{k}\Omega$    $R_F = 100\,\text{k}\Omega$
> $V_{CC} = 15\,\text{V}$       $V_{EE} = -15\,\text{V}$     $V_{DC} = 34\,\text{V}$ (or any other
> $V_{SIG} = 6\,\text{V}$ peak                            value you prefer)

Set up an appropriate waveform analysis profile, run your simulation and display your results.

Possible result displays are shown in Figs. 9.2-2 and 9.2-3.

*Comment*

Note the discharge resistor, necessary for the simulation to give correct results. If not used HSpice produces capacitor (and output) voltages which (slightly) exceed the peaks at the output of **OPAMP 1**. This is equivalent to a (very small) leakage or bias current *into* the capacitor.

The circuit shown in Fig. 9.2-1 is built (without $R_{DIS}$) and tested by UMIST undergraduates using **TL071 CP** op-amps and **BAT 85** diodes. Satisfactory operation for $V_{SIG}$ frequencies up to $500\,\text{kHz}$ is achievable.

# Appendix A
# Control Codes

These are two key combinations used to perform special functions. For all of them the Control (**CTRL**) key is *held down* while a second key is pressed.

**Screen presentation**

| | |
|---|---|
| Screen refresh (refresh) | **CTRL-R** |
| Screen redraw without grid | **CTRL-X** |

**Output to printer**

| | *System Driver* | *ISL Driver* |
|---|---|---|
| Partial screen dump | **CTRL-D** | **CTRL-V** |
| Full screen dump | **CTRL-F** | **CTRL-W** |

**Editing**

When text editor is active (i.e. when you can type text):

| | | |
|---|---|---|
| Character delete | **CTRL-H** | (or the **Backspace** key) |
| Line of text delete | **CTRL-U** | |

**Calculator**

| | |
|---|---|
| Invoke calculator | **CTRL-E** |

# Appendix B
# HSpice DISCRETE
# COMPONENTS LIBRARY

The information tabulated below is presented solely for the guidance of undergraduates and other first time users of the MINNIE/HSpice simulation package. Though care has been taken to minimize errors, inaccuracies may persist. No responsibility can be accepted for consequent problems.

Circuit designers should consult the manufacturer's data books for reliable information.

**Table 1**  Voltage reference diodes

| Type | Nominal voltage | Type | Nominal voltage | Type | Nominal voltage |
|------|------|------|------|------|------|
| 1N5333B | 3.3 V | 1N5352B | 15 V | 1N5371 | — |
| 1N5334B | 3.6 | 1N5353B | 16 | 1N5372 | 62 V |
| 1N5335B | 3.9 | 1N5354B | — | 1N5373 | 68 |
| 1N5336B | 4.3 | 1N5355B | 18 | 1N5374 | 75 |
| 1N5337B | 4.7 | 1N5356B | — | 1N5375 | 82 |
| 1N5338B | 5.1 | 1N5357B | 20 | 1N5376 | — |
| 1N5339B | 5.6 | 1N5358B | 22 | 1N5377 | 91 |
| 1N5340B | — | 1N5359B | 24 | 1N5378 | 100 |
| 1N5341B | 6.2 | 1N5360B | — | 1N5379 | 110 |
| 1N5342B | 6.8 | 1N5361B | 27 | 1N5380 | 120 |
| 1N5343B | 7.5 | 1N5362B | — | 1N5381 | 130 |
| 1N5344B | 8.2 | 1N5363B | 30 | 1N5382 | — |
| 1N5345B | — | 1N5364B | 33 | 1N5383 | 150 |
| 1N5346B | 9.1 | 1N5365B | 36 | 1N5384 | 160 |
| 1N5347B | 10 | 1N5366B | 39 | 1N5385 | — |
| 1N5348B | 11 | 1N5367B | 43 | 1N5386 | 180 |
| 1N5349B | 12 | 1N5368B | 47 | 1N5387 | — |
| 1N5350B | 13 | 1N5369B | 51 | 1N5388 | 200 |
| 1N5351B | — | 1N5370B | 56 | | |

### Voltage reference diodes

The HSpice `Discrete Components` library contains a large number of voltage reference (Zener) diodes. This is because in each family of devices there will be a range of available reference voltages. Typical is the `1N5333–1N5388` family. These are 5 W devices available (with B after the type number) from a number of suppliers.

### Bi-polar transistors

This data was taken from *Towers' International Transistor Selector*, Revised Edition Update Four, 1990, published by W. Foulsham & Co. Ltd., and is reproduced with their permission.

**Table 2**   NPN Devices

| Type | Power (mW)* | $I_C$ (mA) | $V_{CB}$ | $V_{CE}$ (Volts) | $V_{EB}$ | $T_J$ (°C) | $h_{fe}$ ** | at $I_C$ (mA) | $f_T$ (MHz) | $C_{BC}$ (pF) | Similar device |
|------|------|------|------|------|------|------|------|------|------|------|------|
| 2N706 | 300 | 200 | 25 | 20 | 3 | 150 | 20 | 10 | 200 | 6 | 2N2369 |
| 2N708 | 300 | 200 | 40 | 15 | 5 | 200 | 30/120 | 10 | 300 | 6 | 2N2369 |
| 2N918 | 200 | 50 | 30 | 15 | 3 | 200 | 20 | 3 | 600 | 1.7 | BFX73 |
| 2N930 | 300 | 30 | 45 | 45 | 5 | 200 | 100 | 0.01 | 30 | 6 | BC109 |
| 2N2102 | 1 W | 1 A | 120 | 60 | 7 | 175 | 40/120 | 10 | 60 | — | 2N4001 |
| 2N2219A | 800 | 800 | 75 | 50 | 6 | 175 | 100 | 150 | 300 | 8 | BSW54 |
| 2N2222 | 500 | 800 | 60 | 30 | 5 | 175 | 100 | 150 | 250 | 8 | BSW64 |
| 2N2222A | 500 | 800 | 75 | 40 | 6 | 175 | 100 | 150 | 300 | 8 | BSW64 |
| 2N2369 | 360 | 500 | 40 | 15 | 4 | 175 | 40/120 | 10 | 500 | 4 | BSX20 |
| 2N2501 | 360 | 500 | 40 | 20 | 6 | 200 | 50/150 | 10 | 350 | 4 | BSX20 |
| 2N2642 | 600 | 30 | 45 | 45 | 5 | 200 | 100 | 0.01 | 40 | 5 | BFY81 |
| 2N3013 | 360 | 200 | 40 | 15 | 5 | 175 | 30/120 | 30 | 350 | 5 | BSX20 |
| 2N3227 | 360 | 500 | 40 | 20 | 6 | 200 | 100 | 10 | 500 | 4 | BSX20 |
| 2N3501 | 1 W | 300 | 150 | 150 | 6 | 200 | 100 | 150 | 150 | 8 | BSW67 |
| 2N3742 | 1 W | 50 | 300 | 300 | 7 | 200 | 20/200 | 30 | 30 | 6 | BF337 |
| 2N3866 | 5 W$^A$ | 400 | 55 | 30 | 3 | 200 | 10/200 | 50 | 500 | 3 | — |
| 2N3946 | 360 | 200 | 60 | 40 | 8 | 175 | 45 | 1 | 250 | 4 | BC107 |
| 2N3947 | 360 | 200 | 60 | 40 | 6 | 175 | 100 | 10 | 300 | 4 | BC107 |
| 2N5058 | 1 W | 150 | 300 | 300 | 7 | 200 | 30/150 | 30 | 30 | 10 | BF259 |
| 2N5179 | 200 | 50 | 20 | 12 | 2 | 200 | 25/250 | 3 | 900 | 1 | BFY90 |
| 2N6341 | 200 W$^A$ | 25 A | 180 | 150 | 6 | 200 | 30/120 | 10 A | 40 | 300 | — |
| 2SC1815 | 400 | 150 | 60 | 50 | 5 | 125 | 70/700 | 2 | 80 | 3.5 | BC182L |
| 2SC1923 | 100 | 200 | 40 | 30 | 4 | 125 | 140 max | 1 | 275 | — | BF369 |
| 2SC2120 | 600 | 800 | 30 | 30 | 5 | 150 | 100 | 100 | 60 | 13 | — |
| 2SC2235 | 900 | 800 | 120 | 120 | 5 | 150 | 80/240 | 100 | 60 | 30 | — |
| 2SC2669 | 200 | 500 | 35 | 30 | 4 | 125 | 40/240 | 2 | 100 | 2 | — |

\* the power ratings assume the device is in free air at 25 °C except where the superscript $^A$ indicates that the case is held at 25 °C.
\*\* $h_{fe}$ given as min/max or as typical values.

**Table 3** PNP Devices

| Type | Absolute maximum ratings | | | | | | $h_{fe}$ ** | at | $I_C$ (mA) | $f_T$ (MHz) | $C_{BC}$ (pF) | Similar device |
|------|-------------------|------|------|------|------|------|------|------|------|------|------|------|
| | Power (mW)* | $I_C$ (mA) | $V_{CB}$ | $V_{CE}$ (Volts) | $V_{EB}$ | $T_J$ (°C) | | | | | | |
| 2N869A | 360 | 200 | 25 | 18 | 5 | 175 | 40/120 | | 30 | 400 | 6 | BSW25 |
| 2N1132A | 600 | 600 | 60 | 40 | 5 | 175 | 30/90 | | 150 | 60 | 30 | BFS95 |
| 2N2605 | 400 | 30 | 60 | 45 | 6 | 200 | 100 | | 0.01 | 30 | 6 | BC179 |
| 2N2894 | 360 | 200 | 12 | 12 | 4 | 200 | 30/150 | | 30 | 400 | 6 | BSW24 |
| 2N2904 | 600 | 600 | 60 | 40 | 5 | 200 | 40/120 | | 150 | 200 | 8 | BFX30 |
| 2N2904A | 600 | 600 | 60 | 60 | 5 | 200 | 40/120 | | 150 | 200 | 8 | BFX30 |
| 2N2905 | 600 | 600 | 60 | 40 | 5 | 200 | 100 | | 150 | 200 | 8 | BFX30 |
| 2N2905A | 600 | 600 | 60 | 60 | 5 | 200 | 100 | | 150 | 200 | 8 | BFX30 |
| 2N2906 | 400 | 600 | 60 | 40 | 5 | 200 | 40/120 | | 150 | 200 | 8 | BSW24 |
| 2N2907 | 400 | 600 | 60 | 40 | 5 | 200 | 100 | | 150 | 200 | 8 | BSW24 |
| 2N2907A | 400 | 600 | 60 | 60 | 5 | 200 | 100 | | 150 | 200 | 8 | BSW24 |
| 2N2945A | 400 | 100 | 25 | 20 | 25 | 200 | 70 | | 1 | 10 | 10 | BCY94 |
| 2N3250 | 360 | 200 | 50 | 40 | 5 | 180 | 50/150 | | 10 | 250 | 6 | BSW24 |
| 2N3250A | 360 | 200 | 60 | 60 | — | 200 | 50/150 | | 10 | 250 | 6 | BSW24 |
| 2N3251 | 360 | 200 | 50 | 40 | 5 | 180 | 100 | | 10 | 300 | 6 | BSW24 |
| 2N3251A | 360 | 200 | 60 | 60 | 5 | 200 | 100 | | 10 | 300 | 6 | BSW24 |
| 2N3467 | 1 W | 1 A | 40 | 40 | 5 | 200 | 40/120 | | 500 | 175 | 25 | BFS95 |
| 2N3546 | 360 | 200 | 15 | 12 | 4 | 200 | 30 | | 10 | 700 | 6 | BSW25 |
| 2N3637 | 1 W | 1 A | 175 | 175 | 5 | 200 | 100 | | 50 | 200 | 10 | — |
| 2N3743 | 1 W | 50 | 300 | 300 | 5 | 200 | 25/250 | | 30 | 30 | 15 | — |
| 2N3906 | 310 | 200 | 40 | 40 | 5 | 135 | 100 | | 10 | 250 | 5 | BC388 |
| 2N3962 | 360 | 200 | 60 | 60 | 6 | 175 | 60 | | 1 | 40 | 6 | BC179 |
| 2N6438 | 200 W^A | 25 A | 140 | 120 | 6 | 200 | 20/80 | | 10 A | 40 | 700 | — |
| 2SA950 | 600 | 600 | 30 | 25 | 5 | 150 | 320 max | | 100 | 60 | 40 | BCW37 |
| 2SA965 | 900 | 800 | 120 | 120 | 5 | 150 | 80/240 | | 100 | 60 | 30 | — |
| 2SA970 | 300 | 100 | 120 | 120 | 5 | 150 | 200 | | 2 | 50 | 4 | — |
| 2SA1015 | 400 | 150 | 50 | 50 | 5 | 125 | 70/400 | | 2 | 80 | 4 | — |

* the power ratings assume the device is in free air at 25 °C except where the superscript ^A indicates that the case is held at 25 °C.
** $h_{fe}$ given as min/max or as typical values.

# Appendix C   Answers

## Section 2.2.1

1. Kirchoff's Voltage Law (KVL): The algebraic sum of the voltage drops around a closed loop in the clockwise (or anti-clockwise) direction equals zero.

   Applying KVL to the circuit in Fig. A.3-1 yields:

   loop 1: $0 = I_1 (R_1 + R_2 + R_3) - I_2 R_2 - I_3 R_3$
   loop 2: $0 = I_1 R_2 - I_2(R_2 + R_4 + R_5) - I_3 R_4 - V_1$
   loop 3: $0 = -I_1 R_3 - I_2 R_4 + I_3(R_3 + R_4 + R_6) - V_1 - V_2$

   In this problem $V_1$ and $V_2$ are known. Solve for $I_1$, $I_2$ and $I_3$. (Note that other loops can be found. As all possible current paths are included in the loops chosen above the others are redundant).

2. Kirchoff's Current Law (KCL): The algebraic sum of the currents entering (or leaving) a node equal zero.

   Applying KCL to the circuit in Fig. A.3-2 yields:

   node A: $0 = (V_D - V_A)/R_1 + (V_B - V_A)/R_2 + (V_C - V_A)/R_5$
   node B: $0 = (V_A - V_B)/R_2 + (V_D - V_B)/R_3 + (V_C - V_B)/R_4$
   $\qquad - V_1/R_4$
   node C: $0 = (V_A - V_C)/R_5 + (V_B - V_C)/R_4 + (V_D - V_C)/R_6$
   $\qquad + V_1/R_4 - V_2/R_6$

   Set $V_C = 0$ (circuit reference or common point) and solve for $V_A$, $V_B$ and $V_D$.

## Section 2.2.2

Using mesh analysis and a pocket calculator the following results were obtained for a 15 V RMS input signal:

1. $I_S = 55.087 \angle 18.656°$ mA
2. $V_L = 30.887 \angle -86.103°$ V
3. $I_L = 59.447 \angle -17.000°$ mA

These results are close to, but not the same as, those obtained using MINNIE/HSpice. The phase of $I_S$ depends on the direction assumed for analysis.

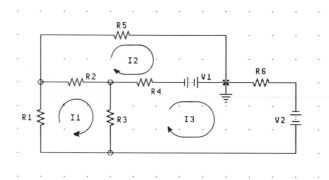

**Fig. A.3-1**   Voltage sources are easy to deal with when applying KVL

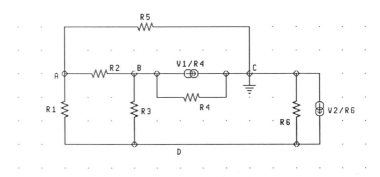

**Fig. A.3-2**   Replacing the voltage sources by equivalent current sources (Thevenin to Norton transformation) simplifies the application of KCL

### Section 5.7.2

Using   $\omega_O^2 = 1/LC$   leads to $C = 101.32\,\text{pF}$ (use $100\,\text{pF}$).

$Q_O = f_O/(\text{bandwidth}) = 10^6/2 \times 10^4 = 50$

$Q_O = \omega_O L/\Sigma R$ leads to $\Sigma R = R_S + R_L + R = 31.4\,\Omega$. Hence as $R_S = 5\,\Omega$ and $R_L = 13\,\Omega$ the additional resistance which must be added to get the required bandwidth is $R = 13.4\,\Omega$ (use $12\,\Omega$).

### Section 5.8.2

$Q_O = f_O/(\text{bandwidth}) = 10.7 \times 10^6/150 \times 10^3 = 71.33$ (maximum).

At resonance the impedance of the tuned circuit will be real, equal to $R_B$ of Fig. 5.8-2(b). Hence the gain at resonance will be (from Equation 5.8-4)

$A_O = 40 I_C Z_L = 40 I_C R_B$

For $I_C = 0.5\,\text{mA}$ and $A_O = 100$ this leads to the equivalent $R_B = 5000\,\Omega$. Then using Equation 5.8-1 leads to

$C = Q_{PO}/(\omega_O R_B) = 212.2\,\text{pF (maximum)}$.

Then   $L = 1/(\omega_O^2 C) = 1.0459\,\mu\text{F}$.

   Also, Equation 5.8-2 leads to $R_A = 0.989\,\Omega$. This is the required resistance of the real tuned inductor.

## Section 6.2

$R_E = 390\,\Omega$,   $533.8\,\Omega$,   $730.6\,\Omega$ and $1000\,\Omega$, with the demarcation lines set at $461.9\,\Omega$,   $632.2\,\Omega$ and $865.3\,\Omega$.

## Section 7.2.4

Refer to Fig. 7.2-1. Let $v_C$ be the collector's AC voltage, $v_O$ be that across the load resistor $R_L$. Then:

$$v_O = \frac{v_C R_L}{R_L + 1/(j\omega_O C_{C2})}$$

and for $f_O = 100\,\text{kHz}$, $C_{C2} = 10\,\text{nF}$ and $R_L = 1\,\text{k}\Omega$

$$v_O = 0.987 \angle{-9.04°} \times v_C$$

and the load voltage lags $9°$ behind the collector voltage. As the frequency is $10\,\text{kHz}$, this represents $0.25\,\mu\text{s}$.

## Section 7.3.1

1. The circuit of Fig. 7.3-2 is a single-sided-output differential amplifier, with a buffered output. However, for high frequency amplification purposes it is more useful to look on it as an **emitter follower** ($T_1$) driving a **common base stage** ($T_2$). A second **emitter follower** ($T_4$) provides buffering for the output while a second **common base** ($T_3$) acts as a current source for $I_{C1}$ and $I_{C2}$ to provide a high **Common Mode Rejection Ratio**.

   Note the *DC feedback path*. When $T_1$ and $T_2$ are both active $V_{B1} \approx V_{B2}$. As $R_{OFFSET}$ is adjusted to set the DC output voltage to $0\,\text{V}$, and $R_{F1} = R_1$ it follows that $R_{F2} \approx R_2 + R_{OFFSET}$ (exact equality requires $I_{B1} = I_{B2}$, not likely with discrete components). Check against the results of your simulation's set-up procedure. This feedback path keeps the DC operating conditions (bias voltages) very stable. The capacitor $C_F$ prevents any AC feedback.

   $I_{C2}$ was chosen to maximize the $f_T$ of the transistors used. For the **BF199** suitable currents lie in the $5–8\,\text{mA}$ range, $5.25\,\text{mA}$ being used here. The current source provides $10.4\,\text{mA}$ to make $I_{C1} \approx I_{C2}$. The nominal DC base voltages are $-4.9\,\text{V}$.

   Assuming $70 \leqslant h_{fe} \leqslant 350$ at $5\,\text{mA}$ leads to a $350–1750\,\Omega$ range for the device $Z_{IN}$. Together with the $R_1$, $R_2$ and $R_{OFFSET}$ biasing components the equivalent circuit input impedance range is $310\,\Omega < Z_{EQ} < 1073\,\Omega$. The $56\,\Omega$ terminating resistor $R_T$ ensures

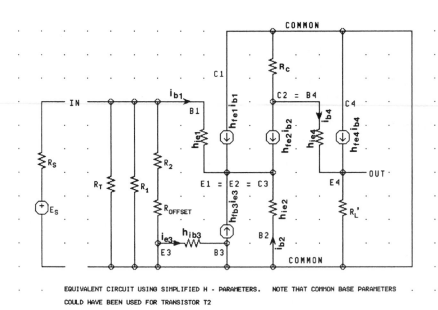

EQUIVALENT CIRCUIT USING SIMPLIFIED H - PARAMETERS.   NOTE THAT COMMON BASE PARAMETERS
COULD HAVE BEEN USED FOR TRANSISTOR T2

**Fig. A.3-3(a)**   The simplified $h$-parameter circuit is used. In effect this means that $h_{re}$ and $h_{oe}$ have been discarded. Note that $h_{ie}$ has two components, $r_{bb'}$ and $r_{b'e}$. Further simplification is based on $r_{bb'}$ being much smaller than $r_{b'e}$, so that $h_{ie} \approx r_{b'e}$. $R'_L$ is the parallel sum of the LOAD, $R_{E2}$ and $R_{F1}$

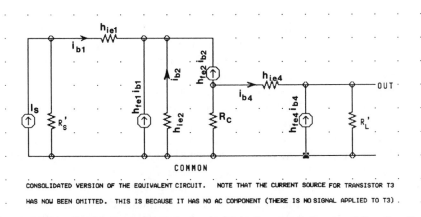

CONSOLIDATED VERSION OF THE EQUIVALENT CIRCUIT.   NOTE THAT THE CURRENT SOURCE FOR TRANSISTOR T3

HAS NOW BEEN OMITTED.   THIS IS BECAUSE IT HAS NO AC COMPONENT (THERE IS NO SIGNAL APPLIED TO T3).

**Fig. A.3-3(b)**   In this consolidated circuit $R'_S$ is the parallel sum of $R_S$, $R_T$, $R_1$, $R_2$ and $R_{OFFSET}$; the source maybe represented by a Thevenin or by a Norton equivalent circuit

that the impedance presented to the $50\,\Omega$ coaxial cable varies in the range $47\,\Omega < Z_{IN} < 53\,\Omega$, thus reducing reflections.

*Note* that under certain conditions these circuits can sustain relaxation oscillations. To avoid them it is desirable to eliminate the possibility of $T_2$ saturating. For this version the maximum possible current in $T_2$ is $I_{E3}$ (when $T_1$ is cut off), so the maximum possible

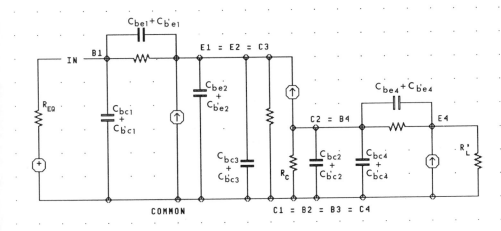

**Fig. A.3-4** As Fig. A.3-3(b) but now showing the base-emitter and base-collector capacitances

voltage drop across $R_C$ is $I_{E3} \times R_C \approx 12.5$. Consequently $V_{B2}$ and $V_{B1}$ should have been designed to be more negative than $-5.5\,\text{V}$. However, the prototype proved quite stable.

2. Fig. A.3-3(a), (b)
4. As the circuit is designed for $I_{C1} = I_{C2}$, $A_V = 0.5$.
5. Fig. A.3-4
6. (a) Base to Collector Capacitances of $T_1$ and $T_2$.

$T_1$ has no base-collector voltage gain ($v_C = 0$), so its $C_{bc}$ and $C_{b'c}$ are not multiplied (no Miller effect). They are simply capacitances between input and common (ground).

The base of $T_2$ is connected through $C_F$ to common (ground). Hence its $C_{bc}$ and $C_{b'c}$ are simply between collector and common, and are not amplified (no Miller effect).

(b) Base to Emitter Capacitance of $T_4$.

The DC current in $T_4$ is approximately $5\,\text{mA}$. Its base-emitter voltage gain is about $0.95$, somewhat lower than for many emitter followers (typical values could be $0.98$–$0.985$–$0.99$ etc.). Its base to emitter capacitance is subject to Miller effect, the effective capacitances being:

(i) between base and common

$$C_{\text{EFF(IN)}} = C_{be}(1 - A) = C_{be}(1 - 0.95) = 0.05 C_{be}$$

(ii) between emitter and common

$$\begin{aligned} C_{\text{EFF(OUT)}} &= C_{be}(1 - 1/A) \\ &= C_{be}(1 - 1/0.95) = -0.053 C_{be}. \end{aligned}$$

Thus the base-emitter capacitance may be replaced by a much smaller value between base and common, and by a much smaller and *negative* value between emitter and common.

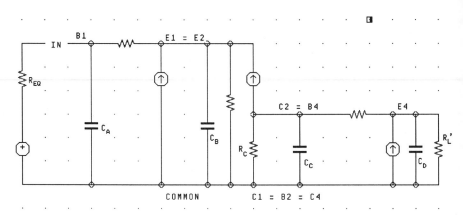

**Fig. A.3-5** *h*-parameter labels omitted for clarity; refer to Fig. A.3-3(b) for details

7. Fig. A.3-5

$$C_A = C_{bc1} + C_{b'c1} + (1 - A_{V1})(C_{be1} + C_{b'e1})$$
$$C_B = C_{be2} + C_{b'e2} + (1 - 1/A_{V1})(C_{be1} + C_{b'e1}) + C_{bc3} + C_{b'c3}$$
$$C_C = C_{bc2} + C_{b'c2} + C_{bc4} + C_{b'c4} + (1 - A_{V4})(C_{be4} + C_{b'e4})$$
$$C_D = (1 - 1/A_{V4})(C_{be4} + C_{b'e4}) + \text{load/probe capacitance}$$

Note that if a terminated $50\,\Omega$ line is used to connect the load to the circuit's output it will present a *resistive* impedance. If not it will be necessary to consider its capacitive loading of the output.

9. Using the approximation $C_{be} \approx 40I_C/\omega_T$ the maximum base-emitter capacitance of $T_4$ is 125 pF for $I_C \approx 5\,\text{mA}$ and $f_T \geqslant 250\,\text{MHz}$.

From question 6. above the corresponding effective capacitance between emitter and common is

$$C_{EFF2} \approx -0.053 \times (125 + 0.2)\,\text{pF} \approx -6.625\,\text{pF}$$

and the total emitter-common capacitance, including the probe, is $C_D \approx 8.4\,\text{pF}$.

The corresponding minimum break frequency is

$$\omega_D \approx |1/(C_D R_{EQ})|$$

where $R_{EQ}$ is the parallel sum of $R_{F1}$, $R_{E2}$ and the load. For the values given $R_{EQ} = 700\,\Omega$, leading to a minimum $f_D \approx 27\,\text{MHz}$.

10. The maximum capacitance $C_C$ may be estimated as

$$C_C = 0.2 + 8 + 0.2 + 8 + (1 - 0.95)(125 + 0.2) \approx 22.45\,\text{pF}.$$

The break frequency is $\omega_C \approx |1/(C_C R'_C)|$. As $R'_C \approx R_C \approx 1.2\,\text{k}\Omega$ the worst case value is $f_C \approx 5.9\,\text{MHz}$.

Note that typical values for $C_{bc}$ (not supplied) would give better agreement with the results of the simulation. Thus if a more typical value is 4 pF the break frequency becomes $f_C = 9.17\,\text{MHz}$.

11. Assume $T_1$ and $T_3$ have the same $f_T$ and the same collector currents. Then, from 8, $C_{b'e1} = C_{b'e2}$. The strays $C_{be1}$ and $C_{be2}$ are also equal. From 4, $A_{v1} = 0.5$, so $C_B$ may be estimated at:

$$C_B \approx (C_{b'e1} + C_{be1})(1 - 1/0.5) + C_{b'e2} + C_{be2} + C_{b'c3}' + C_{bc3}$$
$$\approx C_{b'c3} + C_{bc3} = 0.2\,\text{pF} + 8\,\text{pF}$$

Hence

$$f_B \approx 40\, I_C/(2\pi\, C_B) \approx 40 * 0.005/(2 * \pi * 8.2 * 10^{-12})$$
$$\approx 3.9\,\text{GHz}$$

12. The effective source impedance $R_S'$ is the parallel sum of $R_S$, $R_T$, $R_1$ and $R_2 + R_{OFFSET}$. As the $50\,\Omega$ coaxial cable from the source is properly terminated at both ends (by the effective input impedance $\approx 50\,\Omega$, resistive, see discussion for question 1, and by the signal's source impedance) it presents a $50\,\Omega$ resistive source impedance $R_S$ to the circuit. As $R_1$ and $R_2 + R_{OFFSET}$ are by comparison relatively large $R_S' \approx (R_S R_T)/(R_S + R_T) \approx 26\,\Omega$.

In question 9 it was established that for $I_C \approx 5\,\text{mA}$ and $f_T \approx 250\,\text{MHz}$ the internal base-emitter capacitance $C_{b'e}$ is approximately $125\,\text{pF}$. Hence, as the voltage gain of $T_1$ is $A_{V1} = 0.5$:

$$C_A = 0.2 + 8 + 125(1 - 0.5) = 70.8\,\text{pF}$$

leading to a break frequency $f_A \approx 93\,\text{MHz}$.

### Section 7.4.2

Each power supply provides the current that flows through one of the transistors to the load. These currents, shown in Figs. 7.4-7 and 7.4-8, are half-wave rectified waveforms, each one being just half of the total load current. From the analysis of the half wave rectifier it is known that the average value of each of these currents is $I_P/\pi$ ($I_P$ = peak current). This current discharges the smoothing capacitor.

At 50 Hz the bridge rectifier recharges the capacitor every $1/100\,\text{s}$, so each discharge period lasts for $0.01\,\text{s}$. During this period the capacitor voltage reduction should not exceed 5% of the nominal supply voltages $\pm V_{CC}$. The worst case arises when the signal is maximum, $I_P = 255\,\text{mA}$ in this design. From Fig. 7.4-2 $V_{CC} = 18\,V$. Hence using

$$I = dQ/dt = C\,dV/dt$$

$$C = I\frac{\delta t}{\delta v} = \frac{0.255 \times 0.01}{\pi \times 0.05 \times 18} = 902\,\mu F$$

### Section 7.5.2

$$k = 4 - \sqrt{2}/Q_P = 3.8585786 = 1 + R_B/R_A$$

$$R_B = 2.858\,R_A$$

| $R_A =$ | 1.0 | 1.2 | 1.5 | 1.8 | 2.2 | 2.7 | 3.3 | 3.9 | 4.7 |
|---------|-----|-----|-----|-----|-----|-----|-----|-----|-----|
| $R_B =$ | 2.86 | 3.43 | 4.28 | 5.15 | 6.29 | 7.72 | 9.43 | 11.1 | 13.4 |

$$R_A = \quad 5.6 \quad 6.8 \quad 8.2 \quad 10.0$$
$$R_B = 16.0 \quad 19.4 \quad 23.4 \quad 28.6$$

Hence if $R_A = 5.6\,k\Omega$ then $R_B = 16.0\,k\Omega$.

$$RC = \sqrt{2}/\omega_p = 1/(\sqrt{2}\ \pi\ 250) = 9.003 \times 10^{-4}$$

| $R, k\Omega$ = | 1.0 | 1.2 | 1.5 | 1.8 | 2.2 | 2.7 | 3.3 | 3.9 |
|---|---|---|---|---|---|---|---|---|
| $C, nF$ = | 900 | 750 | 600 | 500 | 409 | 333 | 273 | 231 |

| $R, k\Omega$ = | 4.7 | 5.6 | 6.8 | 8.2 | 10.0 |
|---|---|---|---|---|---|
| $C, nF$ = | 191 | 161 | 132 | 110 | 90.0 |

Hence if $R = 10\,k\Omega$ then $C = 90\,nF$.

$$K = k/(4 - k) = 3.858/(4 - 3.8585786) = 27.28.$$

### Section 7.6.1

(iii) (a) as Equation 7.6-1
(b) $V_O = 0$
(c) $\phi = 0$

# Subject index

# Menus index

(Figure number then page number in brackets)

# Exercise index

# Tutorial index

(Arranged in order of appearance)